ARCHAEOLOGY AT CERROS
BELIZE, CENTRAL AMERICA

David A. Freidel
Series Editor

ARCHAEOLOGY AT CERROS BELIZE, CENTRAL AMERICA

Volume II
The Artifacts

by

James F. Garber

SOUTHERN METHODIST UNIVERSITY PRESS • 1989

ARCHAEOLOGY AT CERROS, BELIZE, CENTRAL AMERICA
VOLUME II, THE ARTIFACTS

Copyright © 1989 by Southern Methodist University Press
Box 415
Dallas, Texas 75275
Printed in the United States of America

The paper in this book meets the standards for permanence and durability
established by the Committee on Production Guidelines for Book Longevity
of the Council on Library Resources.

Library of Congress Cataloging-in-Publication Data

(Revised for vol. 2)

Archaeology at Cerros, Belize, Central America.

    Includes bibliographies and index.
    Contents: v. 1. An interim report / volume editors,
Robin A. Robertson, David A. Freidel; contributors,
Helen Sorayya Carr . . . [et al.] — v. 2. The artifacts /
by James F. Garber.
    1. Cerros Site (Belize) 2. Mayas—Antiquities.
3. Indians of Central America—Belize—Antiquities.
4. Belize—Antiquities. I. Freidel, David A.
II. Robertson, Robin A. III. Garber, James.
F1435.1.C43A73 1986   972.82′1   86-3843
ISBN 0-87074-214-0 (pbk. : v. 1 : alk. paper)
ISBN 0-87074-285-X (pbk. : v. 2 : alk. paper)

COVER ILLUSTRATION: Drawings by Karim Sadr
COVER DESIGN: Marcy Heller

CONTENTS

FIGURES

TABLES

ACKNOWLEDGMENTS

The efforts of many people made this monograph possible. I would like to thank the government of Belize and the Department of Archaeology, including Joe Palacio, Jaime Awe, Elizabeth Graham Pendergast, and Harriot Topsey for encouraging and permitting our research. I would also like to thank the people of Belize, who were gracious hosts throughout the Cerros Project. I became friends with many of the men from Chunox who worked for the project and will always remember many of our conversations and cultural exchanges.

A special thanks goes to David Freidel, director of the Cerros Project, teacher, and good friend. His comments, advice, and insights provided encouragement and inspiration throughout the course of my work. I would also like to thank Payson Sheets and an anonymous reviewer for providing valuable comments on earlier drafts.

Robin Robertson, the assistant project director and project ceramicist, gave many hours to provide ceramic evaluations for many of the excavated lots. Without her advice, many of the chronological assessments of the artifacts would not have been possible. Her efforts are sincerely appreciated.

The detailed analyses of context were made possible through the meticulous work of the project staff: Maynard Cliff, Sorayya Carr, Sue Lewenstein, Beverly Mitchum, and Vern Scarborough.

Michael Holdaway, Art Endress, and Norm McLeod of the Geology Department at Southern Methodist University freely gave of their time to aid in the geologic identification of many of the artifacts.

Eleanor Powers illustrated SF-158, SF-160, SF-161, SF-1469, and SF-1512. The remainder of the artifact illustrations were done by Karim Sadr. His patience is greatly appreciated. Without his keen eye for detail, this monograph would be something less than it is. Robin Robertson inked the maps, and she and Laurie Evans did the layout for the illustrations.

Norman Whalen of Southwest Texas State University generously spent many hours proofreading earlier drafts. The final draft was typed by my student assistants, David Driver and Kenneth Kraft.

Last, but certainly not least, an extra special thanks goes to my wife, Melissa. Her patience, constant encouragement, support, and tolerance are deeply appreciated.

1. INTRODUCTION

This study describes and analyzes some of the artifacts recovered from the Maya site of Cerros in Northern Belize. Included are objects of worked shell, worked bone, reworked sherds, molded nonvessel ceramic pieces, ground stone, polished stone, molded plaster, ground metal, pounded metal, and cast metal. Excluded from this study are artifacts of chipped stone, which are discussed elsewhere (Lewenstein 1984, 1987; Mitchum 1986).

The site of Cerros is located in the Corozal District of Northern Belize, on the south side of Chetumal Bay, which is fed by the New River (Fig. 1). Two distinct settlement zones have been identified at Cerros (Freidel 1979, 1986). The first, Feature 1A, consists of a series of house floors and associated trash dumps. Feature 1A underlies Feature 2A, the main plaza. The northern edge of the Feature 1A settlement zone has been exposed by erosion and extends approximately 65 m east-west along the coastline and is almost a meter thick (Cliff 1982, 1986). The second settlement zone is a dispersed settlement surrounding the ceremonial precinct (Scarborough 1980, 1986; Scarborough and Robertson 1986) (Fig. 2).

The ceremonial precinct of the site consists of pyramids and plazas covering an area of approximately 5.5 ha (Fig. 3). The Late Preclassic component at Cerros has been divided into three ceramic phases (Robertson 1986; Robertson-Freidel 1980) (Fig. 4). The earliest, phase 1, or Ixtabai, coincides with the establishment of the residences of Feature 1A underlying the main plaza. Occupation of the Feature 1A zone continues during phase 2, or C'oh, along with the beginning of dispersed settlement.

Phase 3, or Tulix, witnessed the elaboration and further development of occupation in the dispersed settlement zone. All monumental architecture dates to phase 3 (Freidel 1979, 1986; Robertson-Freidel 1980). The construction of the main plaza during the phase 2–3 transition buried the Feature 1A occupation zone.

Excavations carried out at Cerros have shown that all architecture in the ceremonial precinct appeared during the Late Preclassic period. The site was occupied during the Early Classic and Late Postclassic periods, but no major constructions have been attributed to these later periods.

Early Classic and Late Postclassic period occupation consists of deposits of cultural debris on or just below the surface of structures built during the Late Preclassic. Exceptions to this are Structures 10, 46, and 84, which date to the Early Classic (Scarborough and Robertson 1986).

THE EMERGENCE OF COMPLEX SOCIETY IN THE MAYA LOWLANDS

During the Late Preclassic period (300 B.C. to A.D. 150), many characteristics of Lowland Maya civilization emerged (Adams 1977; Coe 1965b, 1965c). The Late Preclassic in the Maya Lowlands is characterized by tremendous population growth and increased interaction. The most notable evidence for this interaction is the widespread use and manufacture of Chicanel pottery (Ball 1977a; Coe 1965b; Hammond 1977; Sabloff 1975; and Willey, Culbert, and Adams 1967). There was a significant increase in the importation of highland goods such as obsidian and jade as well as expanded circulation of Lowland products such as shell, stingray spines, chert, quartzite, and salt.

During the Late Preclassic period, administrative ceremonial centers were built throughout the Lowlands. Although data from Late Preclassic centers are scarce because of large amounts of Classic period overburden, it is clear that a settlement hierarchy was emerging (Willey 1977). This settlement hierarchy reflects a political hierarchy that replaced the undifferentiated villages of the Middle Preclassic.

The rise of social differentiation and the emergence of an elite class and ruling kinship units are associated with the political hierarchy. Social differentiation is clearly evident in the burials of this time period, with modest burials in the domestic house floors at one extreme and elaborate interments associated with monumental architecture at the other. While the depictions of Classic period kings and their actions are common, the actions of Preclassic kings have been deduced from

1

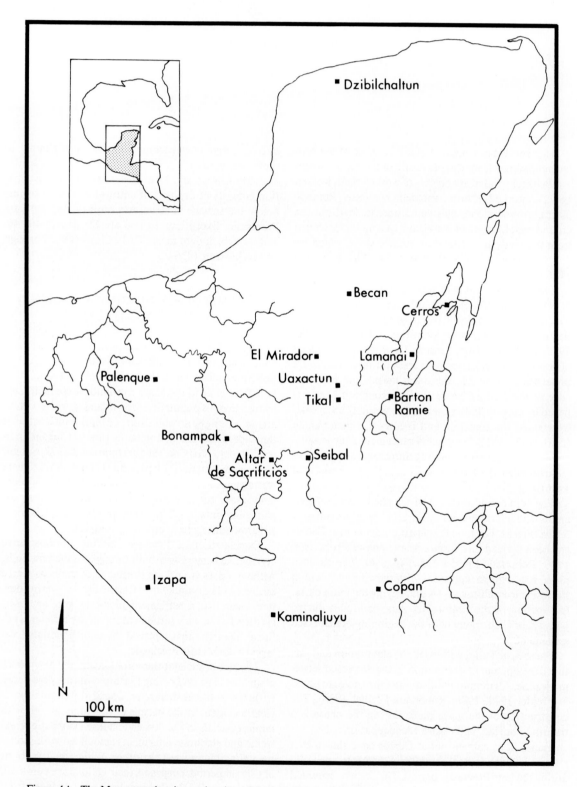

Figure 1A. The Maya area showing major sites of the Late Preclassic Period.

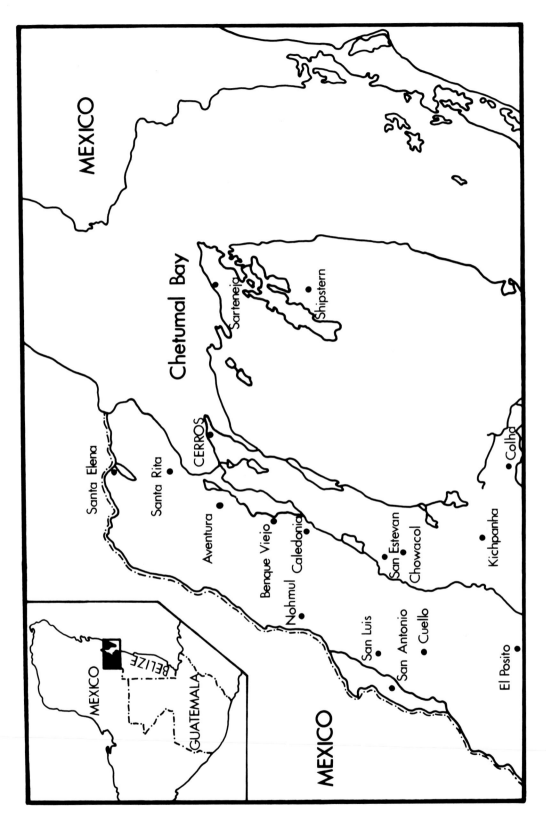

Figure 1B. Northern Belize showing Cerros in relation to other ancient settlements in the area.

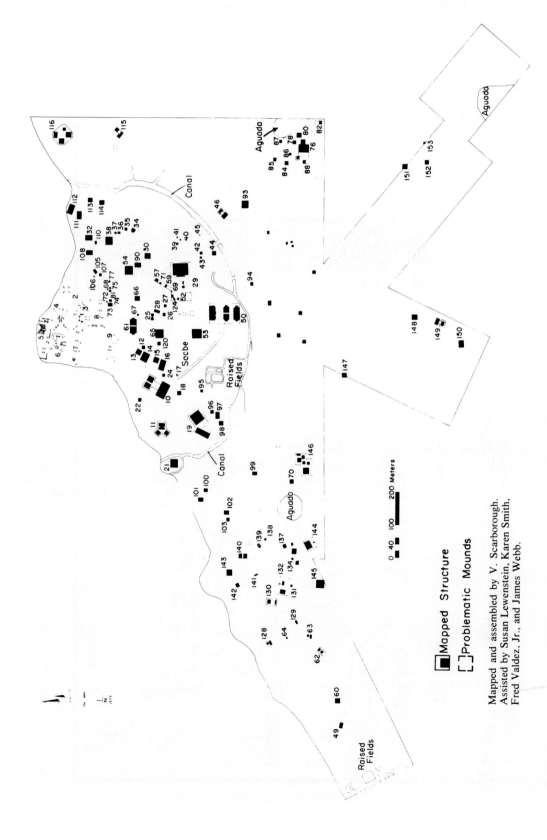

Figure 2. The settlement at Cerros. Mapped small structures in the dispersed settlement zone are conventionally oriented to the cardinal directions unless true orientation is known through excavation. Public buildings such as the ballcourts show true orientation.

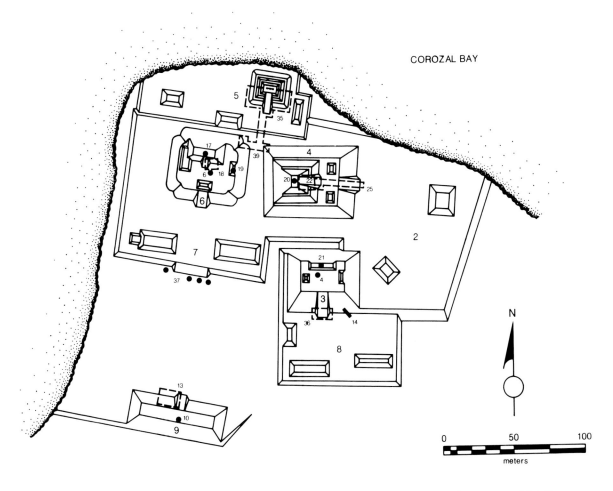

Figure 3. Monumental architecture at Cerros. Deviations from Maler conventions are based on excavated detail.
Key: Dashed lines show major exposures; dots show limited exposures; large numbers designate Structures; small numbers identify Operations.

LATE POSTCLASSIC
(Lobil)

1250 _

EARLY POSTCLASSIC
(New Town)

950 _

LATE CLASSIC
(Tepeu)

550 _

EARLY CLASSIC
(Tzakol)

200 _

AD   Tulix (Phase 3)
- - - - -   0
BC   50 _ _ _ _ _ _ _ _ _ _ _ _ _ _ _ _   LATE PRECLASSIC
                                                           (Chicanel)

             C'oh (Phase 2)
200 _ _ _ _ _ _ _ _ _ _ _ _ _ _ _ _

             Ixtabai (Phase 1)
300 _ _ _ _ _ _ _ _ _ _ _ _ _ _ _ _

Figure 4. Chronology.

their instruments of power and from the contexts in which the actions were performed (Freidel and Schele 1988).

OBJECTIVES

Four objectives of this study are (1) to examine the extent and role of trade at Cerros; (2) to document the changes that Cerros underwent from the Late Preclassic through the Postclassic periods; (3) to examine patterns of artifact consumption and disposal, thus illuminating the behavioral systems that contributed to the configuration of the archaeological record; and (4) to present the Cerros artifactual data in a manner useful for comparative purposes.

Objective 1. Cerros as a Trade Center

The institution of long-distance trade has been posed as one of the major factors contributing to the development of complex society in the Maya Lowlands (Freidel 1978b, 1979; Garber 1981, 1983, 1986; Rathje 1970, 1971, 1972, 1977). A comprehensive analysis of the artifacts from Cerros can shed light on the relationship between trade and the development of complex society.

Research at Cerros has been designed to test the proposition, in addition to several others, that the site functioned as a trading center or, more specifically, as a transshipment point, servicing long-distance canoe traffic. Data collected during six field seasons support this proposition (Freidel 1978b, 1979, 1986; Garber 1981, 1983, 1985, 1986). These include (1) location; (2) the presence of numerous artifacts made from raw materials not available locally; (3) docking facilities; and (4) the cosmopolitan quality of monumental art and architecture.

The presence of numerous brackish-water *Melongina melongina* mollusks in the Feature 1A residential zone and along the coastline strongly suggests that the prehistoric local environment consisted of a slow-moving lagoon fed by the New River. Cerros could have controlled and serviced canoe traffic up and down the coast, as well as up and down the New River.

Hundreds of artifacts recovered during the excavations at Cerros were made from raw materials not available in the immediate vicinity: obsidian, jade, basalt, specular hematite, and quartzite. The nearest source

for all except the last is the highlands of Guatemala. Quartzite is available in the Maya Mountains of Belize.

Feature 2A-Sub.2-1st, adjacent to the nucleated Feature 1A residential zone, may have functioned as a docking facility (Fig. 5) (Cliff 1982, 1986; Freidel 1979). The northern base of this platform is at least 38 m long. The presence of clays at the base of the platform suggests that this feature was constructed at a time when this area was permanently or semipermanently inundated. Along its north-south axis, it extended from dry land into a body of water, possibly a lagoon, river, or bay. The platform, accessible from the water, was made up of trimmed and untrimmed limestone blocks constructed on a bed of sterile clay. Its northern edge consisted of lenses of blue lagoonal clays, sands, and clays containing water-rolled sherds.

Structure 112, to the east of the central ceremonial precinct but within the confines of the encircling canal, has been identified as a port facility, based on its proximity to the shoreline and its ramplike slope rising from the shore to the mound's summit (Scarborough and Robertson 1986). Unlike Feature 2-Sub.2, this docking facility has a spacious summit, which could have been utilized for storage.

Excavations have revealed molded stucco forms decorated in polychrome on four of the five main pyramids. The decorated forms and motifs resemble other Late Preclassic examples of monumental art at Tikal, Uaxactun, Mirador, and Highland Maya sites (Freidel 1977, 1978a, 1978b, 1979, 1986). The overall composition of these decorations is distinctly Lowland Maya and clearly anticipates Classic period conventions. The presence of this monumental art at Cerros implies interaction with contemporary Lowland and Highland Maya centers. Its cosmopolitan nature adequately demonstrates Cerros' participation in a wide-ranging interaction sphere as reflected in the artifactual content of its material culture.

Objective 2. Cerros, a Changing Community

Cerros functioned as a political and economic center during the Late Preclassic period. At the end of the Late Preclassic, it was no longer a locus of power, as evidenced by the lack of monumental constructions of later periods.

Although Cerros declined as a center of political power, it did function as a habitation site in the Early Classic and Late Postclassic periods. Analysis of those

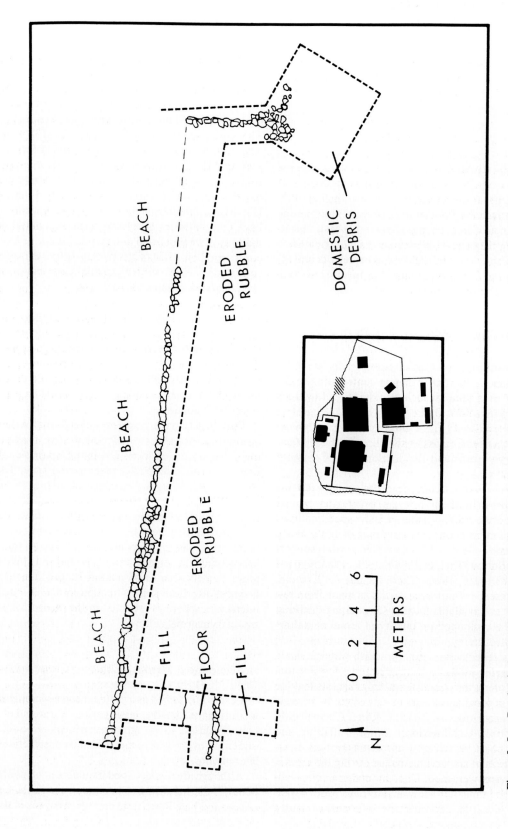

Figure 5. Late Preclassic docking facility at Cerros. Dashed lines refer to limits of excavation. Hatched area on insert notes location relative to monumental architecture.

deposits indicates, however, that the occupation was ephemeral and represented a substantial reduction from Late Preclassic levels (Scarborough and Robertson 1986).

This change in the function of Cerros precipitated changes in the kinds of material culture consumed at the site. During the Late Preclassic period, artifacts made from materials obtained through long-distance trade were used exclusively for ornamental or ritual purposes, never for domestic or utilitarian functions. Utilitarian items were fashioned from materials available regionally, that is, within Belize, but not necessarily from the immediate surroundings of the site. Not until the Classic period were utilitarian objects made from exotic, long-distance trade materials. The significance of this change will be discussed later.

Objective 3. Patterns of Artifact Consumption and Disposal

In this monograph the word "context" refers to depositional context or archaeological setting as defined by associated features, finds, or remains. Patterns of artifact disposal can be recognized by examining the contexts from which the artifacts came. As Butzer (1980: 419) states, "A practical general goal for contextual archaeology would be the study of archaeological sites as part of a human ecosystem. It is within this human ecosystem that communities once interacted spatially, economically, and socially, with the environmental matrix into which they were adaptively networked."

I would like to broaden this statement by using the words "archaeological remains" in place of "archaeological sites." In viewing the goal of contextual archaeology, it is difficult to distinguish it from the theoretical goal for cultural ecology. However, more often than not, cultural ecology, in practice, gets transformed into environmental determinism or some variant, where the physical environment is pivotal and the cultural environment is peripheral. Contextual archaeology, or the study of associations, can be viewed as the methodology to deal with the holistic approach to cultural ecology (Vayda and Rappaport 1968).

The study of the Cerros artifacts differs from previous studies of Maya material culture in that it includes an assessment of context. Contextual designations are not included in a great many artifact descriptions from earlier studies; thus, comparative information on this aspect of the analysis was frequently unavailable.

This assessment of context led to the definition of some previously unrecognized patterns of behavior associated with artifact deposition. One of these has been called "termination ritual," which varies from deposit to deposit but can consist of smashing jade and pottery, the removal of plaster façading, the burning of ceremonial fires, the preparation and consumption of a ceremonial beverage, and the scattering of the smashed artifacts among intentionally deposited layers of white marl (Garber 1983). This activity is associated with the abandonment of monumental architecture prior to succeeding construction, and in some cases, with the abandonment of domestic architecture.

Initially, this activity seemed isolated, but closer examination showed that it was common within the ceremonial precinct of the site. In addition to the many ceramic vessels associated with this activity, a wide range of artifacts was utilized in these rituals, including jade beads, jade ear flares, sherd disks, bone beads, specular hematite mirrors, armatures, doughnut stones, stone disks, stone spheroids, and miscellaneous pieces. Of the Late Preclassic finds at Cerros, 43.1% were recovered from deposits associated with termination ritual (17.8% if the stone disks and spheroids are excluded). These figures indicate that the behavior associated with termination ritual represents a very large investment in time, labor, and material culture.

Objective 4. Presentation of the Cerros Artifact Data

As stated earlier, Late Preclassic data are scarce compared to those of later periods. This is due largely to the great amount of cultural overburden from Classic and Postclassic periods, which overlies earlier remains at most sites. For logistical reasons, earlier deposits are difficult to approach and, as a result, exposures are limited. Such was not the case at Cerros, however, where all monumental architecture and the vast majority of dispersed settlement structures dated to the Late Preclassic period. This resulted in the recovery of a large sample of Late Preclassic artifacts from a wide variety of contexts.

FORMAT OF DATA PRESENTATION

The publication of artifact studies can take one of two basic forms. The traditional approach is a presentation of artifacts, largely in catalog form, organized primarily on the basis of raw material, technology, and artifact form. These studies also include discussions of temporal variability and artifact function. An alternative approach is to analyze artifact collections as assemblages or behavioral units. This entails combining many kinds of artifacts made from a wide variety of raw materials and treating them as a single assemblage or depositional unit. The catalog approach is an inventory of artifact data, whereas the assemblage approach is a contextual analysis of those data. The catalog is a necessary prerequisite to an analysis of context, because factors such as temporal variability, form, and function are critical to analyses of artifact assemblages and behavior associated with artifact deposition.

The objectives of each approach are quite distinct, and each yields different kinds of information. The catalog format cannot accomplish the goals of the assemblage-context approach, just as the assemblage-context format cannot accomplish the goals of the catalog approach. Each format has its own strengths and weaknesses. While a presentation by context provides detailed information on the behavior associated with the deposition of the artifacts, it is limited in utility as a comparative tool or as a means of assessing technological industries, morphological and temporal variability, and artifact function.

The appropriate presentation format depends directly on the objectives of the volume and on the character of the publication series as a whole. The catalog approach is consistent with objectives (1) to examine the extent of trade; (2) to document changes at Cerros through time; and (4) to present artifactual data in a manner useful for comparative purposes. Objective 3, which focuses on an examination of the behavioral systems of artifact deposition, can be accomplished though a modification of the traditional catalog format. This has been achieved by providing a general assessment of depositional context for each artifact. Additionally, presented in Appendix C is a listing of associated artifacts by structure for each major time period and deposit type. This goes beyond the typical catalog approach and minimizes a limitation of the catalog format. Structures with less than ten artifacts are not listed in Appendix C.

TYPOLOGY

The Cerros artifacts are organized into categories on the basis of raw material. They include stone, bone,

shell, clay, plaster, and metal. They are further subdivided according to the technology applied to transform the raw material into final form: chipped stone, ground stone, polished stone, worked bone, worked shell, molded clay, worked sherds, molded plaster, ground metal, pounded metal, and cast metal. The artifact categories correspond to technological industries, which vary according to the material being processed. This organizational scheme is the standard form for describing Maya artifacts and has been used by many investigators (Coe 1959; Dreiss 1982: Garber 1981; Gillis 1982; Hummer 1983; Kidder 1947; Kidder, Jennings, and Shook 1946; Phillips 1979; Proskouriakoff 1962, 1974; Ricketson and Ricketson 1937; Rovner 1975; Sheets 1978, 1983; Smith and Kidder 1951; Willey 1972, 1978; and Willey et al. 1965).

Within each industry, artifacts are then classified according to form. In dealing with the Chalchuapa chipped stone artifacts, Sheets (1978) departs from this procedure and partitions the chipped stone artifacts according to behavioral procedures of the knapper during the stages of production. He also reviews the use of types and typologies in the study of artifacts and compares two schools of thought. On the one hand, Brew (1946) and MacNeish et al. (1967) believe that typologies are defined by an investigator and do not necessarily duplicate a mental template in the minds of the makers; typologies are constructs of the observer. The opposing school of thought (Spaulding 1953) maintains that types can be discovered by an observer. In reference to an artifact collection from Chalchuapa, Sheets asserts: "If the differences in behavior and resultant products in the chipped stone industry have been correctly described, the categories defined were inherent in the collections. Taxonomic distinctions were made based on the differences in procedures used in manufacture" (1978: 82).

In the study of artifacts from Barton Ramie, Willey et al. (1965) used context as a classificatory criterion.

Sheets (1978) criticizes Willey's division of obsidian prismatic blades into two types, ceremonial and utilitarian, on the basis of depositional context. He claims that there are no formal, stylistic, or technological differences between those two types. With reference to depositional context, Sheets states: "A functional inference as weak as this should not be used as such a high-level classificatory scheme device, but should be reserved for the 'comment' section of a type description if it is to be mentioned at all" (1978: 81).

I agree with Sheets that context should not be used as a classificatory criterion in a mainly descriptive typology based largely on form; however, one of the goals of the Cerros artifact analysis is to demonstrate the importance of depositional context in artifact analysis. Context indicates how an artifact functioned within the society. For example, although there are no physical or chemical differences between holy water and ordinary water, to ignore the contextual differences between them would ignore the quite distinct function each has in our own society.

The Cerros artifacts, once organized by industry and form, are discussed in reference to their contexts and patterns of deposition. This involves an analysis of behavior reflected not in the artifacts, but in their deposition. Our approach differs from that taken by Sheets (1978), which focuses on production behavior as reflected in the artifacts. Both are distinct, yet equally viable, avenues of exploration and both are departures from the norm, because they examine not only the artifacts but also aspects of behavior associated with the artifacts.

The description and classification of a site's artifacts into categories and types is all too often the end rather than the beginning of artifact analysis. Typologies are devices to assist analysis; they are not substitutes for analysis.

ARTIFACT DESCRIPTION

As the artifacts came in from the field, each was washed, assigned a Small Find (SF) catalog number, and labeled. An artifact file was compiled consisting of eight-inch by five-inch file cards, one per Small Find. A drawing of each artifact was made on the back of the card. Several kinds of information were recorded on the card: SF number, provenience, artifact type, raw material, and dimensions. Additional items were recorded: form, color, weight, condition, technological variables, and a written description. This recording procedure facilitated manipulation of the artifact data.

The organizational scheme utilized in this study for the presentation of data follows that used in previous studies of Maya artifacts. The artifacts are organized by raw material and industry and then by form and sometimes subform within an industry. This is the most efficient way to present data in a manner useful for cross-comparison. Function is not of prime importance in this typology.

The format of data presentation adopts many techniques from the above-mentioned studies. For each artifact form and subform, several kinds of information are presented, including frequency, raw material tabulations, dating or chronological assessments, and contextual tabulations. Under the heading "Comments," one may find descriptions, summary comments on the chronology or depositional pattern of a particular form or subform, technological observations, and general summary comments regarding the particular form or subform. Figures and tables are grouped according to industry.

A comprehensive comparative treatment of the artifacts was not assembled for this monograph for several reasons. The artifacts included in this study are typical of sites throughout the Maya Lowlands. The Cerros collection is unique, however, in that it represents the largest reported assemblage of Late Preclassic artifacts, yet the majority do not differ greatly from those of later periods. Comprehensive comparative evaluations of Maya artifacts are readily available (Phillips 1979; Sheets 1978; Willey 1972; Willey et al. 1965). The artifacts in the Cerros collection fall within the range of variability represented in those comparative treatments; therefore, extensive comparisons would be restatements of earlier studies. In cases where comparative information yields new insights into the interpretation of a specific artifact or class of artifacts, that information is included in detail.

DATA FORMS

Space limitations, particularly with large collections, require that certain information be condensed or left out of the formal data presentation at the discretion of the investigator. In looking back on his Altar de Sacrificios artifact report (Willey 1972), Willey (1978) states that he feels he left out too much contextual information and provenience data. As a result, in the Seibal artifact report (Willey 1978), he lists provenience, chronological, and contextual data for each artifact. This more complete presentation of recorded information makes the data more usable and understandable to other investigators.

The recognized utility of this system inspired the creation of data forms for the Cerros artifacts, in which many additional classes of information are presented for each artifact. The data forms can be found in Appendix B. Additional information about an artifact that could not be presented on these forms was placed in the "Comment" section for that form or subform. The keys to the alphabetical and numeric symbols used on the data forms appear in Appendix A.

This complete presentation of recorded information will, it is hoped, give other investigators easy access to data not germane to the central issues confronted in this monograph. This monograph is intended to be a contribution to what is known about Maya material culture, and this manner of data presentation is meant to be a methodological contribution that will aid future researchers in dealing with other data sets.

CHRONOLOGICAL PLACEMENT

The dating of the artifacts was made on the basis of associated ceramics. Ceramic evaluations have been made for many of the excavated lots (Robertson-Freidel 1980). Many of the Late Preclassic lots are not ceramically pure with respect to phase. Other lots contained sherds predominantly from one period but with some from another. In those cases, it was difficult to assign a date to artifacts because of uncertainty regarding sherd association. I had to consult with the project ceramicist, Robin Robertson, and the excavators for that operation. After reviewing all of the available data, including associated lots and features, a chronological determination was made. Any of these datings are subject to change, however, as more data become available.

Because of the varying degree of deposit complexity and the incomplete nature of the ceramic evaluations from some of the operations, the reliability of the assigned dates varies. For example, most of the lots from the excavations of the monumental architecture have been carefully reviewed by the project ceramicist, so it is unlikely that the chronological assessments for associated artifacts will change. In contrast, fewer excavated lots from the settlement zone have completed ceramic evaluations. Artifacts from lots that have not been examined by the ceramicist have received chronological assignments on the basis of stratigraphic correlation with the ceramically analyzed test pit in that operation (Scarborough 1980, 1986; Scarborough and Robertson 1986).

The Feature 1A residential zone, which has been analyzed (Cliff 1982, 1986), is a very complex deposit. It contains material from Late Preclassic phases 1, 2, and 3. All of the artifacts recovered from it to date are associated with Late Preclassic sherds.

CONTEXT

A typology of contexts that denotes the behavior associated with artifact disposal has been recognized at Cerros. Some deposits are assigned a contextual designation on the basis of associated features and artifacts. These include cache, burial, habitation debris, pit fill, construction fill with rubble, construction fill without rubble, floor fill, on floor, and termination ritual. Within other deposits the associations with features are absent or unclear, and the nature of the deposit is not well known. These include surface, humus, fall, humus/fall, slump, beach, and beach adjacent to Feature 1A. The variable degree to which each of these two groups of deposits is understood is manifest in the contextual designations. In the poorly understood second group, the contextual designation takes the name of the matrix or provenience, whereas the names in the first group suggest their functions or associations.

A distinction was made between the artifacts found on the beach within 10 meters of Feature 1A and those found farther away on the beach. This distinction was made because the artifact density within Feature 1A is the highest for the site, and in all probability a great many of the artifacts from the beach near Feature 1A have eroded out of this feature.

The surface and humus categories need no explanation. Fall refers to tumble or construction fill that is no longer *in situ*. It can include material originally in the construction fill or material added after the structure began to deteriorate. On the surface or within the humus or fall there may be material that is actually domestic debris or derived from some other context, which may not be readily apparent from associated finds or features. Slump refers to deteriorated plaster, sascab, or marl that has slipped out of place. It may also include material contained in the matrix when *in situ* or material introduced after the slumping began. Slump deposits closely resemble deposits resulting from termination ritual. Termination ritual is defined as the activities associated with the termination or abandonment of a structure or area. It often consisted of the intentional deposition and scattering about of decomposed limestone. This white earth often contains smashed jade, stone spheroids, stone disks, sherd disks, specular hematite mirror fragments, and smashed ceramic vessels, all of which are also associated with the termination activities. The marl frequently contains lenses of charcoal. Both slump and the matrix of termination ritual can be composed of plaster, marl, or sascab. The difference is that the matrix associated with termination ritual is intentionally deposited, whereas slump is the result of natural erosional agents. Termination ritual is discussed at greater length in chapter 3.

A similar approach to context was utilized in the analysis of the Cerros ceramics (Robertson-Freidel 1980). In this analysis six "sources," or contexts, were recognized: cache and burial, primary habitational debris, ritual interment of monumental architecture, secondary habitation debris, construction fill, and surface. Excavators evaluated the deposits on the basis of feature and artifact associations and the general nature of the deposit. Each of the six sources is composed of one or more of the depositional contexts previously outlined.

Contextual information for each piece is lacking from earlier studies with the exception of the analysis of artifacts from caches, tombs, and burials of Piedras Negras (Coe 1959). However, this work deals only with a select sample of artifacts. In a more recent treatment of Maya artifacts, Willey (1978) lists operation numbers and feature provenience for the vast majority of artifacts recovered from the site of Seibal. That information coupled with excavation data can provide a depositional context for each artifact.

2. THE GROUND STONE INDUSTRY

Six hundred and seventy-five artifacts of ground stone were recovered from Cerros. This industry includes all stone artifacts that were manufactured by the processes of pecking or grinding. Using the method adopted by Sheets (1978) in the analysis of the artifacts from Chalchuapa, items that exhibit polish are not included in this classification unless the polish is the result of use, as in the case of some manos and metates. Even though some artifacts, such as jade beads, exhibit polished surfaces and were doubtless pecked and ground, a different technology was involved to obtain the desired smoothness. For this reason, the intentionally polished artifacts are included in chapter 3.

The Cerros ground stone industry includes various raw materials. The raw material identifications of several of the Cerros ground stone specimens were made in 1980 by Art Endress and Norm McLeod, geology graduate students at Southern Methodist University. They helped to compile a raw material–type collection, against which the remaining specimens could be compared. Identifications were based on general appearance, scratch test, and HCl test.

The most frequently used raw material was limestone. Limestone is soft relative to the other raw materials, yet it grades from soft to hard and can easily be shaped by pecking and grinding. Items of dolomite, or dolomitic limestone, are generally somewhat harder than those of limestone.

Fossilized coral is harder than limestone or dolomite and was selected for use as manos and metates, probably because of the porosity of the coral chunks, which made the stones self-roughening, as new holes or channels were constantly exposed as the piece wore down. Marble is also relatively hard but tends to become slick or smooth with use.

Quartzite, harder than the above-mentioned materials, was the most commonly used material for manos and metates. The Cerros quartzite is very granular with numerous crystals visible on the artifact surfaces. Its granular, crystalline nature is particularly evident on the broken faces. Willey (1978) in rediscussing the artifacts from Altar de Sacrificios (1972) remarks that many ground stone pieces recovered from Altar de Sacrificios were initially identified as "crystalline limestone" but were later recognized as quartzite. Many Cerros quartzite specimens met the description of the Altar de Sacrificios specimens initially identified as crystalline limestone.

Volcanic stones used at Cerros include vesicular andesite, rhyolite, and pumice. The availability of these ground stone raw materials and their relationship to trade is discussed in chapter 8.

ARTIFACT FORM:	Mano	
SUBFORM:	Plano-convex and oval (Fig. 6b, f, g)	
FREQUENCY:		33
MATERIAL:	Quartzite	20
	Fossil coral	4
	Marble	4
	Dolomite	3
	Limestone	1
	Chert	1
DATING:	Late Preclassic	17
	Early Classic	2
	Late Postclassic	9
	Unknown	5
CONTEXT:	Construction fill with rubble	6
	Beach	5
	Surface	5
	Humus/fall	5
	Domestic debris	4
	In floor	2
	Pit fill	2
	Humus	1
	Termination ritual	1
	Burial	2

COMMENT: The most common cross-sectional subforms of the manos from Cerros are oval to plano-convex in section. These two varieties are not distinct but intergrade with each other. The defining criteria and separation are subjective. If the curvature of the dorsal and ventral surfaces, both of which often show use polish, is approximately the same, then the piece is referred to as oval (Fig. 6b); however, if one surface

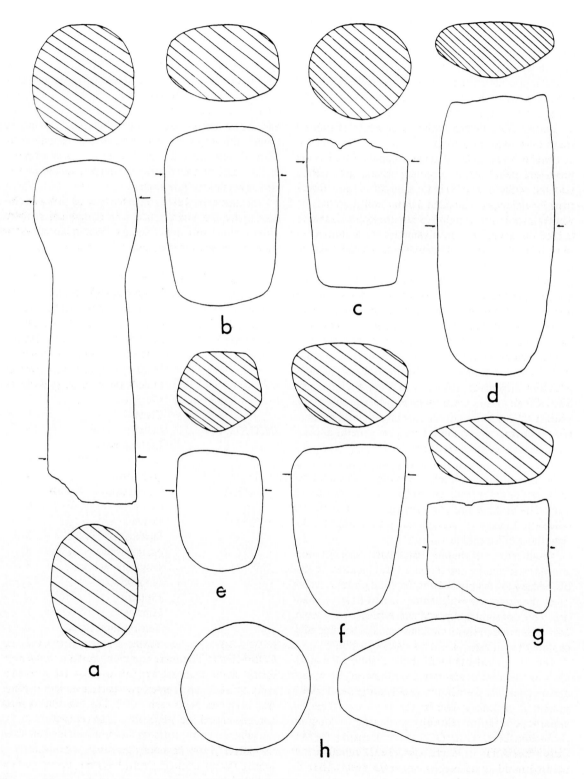

Figure 6. Mano outlines and cross-sections. a, h, overhang; b, oval; c, circular; d, triangular; e, pentagonal; f, g, plano-convex.

shows a noticeably greater degree of curvature than the other, it is classified as plano-convex (Fig. 6f, g). Usually, the "plano" ventral surface is also somewhat convex but much less than the dorsal surface.

Both oval and plano-convex forms have sides that taper toward the ends. The ends vary from flat to slightly rounded to rounded and are usually rough compared to the working surfaces, which often exhibit sheen from use.

SF-956 is unusual in that it is the only whole mano recovered from Cerros. It is truly plano-convex in section in that the "plano" surface is very flat. It is of pink marble and appears to have been a river cobble. Its working surface is unusual in that it is quite smooth except for occasional scratch marks, but shows no signs of pecking or any other attempt to roughen or sharpen the working face. Its flatness and extreme smoothness suggest that it might not have been used as a grinder or mano in conjunction with a metate; it may have functioned as a plaster polisher. Specimens SF-1050, SF-1095 and SF-1350, all composed of marble and very flat and fairly smooth, may have served a similar function.

ARTIFACT FORM:	Mano	
SUBFORM:	Circular (Fig. 6a, c)	
FREQUENCY:		13
MATERIAL:	Dolomite	5
	Andesite	3
	Limestone	2
	Chert	1
	Quartzite	1
	Fossil coral	1
DATING:	Late Preclassic	4
	Early Classic	3
	Late Postclassic	4
	Unknown	2
CONTEXT:	Humus/fall	3
	Humus	2
	Construction fill with rubble	2
	Construction fill without rubble	1
	Surface	1
	Beach near Feature 1A	1
	Beach	1
	Pit fill	1
	Fall	1

COMMENT: Four of the specimens, SF-559, SF-1013, SF-1032, and SF-1714, are of the overhang variety (Fig. 6a). The ends of these specimens appear to

have extended over the edge of the metate during use. All of these overhang forms are of dolomite or limestone. SF-1013 and SF-1332 have midsections that are plano-convex to oval from use. Both have a bulbous end, which is circular in section. Both pieces taper slightly toward slightly rounded ends. In all likelihood, they were originally circular in section, with everything but the ends or "overhang" portion being ground down to a plano-convex or oval shape. Items SF-1013 and SF-1332 are broken but are approximately half complete. SF-559 appears to be an end portion of a similarly shaped mano (Fig. 6h). These manos must have been used on a metate that was flat in at least the dimension across which the mano lay.

SF-1714 is also an overhang variety, but of a different nature. This broken mano is circular in section and expands in diameter toward its flattened end. This wear pattern suggests that this mano could have been used with more lateral shifting than were other overhang forms, since its pronounced bulbous ends would permit more lateral movement. This mano is extremely similar to S-30, a mano fragment from the site of Seibal (Willey 1978: 76). All of the overhang forms in the Cerros collection were listed as circular in cross-section even though their working portions were oval to plano-convex.

ARTIFACT FORM:	Mano	
SUBFORM:	Rectangular	
FREQUENCY:		7
MATERIAL:	Quartzite	3
	Limestone	2
	Dolomite	2
DATING:	Early Classic	3
	Late Postclassic	3
	Unknown	1
CONTEXT:	Surface	2
	Humus/fall	2
	Humus	1
	Fall	1
	Unknown	1

COMMENT: Those manos that are rectangular in section are also rectangular in plan. One surface of SF-214 appears to have been used as a small grinding basin. SF-1377 appears to have been used as a grinder after portions had broken off. No rectangular manos were recovered from Late Preclassic contexts.

ARTIFACT FORM:	Mano	
SUBFORM:	Triangular (Fig. 6d)	
FREQUENCY:		1

MATERIAL: Marble
DATING: Late Preclassic
CONTEXT: Domestic debris
COMMENT: SF-95 is made of a rose-colored marble. Its one whole end is rounded and its sides taper toward the ends. It is approximately 80% complete. All three surfaces show signs of use.

ARTIFACT FORM: Mano
SUBFORM: Pentagonal (Fig. 6e)
FREQUENCY: 1
MATERIAL: Limestone
DATING: Unknown, although a fair amount of Late Postclassic debris was observed in the area of this find
CONTEXT: Beach
COMMENT: The piece is heavily weathered and appears water rolled. Its end is rounded.

SUMMARY: Manos
MATERIAL: Total of all subforms
            Quartzite   27
            Dolomite   11
            Limestone   7
            Fossil coral   5
            Marble   5
            Andesite   3
            Chert   2

Three manos from the Cerros collection, SF-378, SF-807, and SF-1448, are of vesicular andesite, a volcanic stone not available in the vicinity of Cerros. The nearest source of this stone is the highlands of Guatemala and El Salvador (Sidrys and Andresen 1976). None of these volcanic specimens are of Late Preclassic date and all are circular in cross-section.

All of the quartzite manos possess natural pits where crystals have detached. Like the vesicular bubbles in volcanic stone, these pits make the quartzite self-roughening.

The chert, limestone, and dolomite manos show signs of having been pecked. This would be necessary to keep them rough. The chert manos are relatively hard, whereas the limestone and dolomite specimens are soft.

Fossil coral manos are fairly hard and did not need to be pecked to maintain abrasiveness, as channels between the polyp colonies were constantly exposed as the piece was worn down.

Tables 1 and 2 show a comparison of raw material percentages between manos and metates.

TABLE 1

Mano and Metate Raw
Material Percentages

Material	% of Metates	% of Manos
Quartzite	71.4	45.0
Dolomite	14.4	18.3
Fossil coral	2.9	18.3
Rhyolite	2.9	0.0
Andesite	2.9	5.0
Chert	0.0	3.3
Limestone	1.4	11.7
Marble	1.4	8.3
Pegmatite	1.4	0.0
Unknown	1.4	0.0

TABLE 2

Mano and Metate Raw Material
Percentages Condensed

Material	% of Metates	% of Manos
Quartzite	71.4	45.0
All limestone	20.0	46.6
Rhyolite	2.9	0.0
Andesite	2.9	5.0
Chert	0.0	3.3
Pegmatite	1.4	0.0
Unknown	1.4	0.0

DATING: Late Preclassic   23
           Early Classic   10
           Late Postclassic   17
           Unknown   10
CONTEXT: Humus/fall   12
           Surface   9
           Construction fill with rubble   9
           Beach near Feature 1A   7
           Domestic debris   6
           Humus   4
           Pit fill   3
           Construction fill without rubble   1
           Fall   2
           In floor   2
           Burial   2
           Termination ritual   1
           Beach   1
           Unknown   1

As can be seen from the above list, the manos from Cerros came from a wide range of depositional contexts. One can expect to find broken manos in deposits of domestic debris and pit fill (trash pits). Those contexts listed as surface accumulation, humus, and humus/fall, although not associated with any preserved floors or household features, are more than likely domestic debris as well. Many mano and metate fragments came from within the rubble construction fill of many of the mounds and plazas. These manos were broken and some showed signs of reuse. It does not appear that these manos were deposited within the mounds as a result of domestic trash being dumped in with the rubble, because of a paucity of other kinds of domestic debris, such as broken pottery, within the rubble fill. The inclusion of only ground stone tool fragments in the construction fill without other domestic debris was unexpected. It would appear that broken manos and metates were selected out of domestic debris to be included in construction fill, possibly as votive offerings from the laborers who constructed the mounds and plazas.

Table 3 shows a comparison of percentages of the contexts that yielded the Cerros manos and metates.

TABLE 3

Mano and Metate Context Percentages

Context	% of Metates	% of Manos
Humus/fall, humus, surface, fall	58.6	45.0
Construction fill with rubble	15.7	15.0
Domestic debris	11.5	10.0
Beach	5.7	1.7
Beach near Feature 1A	1.4	11.7
Termination ritual	1.4	1.7
Cache	1.4	0.0
Pit fill	1.4	5.0
Unknown	1.4	1.7
Burial	1.4	3.3
In floor	0.0	3.3
Construction fill without rubble	0.0	1.7

ARTIFACT FORM: Metate (Fig. 7)
SUBFORM: Basin
FREQUENCY: 57
MATERIAL:
Quartzite	47
Dolomite	4
Rhyolite	2
Fossil coral	1
Limestone	1
Pegmatite	1
Unknown	1

DATING:
Late Preclassic	22
Early Classic	16
Late Postclassic	9
Unknown	10

CONTEXT:
Humus/fall	12
Construction fill with rubble	10
Domestic debris	7
Surface	7
Humus	6
Fall	5
Beach near Feature 1A	4
Beach	2
Burial	1
Cache	1
Pit fill	1
Unknown	1

COMMENT: The basin-shaped metate is also known as the turtle back metate and is common throughout the Maya Lowlands (Willey 1978). Attempts to subdivide basin metates on the basis of size, outline, and rim form (Willey 1972; Willey et al. 1965) have been rejected because of the intergradation among the forms (Willey 1978).

One whole basin metate, SF-1762, was recovered. It is made of dolomite and probably dates to the Early Classic. Its basin can be described as a trough, since both sides are fairly steep; however, neither end is open. Its back is rough and only crudely shaped and would not have been recognized as a metate had it not been turned over, revealing its grinding surface.

Although the remainder of the Cerros metates are broken and can only be partially reconstructed as to form, the vast majority differ in several respects from the whole example, SF-1762. That specimen was made from considerably softer material than the other basin metates, even those that were also of dolomite. SF-1762 is the only specimen that exhibits a troughlike straight side basin. This is probably due to the softness of the stone. The remaining metates exhibit much shallower basins. Basin depth varies and is often difficult to assess, given the fragmentary condition of many of the finds. Some basins are as shallow as 1 cm.

SF-1903 is of dolomite and appears to have been rectangular in outline. At the one complete end is a 5-cm-wide flattened area at the edge of the basin. The remainder are either basin fragments with no rims present or are rims to which the basin extends with no surrounding flattened areas.

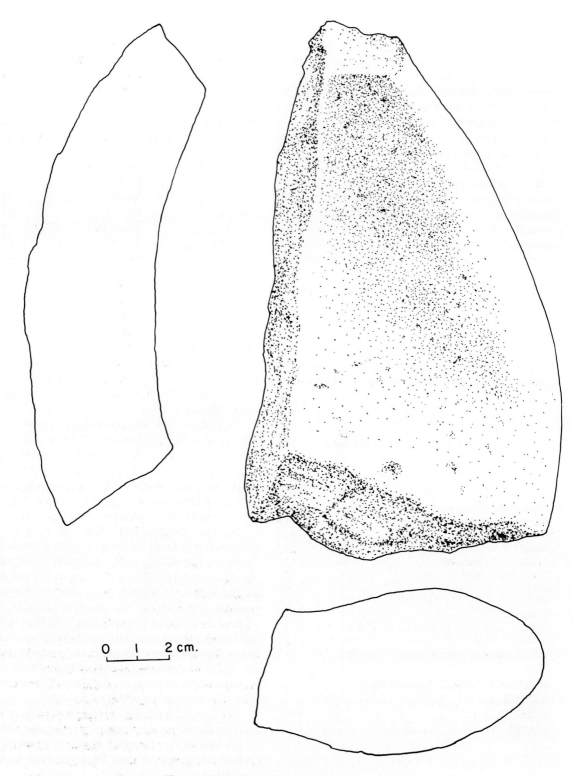

0 I   2 cm.

Figure 7. Basin metate fragment, SF-1770.

The majority of the Cerros basin specimens differ from the complete specimen in that they exhibit extensive working and shaping and in most cases smoothing on their backs, as opposed to the rough back of SF-1762.

Two fragments, SF-538 and SF-1208, are of particular interest in that they are quite narrow compared to the typical Maya metate. SF-538 consists of fossil coral and is 14 cm wide; SF-1208 is rhyolite and is 13 cm wide. Although both are incomplete specimens, both of these measurements are complete width dimensions. Given the nature of the basins, they could be used only in conjunction with a mano no longer than 11 cm.

Several metate fragments show signs of reuse. Thus, the pattern of disposal for these pieces may not be typical of broken metates. SF-368, SF-1613, SF-1867, and SF-1891 all show signs of reuse as pounders after the initial breakage occurred. Evidence of reuse consists of contusions and rounding on a projection or broken corner. SF-383 and SF-630 show signs of having been lightly reused as hand-held grinders. SF-1461, SF-1516, and SF-1760 were reused as grinders and pounders. SF-368 is of an unknown dense material and the other reused fragments are of quartzite. These pieces were no doubt selected because of their hardness.

ARTIFACT FORM:	Metate	
SUBFORM:	Slab	
FREQUENCY:		11
MATERIAL:	Dolomite	5
	Quartzite	3
	Fossil coral	1
	Marble	1
	Andesite	1
DATING:	Late Preclassic	4
	Early Classic	6
	Unknown	1
CONTEXT:	Humus/fall	4
	Fall	3
	Surface	1
	Humus	1
	Construction fill with rubble	1
	Domestic debris	1

COMMENT: Slab metates are defined by the presence of a grinding surface that is flat along at least one dimension. In other words, a grinding surface could be concave along one dimension and straight along another and still be considered a slab. None of the slab specimens are whole, and it is entirely possible that some or all of the fragments may actually have come from legged metates; therefore, the comparisons between the numbers of legged versus nonlegged slab forms are not necessarily valid or meaningful, but this division has been followed for the sake of description.

All of the slab metate fragments appear to have come from slabs that were straight along two dimensions. None were large enough to indicate the shape of the complete form.

SF-976 shows batter marks on a broken edge, which suggests its use as a pounder after breakage.

All of the working faces on the dolomite specimens show signs of pecking. No doubt this was done to maintain abrasiveness. The quartzite, fossil coral, and andesite specimens do not show signs of pecking, as the constant exposure of pits and channels as the surfaces wore down would keep them abrasive. The one marble fragment is smooth and exhibits numerous scratches and only light peck marks.

ARTIFACT FORM:	Metate	
SUBFORM:	Legged Slab	
FREQUENCY:		2
MATERIAL:	Andesite	1
	Dolomite	1
DATING:	Early Classic	1
	Late Postclassic	1
CONTEXT:	Surface	1
	Humus/fall	1

COMMENT: As stated in the comment section of the slab metates, fragments from legged metates may have been included in the category of slab metates because a particular fragment may not be from a leg area. Thus, the number of legged slabs may be underestimated and the number of slabs overestimated.

SF-623 is a leg from what was probably a tripod metate. It is composed of vesicular andesite. It is 16.5 cm from the leg base to the grinding surface, which is steeply slanted and shows sheen from use. The leg tapers toward the base. In horizontal cross-section the leg has a right angle corresponding to the corner of the metate. The outside of the leg is composed of two perpendicular planes, while the inside is convex or quarter round. This leg was found on the surface of the main plaza, Feature 2A, and is probably Late Postclassic in date, based on the amount of Late Postclassic surface sherds associated with it.

SF-1613 is a dolomite slab fragment with a single leg toward the corner of the piece. Its dorsal working face is flat. The ventral surface is convex with edges beveled toward this underside. The leg is rectangular in outline when viewed from the bottom and tapers toward the base. A groove extends along the side of the piece 1.5 cm down from the dorsal surface. Portions of the corner are broken away, but it appears that this groove once extended around the corner. The corner forms a right angle. The dorsal surface is regular and smoothed through use, but numerous solution pits can be observed on this face. The ventral face has been shaped by pecking and grinding. The complete length and width dimensions are unknown, but it is 5.6 cm from the base of the leg to the grinding surface.

SUMMARY:	Metates	
FREQUENCY:	Total of all subforms	70
MATERIAL:	Quartzite	50
	Dolomite	10
	Fossil coral	2
	Rhyolite	2
	Andesite	2
	Limestone	1
	Marble	1
	Pegmatite	1
	Unknown	1

Four metate fragments, SF-623 and SF-1578 (andesite), and SF-1208 and SF-1734 (rhyolite), are of raw materials that are not available in Belize (Sidrys and Andresen 1976). Only one of these, SF-1734, is from a Late Preclassic context. The rest are of an unknown or later date.

Tables 1 and 2 show a comparison of raw material percentages between manos and metates.

DATING:	Late Preclassic	26
	Early Classic	23
	Late Postclassic	10
	Unknown	11
CONTEXT:	Humus/fall	17
	Construction fill with rubble	11
	Surface	9
	Domestic debris	8
	Fall	8
	Humus	7
	Beach near Feature 1A	4
	Beach	2
	Burial	1
	Cache	1
	Pit fill	1
	Unknown	1

Like the manos, the metates from Cerros come from a wide variety of contexts. Table 3 shows a comparison in percentages of the contexts from which the Cerros manos and metates have been recovered.

Like the mano fragments, many of the Cerros metate fragments came from the dry laid rubble construction fill of the mounds and plazas. This fill did not contain other kinds, or the full range of, domestic debris. It appears that broken metates, like manos, were selected from domestic debris to be included in the construction fill of monumental architecture, possibly as votive offerings from the laborers who constructed the mounds.

GROUND STONE FRAGMENTS

FREQUENCY:		8
MATERIAL:	Quartzite	5
	Dolomite	1
	Rhyolite	1
	Unknown	1
DATING:	Late Preclassic	4
	Early Classic	1
	Unknown	3
CONTEXT:	Domestic debris	2
	Construction fill with rubble	1
	Construction fill without rubble	1
	Humus/fall	1
	Beach near Feature 1A	1
	In floor	1
	Unknown	1

COMMENT: The quartzite pieces are of the same raw material as many of the manos and metates. Some pieces show small areas of polish from use but are so fragmentary that an assessment of artifact form cannot be made. Because of similarities in raw material used to make manos and metates, the presence of use-polished surfaces and similarities in the contexts of these pieces and the contexts of manos and metates, these specimens most likely represent mano and/or metate fragments.

ARTIFACT FORM:	Armature (Figs. 8, 9, and 10a)	
FREQUENCY:	19 (at least 20 others were not cataloged)	
SUBFORM:	Oval	11
	Rectangular	5
	Circular	2
	Square	1

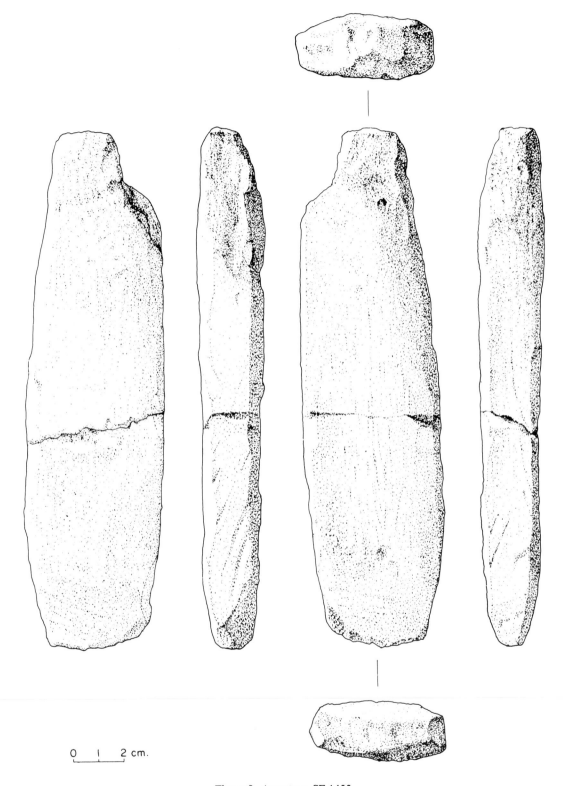

Figure 8. Armature, SF-1455.

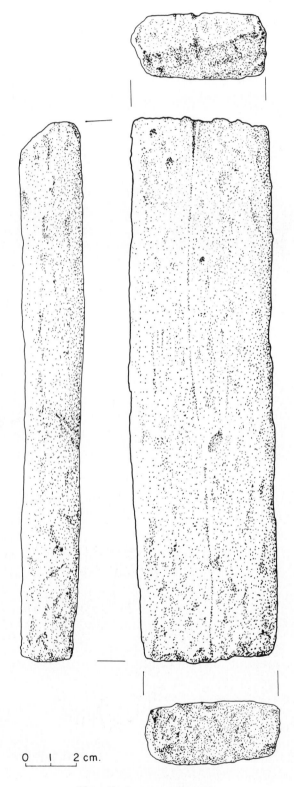

0   I   2 cm.

Figure 9. Armature, SF-1454.

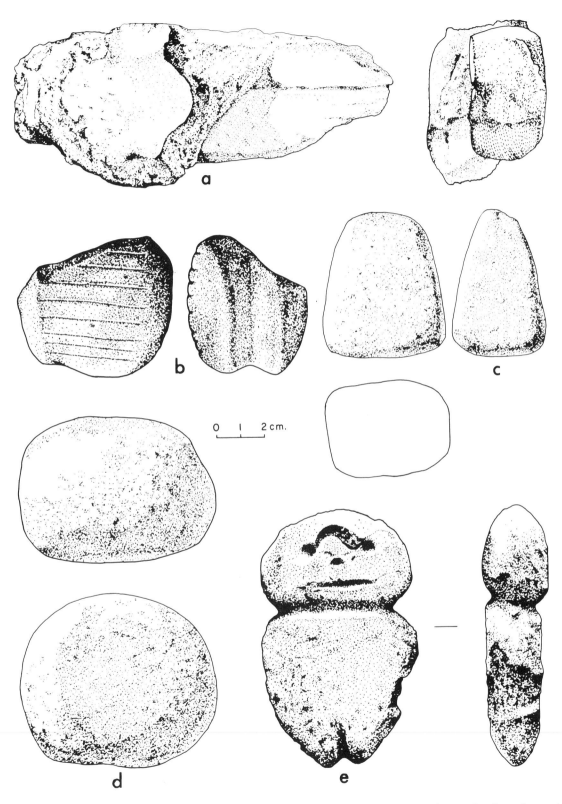

Figure 10. Ground stone artifacts. a, armature with attached plaster; b, bark beater; c, pestle-pounder; d, anvil-pounder; e, figurine.

MATERIAL: Limestone
DATING: Late Preclassic
CONTEXT: Terminal ritual   11
                   Fall   5
                   Humus   2
                   Humus/fall   1

COMMENT: Artifacts of this type have not been reported from other sites, although Eaton (personal communication 1983) found over two hundred similar Late Classic specimens at the site of Chicanna. They are elongated objects of stone that were intentionally shaped by pecking yet show no signs of use. Only two of the Cerros armatures are whole. One, SF-1454, is 20.6 cm by 5.8 cm by 3.1 cm and is rectangular in plan and section. SF-1504 is 15.0 cm by 3.5 cm by 2.7 cm and is oval in section. Other finds have some dimensions that are complete; these are listed on the armature data form, Appendix B-4.

The quality of the limestone used to make the pieces ranges from soft and chalky to hard and dense. The rectangular forms tend to be of harder stone. Those that are circular in section tend to be the softest.

The quality of workmanship also varies. The rectangular specimens are carefully shaped, as opposed to the oval and circular ones, which are somewhat haphazard.

All of the specimens were recovered from Feature 29B, an 11-m-high structure within the settlement zone. Excavations at the summit revealed several painted plaster masks and earplug panels. Excavation produced evidence of termination ritual that included the partial tearing down of molded painted plaster masks and panels, the burning of ceremonial fires, the smashing of ceramic vessels, and the scattering about of much white marl.

Several of the cataloged specimens and most of those not cataloged were recovered from within or immediately above the white marl. One was retrieved from the base of the mound in some marl associated with an interior construction phase, which clearly shows the function of this artifact type. Adhering to, and wrapping partially around, SF-1729 (Fig. 10a), is a painted, molded chunk of plaster. These stones functioned as armatures for the low-relief plaster designs. No armature stones of this type have been found on any of the other three mounds at Cerros that are known to have plaster masks and panel designs. Eaton (personal communication 1983) notes that manolike armatures with red painted stucco adhering to them were recovered from Structure 2 at Chicanna.

Several pieces exhibit scoring lines that run the length of the piece (Figs. 9, 10a). These lines most likely aided in the adhesion of the plaster to the stone.

ARTIFACT FORM: Doughnut stones (Fig. 11a)
FREQUENCY: 27
MATERIAL: Limestone
DATING: Late Preclassic   23
                   Unknown   4
CONTEXT: Construction fill with
                       rubble   9
                   Termination ritual 6
                   Domestic debris   5
                   Fall   2
                   Beach   2
                   Humus/fall   1
                   Pit fill   1
                   Unknown   1
METRIC DATA:

	Range	Mean	Standard Deviation
Diameter	12.4 cm to 6.3 cm	9.5	1.69
Hole diameter	1.6 to 0.5	1.1	0.29
Thickness	4.0 to 1.9	3.0	0.58

COMMENT: The terms "doughnut stone" and "ring stone" have been used to describe a wide variety of biconically drilled, centrally perforated stones. Their occurrence is widespread in the Maya area (Dillon 1977; Hammond 1975; Kidder, Jennings, and Shook 1946; Longyear 1952; Phillips 1979; Ricketson and Ricketson 1937; Sheets 1979; Stone 1957; Willey 1972; Woodbury 1965; Woodbury and Trik 1953; Zier 1980). An examination of the metric variability of these stones seems to indicate that at least two distinct artifact types are represented. Type 1 specimens have a thickness that is close to their diameter. These relatively thick perforated stones often exhibit cogs, incisions, or other designs on their surfaces (Hummer 1983; Sheets 1979; Stone 1957; Willey 1972, 1978). Type 2 disks have a thickness that is generally less than one-half of their diameter. These two forms do not grade into each other in terms of diameter-to-thickness ratio. Within Type 2 there is considerable variation in the diameter of the central hole. This probably represents two distinct subtypes with distinct functional orientations.

For years Mayanists have speculated on the function of doughnut and ring stones. Suggestions include digging stick weights, maize shellers, counterweights for doors, banner holders, club heads, and spear shaft

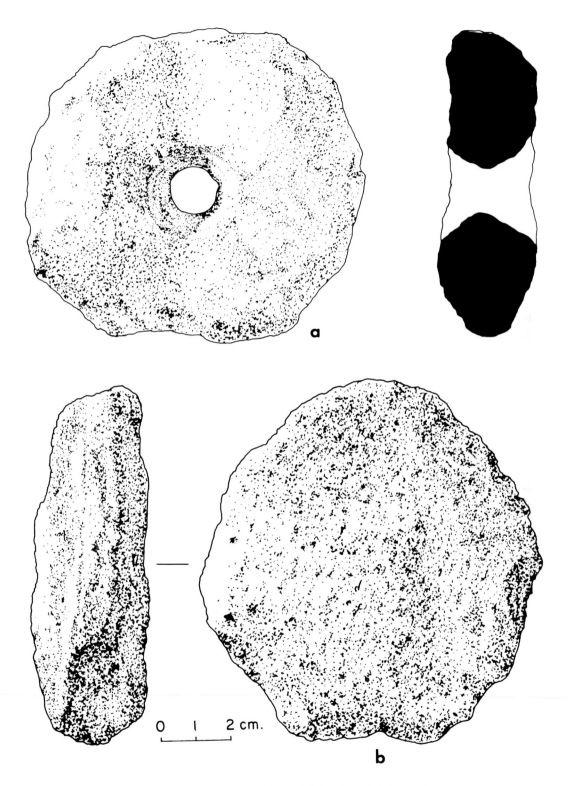

Figure 11. Doughnut stone and burned disk. a, SF-747; b, SF-1593.

weights (Kidder, Jennings, and Shook 1946; Sheets 1979; Willey 1972). This speculation has relied on suitability of form, as good contextual data and *in situ* doughnut stones were lacking.

More recently, two perforated stones, a Type 1 relatively thick cogged specimen and a relatively thin Type 2 plain one, were reported from the site of Cerén in El Salvador (Hummer 1983; Sheets 1979; Zier 1980, 1983). In the course of excavations at that site, the remains of a Classic period farmhouse and associated cornfield were preserved by volcanic ash from the eruption of a nearby volcano. Zier presents a case from this contextual information that the thin (Type 2) specimen recovered from the farmhouse functioned as a digging stick weight. It was found upright along a collapsed wall. Its upright position and casts near the hole indicate that the stone was on a wooden stick when the wall collapsed. The diameter of the central hole is 2.8 cm. This is considerably larger than most of the Cerros specimens, which have an average hole diameter of 1.1 cm. The thicker cogged specimen (Type 1) from Cerén was recovered in an area associated with pottery manufacture, and its function remains enigmatic (Hummer 1983).

All of the Cerros specimens are of the Type 2, relatively thin, form. The Cerros doughnut stones were roughly shaped by pecking; only one specimen shows any signs of smoothing. The central holes were biconically drilled to an approximately equal depth from each side. The diameter of the drill cone is often twice the diameter of the actual opening.

Five of the Cerros specimens come from deposits of domestic debris originating from the dispersed settlement zone (Fig. 2) and Feature 1A, the residential zone underlying the main plaza (Fig. 3). Because the Cerros perforated stones have significantly smaller central holes than the Cerén example, they probably did not function as digging stick weights. A possible function is net weights, as lighter ceramic net weights for throw nets are often found in association with the doughnut stones recovered from these domestic deposits.

Nine of the Cerros doughnut stones have been recovered from dry-laid construction fill. As was the case with the construction fill deposits from which mano and metate fragments were recovered, the construction fill from which doughnut stones were recovered showed a general lack of other kinds of domestic debris, especially sherds. Doughnut stones from construction fill, whatever their original function, probably were deposited by laborers into construction fill as votive offerings.

Six of the Cerros doughnut stones come from a deposit, clearly not of domestic origin, on Structure 5C. These deposits of white marl are interpreted as the remains of a termination ritual (Garber 1983).

Structure 5C is a 6-m-high, two-tiered structure. Two construction phases occurred on this structure, both of which date to the Late Preclassic period. Both phases exhibit the remains of molded and painted plaster masks and panels. The earlier construction phase, 5C-2nd, is extremely well preserved and was intentionally buried to be preserved (Freidel 1977, 1986).

The final phase is poorly preserved, partly because of its proximity to the surface and partly because at the time of abandonment, the termination ritual included the smashing of masks and panels and the deposition of some of the molded plaster chunks in holes along the base of the first tier. The remainder of the termination ritual consisted of spreading quantities of white marl on and about the structure, the burning of several ceremonial fires, and the smashing of several vessels on and about the structure.

From this mixture of white marl, smashed vessels, chunks of molded painted plaster, and charcoal lenses, many of the Cerros doughnut stones have been recovered. This is not a domestic deposit, yet these doughnut stones are virtually indistinguishable from those recovered from domestic debris.

Because the doughnut stones from this deposit are associated with the removal of plaster façading, and one, SF-714, was recovered from one of the pits into which some of the molded chunks were deposited, it is hypothesized that these stones might have functioned as architectural decorations or armatures for molded pieces. The central hole would facilitate attachment to the mound with a wooden peg.

Twelve of the twenty-seven doughnut stones from Cerros are completely or partially discolored from burning. There is a very high correspondence between those that are burned and those that were found in association with monumental architecture. Within the white marl are numerous extensive charcoal lenses that are interpreted as the remains of ceremonial fires. Perhaps this is how the doughnut stones were discolored. It is interesting to note that SF-714, recovered from one of the pits where plaster chunks were deposited, shows no evidence of burning. This, most likely, is because the plaster chunks and doughnut stone were removed and buried in the hole prior to the scattering of white marl and ignition of the fires.

The Temple of the Seven Dolls at the site of Dzibilchaltún in Yucatán, Mexico, exhibits a frieze consisting of stone armatures coated with molded plaster (Andrews 1959: 101). Several doughnut stones are incorporated into the designs of the preserved portions of that temple frieze.

At the site of Palenque, in Chiapas, Mexico, are several stucco friezes, one of which displays doughnutlike elements in the surrounding border (Digby 1964, pl. 1).

Thus, it appears that some of the doughnut stones from Cerros functioned in a subsistence fashion and were eventually discarded with domestic debris, while others functioned in an ornamental fashion, as did those from Dzibilchaltún and Palenque.

As stated earlier, those associated with domestic debris and those associated with monumental architecture are indistinguishable. Perhaps the Maya who provided the labor for the construction of the mounds provided their utilitarian items as votives, which were incorporated into the religious symbolism of the architectural decorations.

The use of a domestic item as an element in iconographic religious designs represents a symbolic link between that which is ordinary or profane and that which is revered or sacred.

Maya hieroglyphic and iconographic studies have revealed a close association and affinity among the representations for corn, water, and jade (Thompson 1950, 1954). The glyphs for each are closely related and sometimes interchangeable. The Chilam Balam of Chumayel refers to the creation and birth of corn. In that allegorical account, the word for jade is sometimes substituted for that for corn (Roys 1933).

Thompson (1954: 191) remarks that, because both water and jade are precious and green, the Maya used a jade bead to signify water. The symbol for water and jade may also be interpreted as a doughnut stone. In the Codex Dresden, there is a serpent decorated with what Thompson calls "jade disks" (1950, fig. 14). The doughnut stones in the frieze on the Temple of the Seven Dolls at Dzibilchaltún also decorated the bodies of serpents or snakes. Serpents or snakes of this kind have been viewed as celestial rain monsters and, as expected, show associations with signs for the sky (Thompson 1950, 1954). It seems evident that the symbolism in Maya glyphic and iconographic representations is extremely complex in that any one sign may have one or several related meanings.

The use of doughnut stones as elements in iconographic decorations during the Late Preclassic period at Cerros is important in that its use as a symbolic element, which during the Classic period was incorporated into several glyphs, is actually functioning as a protoglyph.

The use of domestic items as elements in iconographic representations on monumental architecture is significant not only because it can aid in the decipherment of the multisymbolic nature of some Maya glyphs, but also because it represents a link between the sacred and the profane of Maya society. The inclusion of a domestic, utilitarian, profane item such as a digging stick weight or net weight, into the design of a monumental structure presents to the lower levels of Maya society an observable, understandable part of sacred iconographic representations, frequently associated with the elite.

ARTIFACT FORM:	Abrader (Fig. 12f)	
FREQUENCY:		15
MATERIAL:	Pumice	13
	Sandstone	2
DATING:	Late Preclassic	9
	Late Postclassic	3
	Unknown	3
CONTEXT:	Domestic debris	8
	Fall	2
	Construction fill with rubble	2
	Beach near Feature 1A	1
	Humus/fall	1
	In floor	1

SUBFORM: Several abrader subforms were recognized, but because each piece was distinct, no attempt was made to create formal groupings.

SF-76 is a pumice fragment plano-convex in section. This cross-section very closely resembles many of the Cerros manos in shape and size. This piece is broken and shows no definite sign of reuse after the breakage occurred.

SF-814 is triangular in outline and oval in section. Bisecting the piece at the apex is a groove 4.0 cm long, 2.0 cm wide and 1.0 cm deep. The groove is V-shaped in section. The groove may have resulted from use of the piece as a sharpener for wood or bone spikes.

SF-969 is oblong ovate in outline and plano-convex in section. The ends are rounded. One surface exhibits seven striations, which cross the piece diagonally. They vary in width from 0.1 cm to 0.5 cm., in length from 1.5

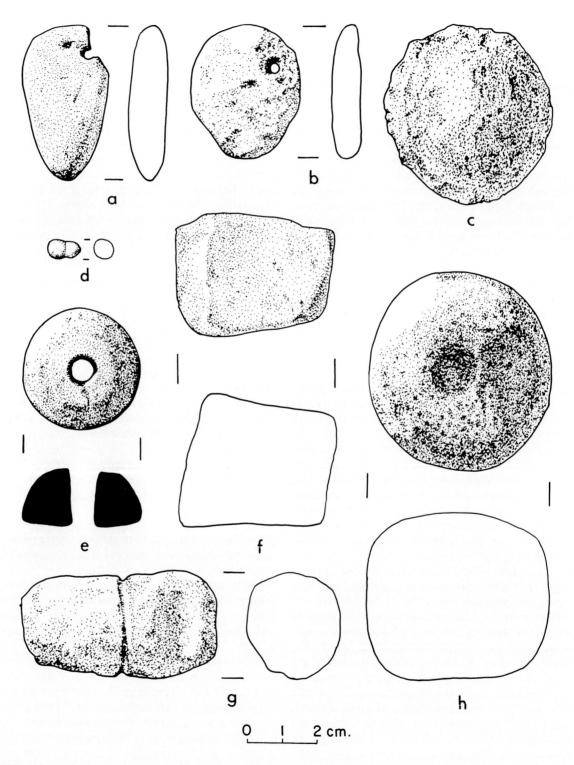

Figure 12. Ground stone artifacts. a, b, pendants; c, spheroid; d, g, girdled stones; e, spindle whorl; f, abrader; h, stone with hemispherical depression.

cm to 5.5 cm, and are 0.3 cm deep. They are U-shaped in section and may have been sharpening grooves for pointed objects.

SF-1051 is ovoid in plan view and plano-convex section. All surfaces are rounded.

SF-229 is a pumice piece that exhibits an irregular shape and shows only one smoothed surface. It appears to be broken.

SF-1195 is a broken pumice piece that had one convex smoothed face. The others are irregular and broken.

SF-1236 is an irregular pumice piece that shows some rounding and smoothing of broken faces. It also has a slice across one face. This slice is 3.3 cm long, 0.5 cm wide, and 0.3 cm deep. This may be a sharpening groove.

SF-1275 is a fragment of what might have been a basin metate; however, all the surfaces have been smoothed from reuse except one, which is concave.

SF-1860 is a complete pumice specimen. It is oval in plan view and rectangular in section. All surfaces show rounding.

SF-1932 is a broken pumice piece that exhibits one face that is smoothed from use. The opposite face is rounded and irregular and shows no signs of reuse after breakage.

SF-1422 and SF-1145 are both made of pumice and are egg-shaped. SF-1422 is somewhat flattened and has five small cut marks on one end. These may be string or blade cuts.

SF-68 is a broken piece of very fine-grained sandstone. The two working faces are opposite each other and are slightly concave and smoothed from use (Fig. 12f).

SF-66 is also of very fine-grained sandstone. It is broken, possibly fire-cracked, so complete dimensions could not be taken. Its two smoothed faces are perpendicular to each other.

COMMENT: Pumice was not formed in the Lowlands; however, it does float in from highland source areas and is common on the Belize coast and on the cays (Graham 1987; Phillips 1979). Pumice could have been imported, but the utilization of pieces that have washed in from other source areas is supported in that all pieces show rounding of edges, some due to use but others probably from water rolling and weathering.

These artifacts have been referred to as abraders because of their suitability for this purpose, particularly those made of pumice.

ARTIFACT FORM:	Stone disk (Fig. 11b)	
FREQUENCY:		101
MATERIAL:	Limestone	
DATING:	Late Preclassic	91
	Early Classic	4
	Late Postclassic	5
	Unknown	1
CONTEXT:	Termination ritual	73
	Fall	7
	Humus/fall	7
	Domestic debris	6
	Construction fill with	
	rubble	5
	Surface	1
	Pit fill	1
	In floor	1

COMMENT: The stone disks range from 20.2 cm to 6.9 cm in diameter. They also show considerable variability with respect to degree of shaping. Most are crudely shaped by pecking, although some show signs of careful shaping and grinding.

Limestone disks occur throughout the Maya area, and numerous functions for them have been proposed. For years they have been referred to as pot-lids (Proskouriakoff 1962; Ricketson and Ricketson 1937; Willey 1972). Very few have been recovered in association with pots; thus this function seems unreasonable. Thompson (1963), drawing a parallel to a ceremony in the ethnographic present using tortillas, similarly shaped objects, suggests that some might relate to curing. More recently, several investigators have compiled a convincing body of evidence, both archaeological and ethnological, to support the proposition that these disks functioned as end plugs for beehives (Andresen 1986; Freidel 1976; Phillips 1979; Sidrys 1976).

The Cerros specimens are very similar to those recovered from Cozumel (Phillips 1979) and Chan Chen in Northern Belize (Sidrys and Andresen 1976); however, based on an analysis of context, the Cerros specimens functioned in quite a different manner (Garber 1981,1986; Walker 1986).

Of all the stone disks, 76.2% were burned. The burned disks are quite uniform in size. Table 4 gives the means and standard deviations of the diameters and thicknesses for burned and unburned disks. This table shows that unburned specimens not only are more uniform in size, but also tend to be smaller in diameter. The burned specimens are a dark- to medium-gray color and show no signs of having been

TABLE 4

Metric Data for Stone Disks

	Burned		Unburned	
	Diameter	Thickness	Diameter	Thickness
Range	6.9–15.9	2.1–6.4	4.8–20.2	1.5–7.0
Mean	9.8	3.9	12.8	4.2
Standard deviation	1.3	0.7	4.4	1.6

shaped by grinding, as the surfaces are regular in shape yet rough, pocked, and pecked.

Nine of the seventy-seven burned specimens came from fill directly overlying the marl deposits that characterize the termination ritual. The ritual consists of the removal of plaster façading, the smashing of vessels and jade, the burning of ceremonial fires, and the scattering about of white marl.

The great majority of the burned disks come from the white marl associated with the termination of Structure 2A-Sub.4-1st. Structure 2A-Sub.4-1st is a two-terraced platform, 2.3 m high, with an outset staircase and apron moldings. The structure is fronted by a plaza and is associated with some of the residential loci of Feature 1A (Cliff 1982, 1986). Structure 2A-Sub.4-1st was abandoned with much ceremony prior to being buried by Feature 2A, the main plaza. Associated with the burned disks from this deposit are numerous lenses of smashed vessels and charcoal.

Because such a high percentage of the disks from certain contexts are burned, burning might have something to do with the primary function of these artifacts; in fact, they may have been burned during use and not after disposal. A possible function for these disks might be rests for cooking pots or censer supports. Within this deposit are the remains of numerous "beer mugs," which Robertson-Freidel (1980) has suggested were used as drinking utensils. Numerous sherd disk lids have also been recovered from this deposit, which could have kept warm or dust free whatever was put into the drinking mugs. The association of disks, beer mugs, lids, and burning is indirect evidence that the stone disks functioned as pot rests.

The suggestion that the disks functioned as pot rests in association with termination ritual is further supported by the presence of five stone subspheroids, or fat disks, from a deposit on Structure 4B. These burned stones were found arranged in a semicircle on the floor of the 4B superstructure (Fig. 13). Much charcoal was recovered from immediately above this cluster of stones. Their configuration and the presence of a lot of charcoal support the proposed pot rest function.

Within this deposit were several smashed censers and fragments of copal incense (Walker 1986). Subspherical stones and stone disks, as well as spheroids (see comments on spheroids), are found within the matrix of termination activities conducted on monumental architecture. These stones do not occur in domestic debris; thus, it can be said that these kinds of stones, more than likely, were utilized as pot rests as a part of abandonment or termination ritual. Identification of the burned, cooked, or boiled contents of the vessels is opened to speculation.

Twenty-four of the Cerros stone disks were not burned. The unburned disks show greater variability in size and fineness of manufacture than do the burned specimens. Some show signs of having been carefully ground, whereas others are only crudely flaked and pecked. It is possible that some of the cruder specimens were actually building stones with a discoid rather than rectangular shape. The majority of the unburned disks, however, are too finely made to be construction stones.

SF-1623, SF-1726, SF-1800, and SF-1812 were all associated with the Structure 50 group, which has been identified as a Late Preclassic ball court (Scarborough 1980; Scarborough et al. 1982). These stones show careful shaping and may have functioned as portable ball court markers. Finely carved stones called *hachas,* or thin stone heads, are associated with the Classic period ball courts of Vera Cruz (Proskouriakoff 1954). See the stone disk data forms for the dimensions of the Structure 50 group stone disks. The function of the stone disks associated with the other structures is not readily apparent. This discussion clearly illustrates the importance of context in an analysis of Maya artifacts.

ARTIFACT FORM:	Stone spheroid (Fig. 12c)	
FREQUENCY:		357
MATERIAL:	Limestone	
DATING:	Late Preclassic	349
	Early Classic	4
	Late Postclassic	1
	Unknown	3
CONTEXT:	Termination ritual	336
	Construction fill with rubble	10
	Humus/fall	4

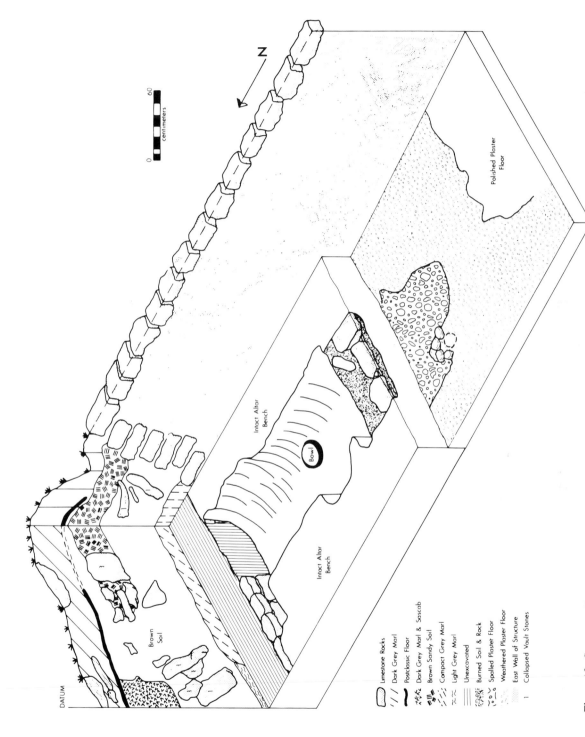

DATUM

Brown Soil

Bowl

Intact Altar Bench

Intact Altar Bench

Polished Plaster Floor

N

0
60
centimeters

Limestone Rocks
Dark Grey Marl
Postclassic Floor
Dark Grey Marl & Sascab
Brown Sandy Soil
Compact Grey Marl
Light Grey Marl
Unexcavated
Burned Soil & Rock
Spalled Plaster Floor
Weathered Plaster Floor
East Wall of Structure
1 Collapsed Vault Stones

Figure 13. Structure 4B superstructure.

Humus	4
In floor	2
Fall	1

METRIC DATA:

Diameter range: 3.1 cm
to 6.3 cm
Mean diameter: 3.8 cm

COMMENT: The most striking feature of these artifacts is their uniformity in size, shape, and appearance. Some are slightly flattened. Ninety-eight percent are burned. The burned specimens are discolored and charred to the same degree as the burned disks and both have the same surface appearance. Even though some of the spheroids are slightly flattened, the spheroids and disks represent two distinct typological forms. The only exceptions are the five flattened spheroids recovered from the 4B superstructure floor (see comments on stone disks). These specimens date to the Early Classic and consequently are temporally distinct from the vast majority of the stone disks and spheroids. In size, they fall within the range of stone disks, but in shape they more closely resemble spheroids.

Unfortunately, those stones from the 4B superstructure were not brought in from the field or cataloged at that time, since they were not recognized as artifacts. As a result, only approximate measurements and field descriptions are available. All were about 8.0 cm to 10.0 cm in diameter and all apparently were discolored from fire. Fortunately, they were mapped and photographed in place, and it is from the configuration of these stones that the function of the disks and spheroids has been assumed. Because the burned stones from the ritual deposit on Structure 4B were situated in such a manner as to accommodate a vessel, it is reasonable to assume that similar stones no longer in their functional position in a ritual deposit once performed in a similar fashion.

The great majority of the burned disks and spheroids come from a deposit resulting from termination ritual on Structure 2A-Sub.4-1st. The disks, spheroids, or large spheroids (from 4B) may each accommodate a different vessel form. The disks and spheroids from Structure 2A-Sub.4-1st are of a Late Preclassic phase 2/3 transitional date (Robertson-Freidel 1980). The large spheroids from Structure 4B are Early Classic (Walker 1986). The change in vessel rest form suggests a change in the vessel types used in termination ritual.

In structures 3A, 3B, 5A, 5C, 6B, 10C, 18A, 50A, 50B, and 50D, burned spheroids appeared in small quantities totaling three or less, in stark contrast to the large numbers found on Structure 2A-Sub.4-1st. Here, too, they may signify a termination ritual, since they do not occur in domestic debris.

Unburned spheroids are found on or in Features 1A, 2A, and Structures 50D and 50C. The function of these finds is unclear, although those few from 2A-Sub.-1 were found with the burned ones and probably represent unused specimens.

ARTIFACT FORM: Bark beater (Fig. 10b)
FREQUENCY:		2
MATERIAL:	Hard limestone	
DATING:	Unknown	2
CONTEXT:	Beach near Feature 1A	1
	Beach	1

COMMENT: When whole, SF-1018 was probably rectangular with rounded corners. The side and end are slightly convex and contain the hafting groove. This groove, shallow U in section, varies from 1.1 to 1.7 cm wide and is 0.3 to 0.4 cm deep. Both faces are striated. The striations do not seem to vary significantly from side to side. The cut grooves are straight to slightly curved and vary from 0.1 cm to 0.2 cm wide and are 0.3 cm to 0.4 cm apart, from center to center. The flat area between grooves averages 0.2 cm. The piece shows possible signs of reuse as a hammer stone, as numerous batter marks are present on the corner area of one face.

SF-1447 was also probably rectangular with rounded corners and ends (Fig. 10b). The side is slightly convex. Both faces, when viewed from the end, are convex. A hafting groove is present on the side and extends around the corner to the end. This groove is 1.5 cm to 1.7 cm wide and is 0.2 cm to 0.4 cm deep. This groove is a shallow U in section. One of the surfaces is plain, the other is striated. These striations are straight. The grooves vary from 0.1 cm to 0.2 cm in width and are 0.1 cm deep. From center to center the grooves vary from 0.6 cm to 0.4 cm apart. The artifact appears to be water rolled.

ARTIFACT FORM:	Girdled stone (Fig. 12d, g)	
FREQUENCY:		4
MATERIAL:	Limestone	
DATING:	Late Preclassic	3
	Late Postclassic	1
CONTEXT:	Domestic debris	2
	Construction fill with rubble	1
	Humus	1

COMMENT: SF-977 is considerably smaller than the other girdled specimens. It is 1.0 cm long and 0.5 cm to 0.6 cm in diameter. This piece is bilobed, with each lobe roughly spherical (Fig. 12d). The two lobes are defined by a V-shaped groove, which encircles this specimen. At each end is a very small protrusion or nipple. This find was associated with Late Postclassic sherds and may have functioned as a toggle for clothing (Robertson-Freidel, personal communication 1980).

SF-806, SF-1052, and SF-1261 are considerably larger than SF-977. SF-806 and SF-1052 are approximately cylindrical in shape with rounded ends. At the midsection of each is a 0.2 cm to 0.3 cm deep, U-shaped in section, encircling groove. SF-1261 is somewhat irregular but generally barrel-shaped in outline. At the midpoint is a U-shaped, partially encircling groove. These may have functioned as weights.

ARTIFACT FORM:	Stone spindle whorl (Fig. 12e)	
SUBFORM:	Stone	
FREQUENCY:		2
MATERIAL:	Limestone	
DATING:	Late Postclassic	1
	Unknown	1
CONTEXT:	Humus	1
	Beach	1

COMMENT: SF-190 has a flat base with a domed top (Fig. 12e). The dome is flattened at the top and surrounds the central hole, which appears to have been drilled from the top. The surfaces have been carefully ground. The limestone is off-white, with a reddish purple area on the top of one side. Because it is heavier than ceramic spindle whorls, it may have functioned on a pump drill or some spindle that required greater weight than that used for spinning cotton thread.

SF-1335 is oval in plan view. The dorsal and ventral surfaces are not parallel but are at a slight angle to one another. The sides vary from rounded to beveled. The hole is not biconical but cylindrical and is slightly off-center. As evidenced by its oval shape and off-center hole, it may have been a pendant rather than a spindle whorl.

ARTIFACT FORM:	Ground stone pendant (Fig. 12a, b)	
FREQUENCY:		3
MATERIAL:	Limestone	
DATING:	Late Preclassic	2
	Late Postclassic	1

CONTEXT:	Humus	1
	Domestic debris	1
	In floor	1

COMMENT: SF-576 is J-shaped in outline and circular in section. The hole has been drilled from two directions, one from the top edge and the other in toward the center from the side edge. Initially it may have been a water-rolled pebble. Willey et al. (1965) report a similar find from Barton Ramie.

SF-902 (Fig. 12b) is ovoid in outline and lenticular in section. The biconically drilled hole is 0.7 cm from the edge. It may also have been a water-rolled pebble.

None of these items show any signs of polish; for that reason and the fact that all are of soft stone, they have been classified with the ground stone industry rather than with the polished stone industry. Objects in the polished stone industry are made from harder materials and require a different technology to work.

ARTIFACT FORM:	Pestle-pounder (Fig. 10c)	
FREQUENCY:		2
MATERIAL:	Sandstone	1
	Quartzite	1
DATING:	Late Preclassic	2
CONTEXT:	Domestic debris	1
	Fall	1

COMMENT: SF-707 is made from an orangish-buff hard, dense sandstone. The pounding surface is convex and rectangular, with sides roughly trapezoidal in shape, tapering toward the top (Fig. 10c). Possible functions include pot burnisher, plaster smoother, and pigment or herb grinder. It is similar in shape to present-day chile grinders of volcanic stone sold in markets throughout Mexico.

SF-957 is considerably larger than SF-707. The base is slightly convex. The top is rounded and the uppermost quarter portion of the piece is sharply tapered. It resembles very closely the overhang portion of the Cerros overhang manos and may have been a reworked mano used as a pestle.

ARTIFACT FORM:	Stone with hemispherical depression (Fig. 12h)
FREQUENCY:	1
MATERIAL:	Marble
DATING:	Late Preclassic
CONTEXT:	Domestic debris

COMMENT: SF-317 is subspherical in shape with a hemispherical concavity 1.3 cm deep on one of the flattened surfaces. All of the surfaces have been ground and pecked, making it regular in shape and carefully formed. It may have been used as the distaff or object held in the hand while using a bow drill.

ARTIFACT FORM: Anvil-pounder-grinder
                   (Fig. 10d)
FREQUENCY: 1
MATERIAL: Marble
DATING: Late Preclassic
CONTEXT: Construction fill with rubble

COMMENT: SF-1130 is subspherical in shape with one flat surface. Batter marks can be observed on all surfaces. The batter is heaviest on the edges and protrusions. The flat surface is approximately 4.5 cm in diameter and exhibits pecks, cuts, scratches, and light polish. It seems to have functioned as an anvil, pounder, and polisher.

ARTIFACT FORM: Weight with suspension
                   hole
FREQUENCY: 2
MATERIAL: Limestone
DATING: Late Preclassic   1
                   Unknown   1
CONTEXT: Domestic debris   1
                   Surface   1

COMMENT: SF-1599 is a complete specimen weighing 1.8 kg and is irregular in shape. It appears to be a water-rolled stone. The hole, located toward the narrow end, has been biconically drilled. Peck marks appear on all surfaces except inside the hole. The reason for the peck marks is unclear.

SF-1851 is a broken water-rolled specimen that closely resembles a portion of the preceding find. The hole on this broken piece is three-quarters present and is also biconical.

ARTIFACT FORM: Ground stone figurine
                   (Fig. 10e)
FREQUENCY: 1
MATERIAL: Limestone
DATING: Early Classic
CONTEXT: Humus/fall

COMMENT: This figurine is bilobed, with the upper lobe representing the head and the lower lobe the body. The two lobes are defined by a U-shaped groove that encircles the specimen. On the front the groove is 0.7 cm wide; on the back it is 0.4 cm wide; on the sides it is 1.5 cm to 2.0 cm wide. Individual cut marks can be observed in this groove.

The head is a flattened oval in outline, with the flattened side being formed by the neckline or encircling groove. Each eye is 0.7 cm in diameter and is formed by a rounded depression. The nose is 0.4 cm in diameter and is also a rounded depression. The mouth is formed by a straight 2.7 cm groove, which is 0.3 cm wide and 0.1 cm to 0.3 cm deep. Individual cut marks can be observed in this groove. The body is generally triangular in outline. At its base is a groove, U-shaped in section, which extends 2.0 cm up the front and 0.9 cm up the back. The front of the body is flat, presumably from grinding. The back of the head and body is flattened yet rough and irregular when compared to the front. Front and back surfaces are parallel. Broken areas include the brow area and the right side. Freidel (personal communication 1980) has suggested that the figurine has characteristics of both sexes, as the general outline is penis-shaped and the groove at the base represents a vagina. The piece may have functioned as a fertility symbol (Freidel, personal communication 1980).

3. THE POLISHED STONE INDUSTRY

The polished stone industry includes all stone artifacts that exhibit intentional polish. The vast majority of these stone artifacts are of a group of materials referred to as greenstones. Some of the Cerros polished stone pieces are referred to as jade, although it is likely that not all of these are true jadeite.

Two hundred and forty-two jade pieces have been recovered from the excavations at Cerros. Many of the pieces are broken, and some fit together. Others are similar enough in color, surface contour, and degree of polish to be fragments from the same piece. Table 5 shows the number of each form represented.

In addition to a catalog number, each jade piece received a form number. This number indicates the piece form, the feature or structure from which the piece came, and the piece number of that form from that feature or structure. For example, Bead 4B-6 means that the piece or pieces are from bead 6 of Structure 4B. Each form has its own set of numbers for each feature or structure. Because of the fragmentary condition of so many of the jade finds, and because these were often found scattered about, it was necessary to devise this system in order to assess the number of jades associated with each structure. Table 6 lists by structure the form numbers and the Small Find catalog numbers of the jade pieces that are represented by more than one fragment.

As the analysis of the Cerros jades proceeded, some very distinct patterns of consumption and disposal

TABLE 5

Polished Stone Forms

Form	Frequency
Beads	108
Flares	22
Mosaics	12
Ground fragments	5
Head pendants	5
Spangles	1
Celts	8
Unidentifiable fragments	33

TABLE 6

Multiple Fragment Jade Pieces

Form Numbers	SF Catalog Number
Bead 1A-15	SF-1074A, B; SF-1077B, C
Bead 1A-17	SF-1083A; SF-1112A
Bead 1A-24	SF-995E, F
Bead 1A-25	SF-1114A, B, C
Bead 1A-26	SF-1114D, E, F
Bead 1A-27	SF-1114G, H, I, J, K, L, M
Bead 1A-28	SF-1172D, E, F, G
Bead 1A-29	SF-1172H, I, J, K, L, M, N, O
Bead 2A-4	SF-1787A, B
Flare 1A-3	SF-1079A; SF-1172A, B, C
Flare 2A-1	SF-1737D; SF-1780A, B, SF-1782; SF-1783; SF-1807, SF-1808A, B
Flare 2A-2	SF-1850; SF-1781
Flare 2A-4	SF-1733; SF-1737C

began to emerge. These are discussed at the end of the chapter.

ARTIFACT FORM: Bead

The polished stone beads recovered from the excavations at Cerros vary in the degree of polish from very light to a high sheen. The material used to make the beads varies in hardness from chalky and granular to hard and dense. There does not seem to be a correspondence between hardness or degree of polish and form.

The vast majority of the beads have been biconically drilled. Only disk beads and subspherical beads ever exhibit uniconical drilling. As would be expected, uniconical drilling does not occur on either barrel, tubular, or collared subforms.

Six beads exhibit short, shallow grooves or depressions near the drill hole. They are usually less than 0.1 cm in depth and width and are between 0.1 cm and 0.3 cm long. Some are observable only with the aid of a 10 × hand lens; others are just barely visible to the naked eye. Similar marks are observable on many of the shell beads. It is possible that these grooves were cut or ground into the bead prior to drilling, perhaps to facilitate securing the bead during the drilling process. These grooves never appear on the elongated subforms. One of these grooved beads comes from a Late Preclassic deposit; the remainder are from deposits of an Early Classic date.

Beads are the most common artifact forms among the polished stone artifacts (Table 5). They have been divided according to subform. The criteria defining those subforms appear in the "Comment" section.

ARTIFACT FORM: Bead
SUBFORM: Barrel
FREQUENCY: 33
MATERIAL: Greenstone
DATING: Late Preclassic   24
                   Early Classic   8
                   Late Postclassic   1
CONTEXT: Domestic debris   19
                   Termination ritual   9
                   Beach near Feature 1A   3
                   Cache   2

COMMENT: Barrel-shaped beads taper toward the ends. The length of the drill hole exceeds the diameter of the bead. Should the length be less, the bead is subspherical. Barrel-shaped beads are the most common form at Cerros. Many are represented only by fragments, but are classified as being of the barrel variety based on surface contour relative to the drill hole. The most common depositional context for these beads was domestic debris. This assessment may be misleading, however, in that beads or fragments found in a matrix of domestic debris may actually be there as a result of a termination offering.

ARTIFACT FORM: Bead
SUBFORM: Tubular
FREQUENCY: 24
MATERIAL: Greenstone
DATING: Late Preclassic   13
                   Early Classic   10
                   Late Postclassic   1
CONTEXT: Termination ritual   11
                   Domestic debris   6
                   Beach near Feature 1A   3
                   Cache   2
                   Humus   1
                   Fall   1

COMMENT: Tubular beads are very similar to barrel beads except that a tubular bead's sides do not taper toward the end but are parallel. Both, however, have a

length greater than their diameter. Like the barrel beads, those found in domestic debris probably relate to termination ritual.

ARTIFACT FORM: Bead
SUBFORM: Subspherical
FREQUENCY: 22
MATERIAL: Greenstone   21
                   Marble   1
DATING: Late Preclassic   11
                   Early Classic   8
                   Late Postclassic   3
CONTEXT: Termination ritual   9
                   Cache   7
                   Domestic debris   4
                   Fall   1
                   Construction fill with
                     rubble   1

COMMENT: Subspherical beads are those having a drill hole length less than the diameter. SF-964, the marble specimen, is medium brown in color. It is moderately polished.

ARTIFACT FORM: Bead
SUBFORM: Spherical
FREQUENCY: 7
MATERIAL: Greenstone
DATING: Late Preclassic   2
                   Early Classic   5
CONTEXT: Termination ritual   6
                   Domestic debris   1

COMMENT: Spherical beads are often depicted on Classic period stone sculpture as necklaces on elite personages. Although present in the Late Preclassic, the frequencies indicate a preference for this form in the Classic. This may indicate a change in the technology of bead manufacture.

ARTIFACT FORM: Bead
SUBFORM: Collared
FREQUENCY: 6
MATERIAL: Greenstone
DATING: Late Preclassic   3
                   Early Classic   3
CONTEXT: Termination ritual   3
                   Domestic debris   3

COMMENT: All of the Cerros collared beads are elongated; that is, the dimension from drill hole opening to drill hole opening is greater than the diameter. Collared beads are so named because of a rim or band at or near the bead's end. These beads could be considered a variation of either the barrel or tubular varieties. All six collared beads are broken, intentionally smashed as part of a termination ritual.

ARTIFACT FORM: Bead
SUBFORM: Wedge (Fig. 14b)
FREQUENCY: 4
MATERIAL: Greenstone
DATING: Late Postclassic
CONTEXT: Cache   2
    Humus   2

COMMENT: Wedge-shaped beads are triangular in section and/or plan. Only four were recovered, all from Late Postclassic deposits. These beads may be manufactured from by-products, or wedges, obtained during the manufacture of ear flares (Digby 1964).

ARTIFACT FORM: Bead
SUBFORM: Disk
FREQUENCY: 3
MATERIAL: Greenstone
DATING: Late Preclassic   2
    Early Classic   1
CONTEXT: Beach near Feature 1A   2
    Fall   1

COMMENT: Disk beads have a diameter greater than the length of the drill hole. The difference between a disk bead and a tubular bead is the diameter-to-thickness ratio.

ARTIFACT FORM: Bead
SUBFORM: Rectangular
FREQUENCY: 1
MATERIAL: Greenstone
DATING: Late Postclassic
CONTEXT: Cache

ARTIFACT FORM: Bead
SUBFORM: Flared
FREQUENCY: 1
MATERIAL: Greenstone
DATING: Late Preclassic
CONTEXT: Cache

COMMENT: SF-145 is flared at one end. The material is translucent and light green in color. This bead was found lying directly above the throat of ear flare SF-144. Its shape closely resembles many of the coral flared beads from Cerros. A similar bead was excavated from a Late Preclassic cache at Nohmul in Northern Belize

(Hammond 1975). That bead was also associated with ear flares in a Late Preclassic dedicatory cache.

ARTIFACT FORM: Bead
SUBFORM: Irregular
FREQUENCY: 3
MATERIAL: Greenstone   2
    Turquoise   1
DATING: Late Postclassic
CONTEXT: Cache

COMMENT: SF-737 is irregular in outline but rhomboid in section. SF-739J is now irregular but at one time was probably a rectangular bead. The break was smoothed down, precluding the need to redrill the bead. SF-879 is generally trapezoidal in outline and rectangular in section.

ARTIFACT FORM: Bead
SUBFORM: Unknown
FREQUENCY: 40
MATERIAL: Greenstone
DATING: Late Preclassic   33
    Early Classic   7
CONTEXT: Domestic debris   24
    Termination ritual   12
    Beach near Feature 1A   3
    Construction fill with
      rubble   1

COMMENT: The subform of these pieces is unknown because they are broken to the point that enough of the piece is present to identify them as beads but not enough to recognize the subform. A great many were recovered from domestic debris. They probably were not in this debris as trash, however, but as a part of a termination offering.

SUMMARY: Bead
FREQUENCY: Total of all subforms and
      those of unknown form   144
DATING: Late Preclassic   89
    Early Classic   42
    Late Postclassic   13
CONTEXT: Domestic debris   57
    Termination ritual   50
    Cache   18
    Beach near Feature 1A   11
    Humus   3
    Fall   3
    Construction fill with
      rubble   1

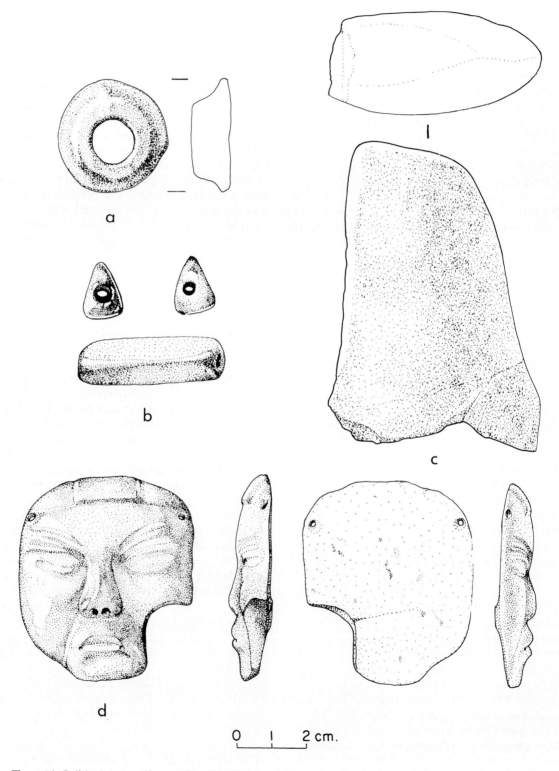

Figure 14. Polished stone artifacts. a, flare SF-144; b, bead SF-1512; c, celt SF-1190; d, Olmecoid pendant SF-162.

Construction fill without
rubble   1

COMMENT: Table 7 illustrates the frequencies and percentages for the various subforms of beads. The elongated subforms (barrel, tubular, and collared) account for 60.6% of the identifiable subforms. That figure is unusually high compared to other Lowland Maya sites. For example, at Cozumel the elongated forms account for only 24.6% (Phillips 1979).

Table 8 lists the percentages of the various subforms of beads for each time period at Cerros. The irregular and wedge subforms are restricted to the Late Postclassic period, which suggests a decline in labor investment in jade working. Spherical beads increase in frequency into the Early Classic period.

TABLE 7

Polished Stone Bead Subforms

Subform	Frequency	%
Barrel	33	31.7
Tubular	24	23.1
Subspherical	22	21.2
Spherical	7	6.7
Collared	6	5.8
Wedge	4	3.8
Disk	3	2.9
Irregular	3	2.9
Rectangular	1	1.0
Flared	1	1.0
Unknown	40	
Total	144	

TABLE 8

Polished Stone Bead Subforms by Period

Subform	Late Preclassic (%)	Early Classic (%)	Late Postclassic (%)
Barrel	42.9	22.9	7.7
Tubular	23.2	28.6	7.7
Subspherical	19.6	22.9	23.1
Spherical	3.6	14.3	0.0
Collared	5.4	8.6	0.0
Wedge	0.0	0.0	30.8
Disk	3.6	2.9	0.0
Irregular	0.0	0.0	23.1
Rectangular	0.0	0.0	7.7
Flared	1.8	0.0	0.0
	n = 56	n = 35	n = 13

The percentage of elongated beads in the Late Preclassic (77.8%) is similar to that for the Early Classic (60.1%). However, there seems to be a preference for barrel subforms in the Late Preclassic as opposed to a preference for tubular subforms in the Early Classic. The percentage of elongated forms in the Late Postclassic is 15.4%.

Of all the bead pieces in the Cerros collection, 75.7% are broken, an extremely high percentage when compared to other Lowland Maya samples. This high percentage results from intentional breakage during termination rituals associated with the abandonment of structures.

ARTIFACT FORM:	Polished stone ear flares (Fig. 14a)	
FREQUENCY:		35
MATERIAL:	Greenstone	34
	Fuschite	1
DATING:	Late Preclassic	27
	Early Classic	6
	Unknown	1
CONTEXT:	Termination ritual	19
	Domestic debris	8
	Beach near Feature 1A	4
	Cache	2
	Construction fill with rubble	1

COMMENT: Only two of the ear flare finds are whole, SF-142 and SF-144 (Fig. 14a). These flares are a matched set and were recovered from Cache 1, a Late Preclassic dedicatory cache on Structure 6B. They are very fine-quality dark green jadeite with light green swirls. Both are irregularly round in outline. The inner surfaces of the flares' throats are highly polished and the outer surfaces are moderately polished. The holes of the throats show light polish.

SF-80 is of particular interest in that its estimated diameter is 10 cm. It was found along the erosion exposure of Feature 1A and was probably once a part of that deposit; it probably dates from the Late Preclassic. This is one of the largest flares reported from the Maya area, the largest being the Pomona flare, which is 18.0 cm in diameter (Digby 1964; Hammond 1986).

SF-995A is made of fuschite, a soft, glistening aqua green material. The flare has a cogged or serrated rim. The V cuts in the rim extend down the exterior surface of the throat, which is deep relative to the diameter. The interior and exterior surfaces show moderate polish.

SF-1172A, B, and C are fragments from the same flare. The flare is round and the interior and exterior surfaces show high polish except on the interior at the base of the throat, where the polish is light. On the exterior surface the flare rim is sharply defined. The base of the throat opening is larger than the middle. This enlarged basal opening has been made by a separate drilling from the rear. SF-1079A is a flare fragment that exhibits this same countersunk characteristic.

The remainder of the flare fragments are too small to determine their complete shape or size. Many are small rim or throat fragments. Most appear to have the same basic shape as the two complete specimens, SF-142 and SF-144. The flares were probably broken intentionally as a part of termination offerings.

ARTIFACT FORM: Head pendant (Fig. 15)
SUBFORM: Bib
FREQUENCY: 4
MATERIAL: Greenstone
DATING: Late Preclassic
CONTEXT: Cache
COMMENT: Freidel and Schele (1988) have presented a detailed iconographic analysis of the bib head pendants from Cache 1 at Cerros. They also present persuasive evidence that the heads functioned as elements of a royal crown. This is especially significant because these head pendants, which are Late Preclassic, are icons of Classic period kingship and power. The following descriptions of the pendants were provided by David A. Freidel and Robin Robertson-Freidel.

SF-158 was carved on a water-rolled pebble (Fig. 15b). The drill hole is biconical and pierces the pendant laterally at the level of the eyebrow incisions. The back is lightly polished and exhibits some uneven pockmarked areas. It is light gray-green in color with mottled areas of dark green.

SF-158 represents a face with an elaborate headdress. It has lateral flanges and a bib, which are distinguished from one another by grooves at the level of the lower lip. The basic technique of shaping was sawing and then grinding the saw cuts. The nose, mouth, and chin form a single trapezoidal ridge defined by two long grooves. The grooves form a wide V in cross-section. The nose is distinguished from the upper lip by another wide V groove. Similarly, the mouth opening and the lower lip-chin juncture are defined by such

grooves. The lower lip-chin groove was ground down on the chin side to lower the chin from the plane of the lips and nose. The top of the nose was ground down, and the nose-mouth area is the highest relief on the piece. The nose is very wide, the lips are thick, and the chin is receding. The cheek–lateral flange juncture is outlined by a long U-shaped groove. The cheeks are rounded on the surfaces and fat. The eye areas comprise wide shallow grooves that were almost entirely ground away, substantially lowering the eye area to a level below the cheek. The eye-brow juncture consists of two curving grooves that meet in the center in a widow's peak. The forehead is prominent and bulges in the center.

There is a horn or topknot protrusion above the forehead, angling off to the left (as one faces the piece). This protrusion is conical and is distinguished from the forehead by a groove running perpendicular to the axis of the protrusion. Two smaller grooves parallel the basal groove higher up on the protrusion. There is a groove on the right side, which defines a small, rounded ridge on the right side of the forehead. The protrusion to the left and small ridge on the right may represent a hairstyle and not a headdress. Freidel and Schele (1988) suggest that this head may represent Venus, the hero twin G1 of the Triad. Hammond (1986) suggests that it represents the Maize God.

SF-159 appears to have been carved on a rounded, water-rolled pebble (Fig. 15d). The suspension hole has been biconically pierced laterally at the level of the eyebrows. The back, lightly polished, is flat and rounded at the edges. The piece is light mottled-green in color. Pockmarks can be observed on the back. Drill holes are notched into the back, giving the upper back a constricted appearance.

The pendant represents a face with lateral and basal flanges. The techniques used to produce the piece were sawing and grinding.

The nose is defined by two curving grooves, U-shaped in section and separated from the upper lip by a groove that is a wide V in section. The lower lip is distinguished from the chin by a very shallow groove. The chin is rounded and full. The nose is trapezoidal in plan and hooked in profile.

The eye regions are sculpted at the bottom by two long, curving grooves outlining the sides of the nose. These grooves curve across the face region and terminate at the edge of the face. They are sharply V-shaped in section. The cheek area below them was ground down. The upper eye region is separated from the forehead by

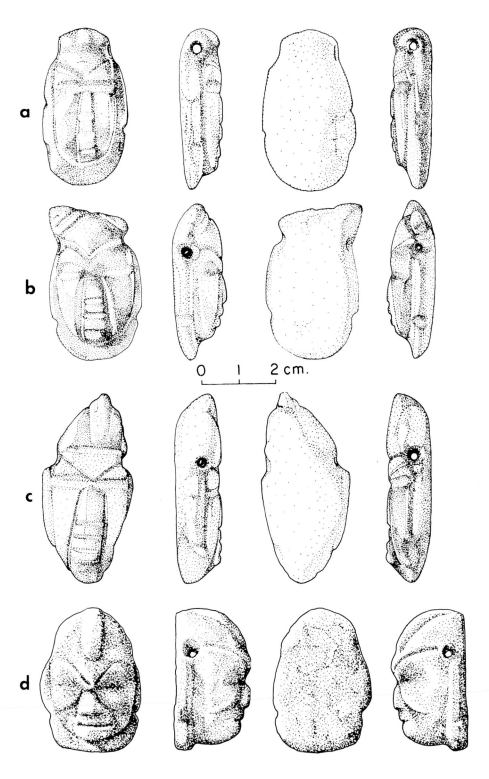

Figure 15. Bib head pendants. a, SF-161; b, SF-158; c, SF-160; d, SF-159.

two long, curving grooves, which are placed symmetrically to the lower grooves. Thus, the eye regions appear as large ovals encompassing the upper cheek and lower forehead areas. The forehead is bulging and prominent. There is a large prominent ridge running down the center of the forehead. This crest has been circumscribed by two wide V grooves, which were completely ground down on the sides, thus substantially raising this central element above the level of the forehead.

The face is framed by two lateral flanges and a basal flange. The lateral flanges are separated from the basal flange by a notch on each side at the level of the mouth. The lateral flanges terminate at the drill holes. The flanges are delineated from the face region by wide grooves, V-shaped in section.

While this piece is stylistically related to the other three bib heads, it is iconographically distinct in the wide, goggle-shaped eye regions and the rounded appearance of the piece. It was found opposite SF-160, which has been identified as the Jester God and may represent a substitute or category analog of God K (Freidel and Schele 1988). Hammond (1986) identifies this pendant as a representation of the god head *akbal,* or "darkness." This goggle-eyed form is the most common head pendant form in the Late Preclassic.

SF-160 appears to have been carved on a water-rolled pebble (Fig. 15c). It is biconically drilled laterally at the level of the headdress groove. The back is lightly polished and exhibits two facets. The piece is mottled light green in color and depicts a face with a three-part headdress. There are small lateral flanges but no basal flange. An irregular conical protrusion near the chin region may be interpreted as a basal flange, beard, or chin. The lateral flanges are distinguished from the cheeks by long grooves. These flanges extend to the drill hole. The techniques used in carving the pendant were sawing and grinding.

The nose-mouth-chin region forms a single trapezoidal ridge delineated on the sides by long lateral grooves that are narrow V-shaped in section. The nose is isolated from the upper lip by a bar formed by two parallel U-shaped grooves. Between the upper and lower lips is a short U-shaped groove parallel to the nose–upper lip groove. A wide V-shaped groove, which was completely ground down on the flange side, segregates the lower lip from the chin.

The nose is flat and wide, the lips thick and fat. There are two distinct eye grooves, which meet at the bridge of the nose. Those grooves are relatively deep and are U-shaped in section. The eyebrows are formed

by two curving grooves that meet in a widow's peak at the bridge of the nose. A long groove parallel to the eye grooves separates the forehead from the headdress-hairpiece area. The headdress hairpiece is divided into three vertical segments by two long grooves.

The face is highly polished on the prominent surfaces but not in the eye grooves. It is a mottled gray-green to dark green color. Because of the three-part headdress, Freidel and Schele (1988) have identified this pendant as the Jester God and note that this was an important symbol of kingship.

SF-161 appears to have been carved on a water-rolled pebble (Fig. 15a). It is biconically drilled just above the level of the eyebrows. The back has been smoothed but not polished. It is mottled in color and exhibits splotches of dark green, gray-green, and light green.

The pendant is of a face with a hairpiece, skull deformation, or helmet. It has two lateral flanges and a basal flange differentiated by notches at the level of the lips. The basal flange is rounded. Techniques employed to produce this pendant were sawing and grinding.

The nose, mouth, and chin form a single trapezoidal ridge enclosed within two long grooves. A short groove, V-shaped in section, separates the nose from the upper lip, which in turn is distinguished from the chin by a wide groove, V-shaped in section. The lateral grooves curl around the chin, giving it a rounded appearance.

At the top of the nose is an eye groove, which is U-shaped in section. This single eye groove extends toward the side of the pendant. The cheek–lateral flange juncture also has a groove U-shaped in section, which has been ground down on the outside, substantially lowering the level of the flange below that of the cheek.

The cheeks, which are rotund, were carefully ground and modeled. Two curving grooves that meet in the center in a widow's peak form the eyebrows. The forehead exhibits a small, shallow groove apparently representing a furrow in the forehead.

Between the forehead and the hair or helmet is a shallow groove running at a slight angle to the eye groove. The hair or helmet region is divided into three parts by two grooves, thus forming three ridges. The central ridge is substantially higher than the two lateral ridges.

The fatness of the face conveys a general Olmecoid impression. The raised central crest of the headdress area also suggests Olmec or Olmec-derived influence. This pendant may represent G3, the Jaguar Sun, one of the Triad Gods (Freidel and Schele 1988).

ARTIFACT FORM: Head pendant (Fig. 14d)
SUBFORM: Olmecoid
FREQUENCY: 1
MATERIAL: Greenstone
DATING: Late Preclassic
CONTEXT: Cache

COMMENT: The detailed description of this piece was provided by David A. Freidel and Robin Robertson-Freidel. Freidel and Schele (1988) suggest that because of its size and style it is appropriate for use as an *ahau* pectoral and may be a prototype of the kind seen in Classic period portraiture. SF-162 was carved on a flat slab. It was biconically drilled at the level of the helmet on each side. The two drill holes are at the very edge of the piece. The back of the piece is smoothed but not polished. It was carefully sawed. There are three distinct sawing planes. The piece is a light gray-green color.

This pendant is of a face surmounted by a helmet. The face is square with fat cheeks and carefully modeled eyes, nose, mouth, and chin. The nose is flat with two very prominent nostrils, which are drill holes. The nose has a very carefully modeled, rounded character, but the shaping grooves that outlined the nose have been completely ground away.

The mouth has been formed by two grooves, one below the nose and the other below the lower lip. These grooves were carefully ground and polished, leaving the mouth prominent but naturalistic. The septum is expressed by a very light groove emanating from between the nostrils and terminating at the upper lip. The lips consist of a wide groove, V-shaped in section. It was ground on both sides, giving the lips a modeled, rounded appearance. There are two distinct drill holes in the corners of the mouth, but they do not relate technically to the shaping of the mouth. Some Olmec carvings exhibit drill holes in the corners of the mouth, which are a stage in the manufacture of the pieces (Covarrubias 1957). It has been noted that on Olmec-derived or Olmec-related pieces, sometimes this characteristic will be present without technically relating to the formation of the mouth (Joesink-Manderville and Meluzin 1976).

The left cheek (facing the piece) is rounded and fat. A depression in the left cheek below the level of the eye gives the cheek a very realistic appearance. The groove between the nose and the cheek continues below the level of the nose to the edge of the chin, thereby outlining the chin-mouth region. The right cheek shows a similar groove, which terminates in a carefully cut out section of the right cheek. The section of the right cheek that has been removed is very carefully curved around the chin and shows saw marks running perpendicular to the plane of the pendant. The removal of the cheek clearly took place sometime after the pendant was finished. It may have been removed to symbolize the death of the person that it belonged to.

The eyes are naturalistic but without pupils. They have upper and lower lids formed by grooves, making each lid a ridge. The eye socket is ground but not polished. Eyebrows are thick, curving bars, formed by sets of grooves, which give the face a frowning appearance.

The forehead is flat, wide, and carefully ground and polished. The border of the helmet consists of a long, shallow groove running straight across the forehead. The helmet is divided into three segments. The central segment is rectangular in plan and is defined on the sides by two grooves. This central section is prominently raised above the other two.

Certain iconographic diagnostics such as the down-turned mouth, drill holes in the corners of the mouth, tight-fitting, rounded helmet, fat cheeks, square face, and frowning expression, support the interpretation of this piece as being Olmec, or Olmec related. The piece is technically superior to the four bib heads recovered with it. This, however, does not mean that the piece was necessarily an heirloom. The technically superfluous drill holes in the mouth corners suggest the passage of some time between Classic Olmec times and the carving of the piece. Hammond (1980) demonstrates the widespread occurrence of bib head pendants in the Maya Lowlands. Easby (personal communication 1980) feels that the bib head pendants are of Maya origin. The more Olmecoid, technically superior pieces may also be of Maya origin but of a different school, one more directly linked to the Olmec. This school may have also influenced the bib head school, implied by some Olmecoid features on bib heads.

Head pendants similar to the Cerros Olmecoid piece have been recovered from Cayo District, Belize (Thompson 1931) and Tabasco, Mexico (Easby and Scott 1970).

ARTIFACT FORM: Polished stone celt
　　　　　　　　(Fig. 14c)

FREQUENCY:		8
MATERIAL:	Greenstone	5
	Chert	2
	Marble	1

DATING:	Late Preclassic	4
	Early Classic	1
	Late Postclassic	1
	Unknown	2
CONTEXT:	Domestic debris	2
	Humus	1
	Humus/fall	1
	Fall	1
	Construction fill without rubble	1
	Pit fill	1
	Beach	1

COMMENT: SF-69 is light green in color, moderately polished, and is probably made of serpentine. Its curved bit edge shows chipping and crushing from use. The piece is broken, with no sign of use after the break.

SF-105 is the distal end of a finely ground and polished dark green chloromelanite axe. The bit edge is curved and shows edge damage. The break edges have been worn smooth, indicating that the tool was used after it was initially broken. This celt was found in a pit designated as Feature 1A-9 (Cliff 1982), along with two antler punches, chert debris, obsidian blades, large sherds, shell, and fish bone.

SF-225 is the butt end of a celt. This end shows some contusions and may have been used in termination ritual to sacrifice other artifacts and was then itself crushed. The piece is blue-green in color, very fine grained, and carefully shaped and polished. Although fashioned from quality material, it shows no sign of reuse.

SF-429 is the poll end of a moderately polished, dark green chloromelanite celt. The poll end is rounded and the bit end is convex. The bit shows signs of heavy use. A large flake is missing from the bit end on one side, but it is still usable. It was carefully shaped. A grinding facet can be observed parallel to its length.

SF-605 is a medium-sized, moderately polished green schist celt, ovate in cross-section and outline. Its poll end is rounded. The bit end has been dulled by heavy use and is broken at one end of the convex edge. It was used after this break occurred.

SF-1190 is a portion of a marble celt (Fig. 14c). In section it is lenticular. When whole, the sides converged toward the end that is flattened. It has a central bulge similar to those on a fully grooved axe. Polish ranges from dull to a high sheen. This artifact was most likely a part of a ceremonial celt.

SF-1545 is a fragment of chert that exhibits a convex, smooth, and highly polished face that shows signs of heat damage. It was probably broken by fire. There is no sign of reuse after having been cracked.

SF-1895 is a chert object with two polished surfaces that intersect to form a V-shaped edge. It may have been part of a grinder or polisher, but the probable bit edge and the lenticular shape suggest that it is a fragment of a celt.

ARTIFACT FORM:	Spangle
FREQUENCY:	1
MATERIAL:	Greenstone
DATING:	Late Preclassic
CONTEXT:	Cache

COMMENT: SF-146 is light green with mottled, dark-green areas. One face is highly polished, the other face has been smoothed. There is a groove on this smoothed side, which appears to be the remains of a biconical drill hole. It is made from a broken or cut up bead and has two tiny biconical drill holes, each 0.1 cm in diameter, along one edge. It could be a reworked fragment of a bead that was sacrificed during a termination ritual and may have functioned as an *am,* or prophecy stone, as noted in ethnohistorical and ethnographic contexts (Freidel and Schele 1988).

ARTIFACT FORM:	Ground jade fragments
FREQUENCY:	5
MATERIAL:	Greenstone
DATING:	Late Preclassic
CONTEXT:	Cache

COMMENT: The five jade fragments that make up SF-147 appear to be partially reworked pieces of broken jade artifacts. One shows polish on both faces, the others on only one. Some edges are rough and broken while others are partially ground down or slightly beveled. They were scattered about in Cache 1 and, despite the slight beveling on some edges, they do not seem to be a mosaic, unless it was dismantled before deposition. These pieces are probably partially reworked fragments from a termination offering. Like the spangle, they might also have been used as prophecy stones.

ARTIFACT FORM:	Jade mosaic	
FREQUENCY:		17
MATERIAL:	Greenstone	
DATING:	Late Preclassic	14
	Late Postclassic	3
CONTEXT:	Cache	14
	Surface	1
	Humus	1
	Humus/fall	1

COMMENT: SF-106 is highly polished on its flat face. The opposite face exhibits concentric areas that resemble a fracture, possibly from heat. All edges are beveled toward the fractured face. Two of the edges are straight, one is convex, and one is concave. The piece is mottled light and medium green. As a mosaic it is complete, but is probably a reworked fragment of something else.

SF-171 consists of five fragments, dark green in color, that fit together to form an elongated bivalve shell in outline. A portion of it is missing. The faces show moderate polish. Some edges are beveled toward the interior, and some edges are beveled toward the exterior. Jagged edges on some indicate that they might be reworked fragments. The pieces were found in the fill at the bottom of one of the Cache 1 vessels on Structure 6B. Willey discovered two similar jade pendants, carved in the shape of bivalve shells, at the site of Barton Ramie (Willey et al. 1965).

SF-813 is dark green and gray-green in color. In outline it is a curved trapezoid. The finished surface is slightly convex. All edges are beveled toward the lightly smoothed exterior surface. This piece is whole as a mosaic, although the curvature of the finished face suggests that it might be a reworked fragment from a large ear flare.

SF-1424 is made up of four pieces that appear to be reworked fragments. Beveling is present on many of the edges, suggesting that they were part of a mosaic.

ARTIFACT FORM:	Unidentifiable fragments	
FREQUENCY:		33
MATERIAL:	Greenstone	
DATING:	Late Preclassic	32
	Unknown	1
CONTEXT:	Domestic debris	27
	Beach near Feature 1A	4
	Fall	1
	Termination ritual	1

COMMENT: The vast majority of these pieces exhibit one polished surface, but because of their small size it is impossible to determine the complete forms. The fragments were parts of artifacts that were intentionally smashed, as discussed in the following section.

PATTERNS OF JADE CONSUMPTION AND DISPOSAL

Several investigators have recognized the importance of jade in Mesoamerica as a material symbol of wealth, power, and prestige (Coe 1965a; Digby 1964; Easby 1961; Proskouriakoff 1974; Ruz Lhuillier 1952; Thompson 1966; and Tozzer 1941). Jades appeared in various contexts in the Maya area, including caches, burials, tombs, and sacrificial offerings. Beads, plaques, pendants, ear flares, inlays, and mosaics are the most common artifact forms (Rands 1965).

Jade recovered from caches, tombs, and dedicatory offerings is usually whole, but sometimes those contexts contain raw or partially worked jade, as, for example, was the case at Kaminaljuyu (Kidder, Jennings, and Shook, 1946) and Seibal (Willey 1978), where jadeite boulders and pebbles were cached in structures presumably as dedicatory offerings.

The unbroken condition of jades from those contexts contrasts sharply with broken jade artifacts excavated at Cerros. The Cerros deposits contain jade artifacts broken as a consequence of termination ritual, which involves removal of plaster facades, burning of ceremonial fires, scattering about of white marl, and smashing of jade and ceramic artifacts (Garber 1981, 1983; Robertson 1983).

During the course of excavations at Cerros, 236 jade artifacts have been uncovered from a variety of contexts and depositional categories, including caches, construction fill, humus, fall, termination ritual, and trash. An approximate functional assessment of each of these categories could be made on the basis of associated features. As the analysis of the Cerros artifacts proceeded, some interesting patterns of jade consumption began to emerge.

With the exception of the jade from marl and trash, the deposition of Cerros jade is quite typical of that reported from other Maya sites. A Late Preclassic dedicatory cache, recovered from the summit of Structure 6B (Fig. 3) (Freidel 1979), contained twenty-eight artifacts of jade, including five head pendants, two ear flares, six beads, five mosaic fragments, nine ground fragments, and one spangle, in addition to seven ceramic vessels, several *spondylus* shells, white shell disks of unknown species, and eighty-six mirror fragments of specular hematite.

Other cached jade artifacts from Cerros include a 4.9-cm-long apple green bead of fine-quality workmanship and material excavated from a Late Preclassic phase 3 dedicatory summit cache in the construction fill of the medial axis of Structure 5C-1st, the final construction phase on Structure 5C. This bead was found with specular hematite mirror fragments in a ceramic vessel covered by an inverted dish (Robertson-Freidel 1980).

Three additional jade beads, found with eight conch shell beads, were recovered from directly on top of a Late Preclassic floor (1A-3-11) within the Feature 1A residential zone. These were lying in such a manner as to suggest that they were strung together, perhaps as a wristlet or necklace. This bead cluster appears to represent a dedicatory cache associated with the construction of the overlying feature, Structure 2A-Sub.12-2nd-D (Cliff 1982, 1986).

What is important about these jade artifacts from dedicatory caches is their condition. All, with the exception of the occasional ground fragments, are whole. As stated earlier, this pattern duplicates dedicatory caches in other parts of the Maya Lowlands.

The remainder of the Cerros jade artifacts are unusual in their condition and depositional context. Of the 221 Late Preclassic and Early Classic jade pieces from Cerros, only 47 are whole or reworked, and of these, 27 are from caches. No jade artifacts were found in association with burials at Cerros, and no tombs were encountered. Consequently, the great majority of the Late Preclassic and Early Classic jade artifacts from Cerros were broken and retrieved from contexts other than dedicatory caches, burials, or tombs.

Table 9 compares percentages of whole versus broken jade artifacts from termination ritual and cache contexts. All of the jade artifacts from the Cerros caches are either whole or reworked, and 92% of those from termination ritual deposits are broken. The intentional destruction of jade artifacts in association with the abandonment of architecture has not been reported elsewhere for sites in the Maya area.

Within the main plaza, Feature 2A at Cerros is a 2.3-m-high two-terraced platform with an outset staircase and apron mouldings. This Late Preclassic platform, Structure 2A-Sub.4-1st, faces east and is fronted by a plaza. The plaza and structure are contemporaneous with at least some of the residential locations within

Feature 1A (Cliff 1982, 1986). Structure 2A-Sub.4-1st was abandoned during the Late Preclassic with much ceremony and ritual just prior to its being buried by the main plaza. The termination ritual consisted of smashing ceramic vessels, burning ceremonial fires, depositing molded, painted plaster in excavated holes at the first terrace junction of the staircase, scattering and depositing much white marl on and about the structure, and smashing and scattering jade artifacts in and among the above-mentioned vessel fragments and marl. In short, this termination ritual was the last activity carried out on this structure prior to complete burial by the construction of the overlying main plaza.

Within this termination ritual deposit on Structure 2A-Sub.4-1st, twenty-one fragments of jade have been recovered. Seven of these are bead fragments and represent six different beads. Thirteen are ear flare fragments and probably represent four separate flares. One fragment was unidentifiable. None of the flares or beads is complete. The deposit was not completely excavated; however, on Structure 4B at Cerros, where a similar termination offering was completely and carefully excavated, many bead and flare fragments were missing. Termination offerings on Structures 5C-1st, 5C-2nd, 3B, and 29B at Cerros, which consist of many smashed vessels deposited in white marl and lenses of charcoal but no smashed jade, show, despite careful excavation, the same pattern of only partially represented vessels (Robertson-Freidel 1980; Robertson 1983).

Thus, it appears that a consistent feature of termination ritual is the deposition or storage of some of the smashed offerings elsewhere. Partially ground jade fragments often found in dedicatory caches are perhaps reworked curated pieces from a termination ritual.

Within the superstructure of Structure 4B at Cerros, the remains of a termination ritual of Early Classic date were recovered (Walker 1986). This ritual consisted of the burning of ceremonial fires, deposition of white marl, smashing of open-bottomed censers, deposition of a whole plate, and the smashing and scattering of many jade fragments. In all, forty-seven pieces of jade were found in this deposit. Six are ear flare fragments, representing six flares. The largest of these flare fragments represents approximately one-eighth of a complete flare. The remaining forty-one jade pieces from this deposit represent thirty beads. Five of these beads are whole; the remainder are incomplete, represented by one to eight fragments. Two of the bead fragments

TABLE 9

Whole and Broken Jade Artifacts

Condition	From Cache (%)	From Termination Ritual (%)
Whole	100.0	8.0
Broken	0.0	92.0
	n = 31	n = 187

exhibit linear contusions or crush marks paralleling the breaks. These are probably the result of a sharp chisel-like tool having been used to break the beads. Similar marks have been reported on fragmented pieces from the Cenote of Sacrifice at Chichén Itzá (Proskouriakoff 1974).

Of the deposits at Cerros containing smashed jade, the most peculiar and difficult to interpret are those from the residential zone, Feature 1A, underlying the main plaza. Smashed jade artifacts were recovered from midden deposits of transposed primary context, or trash (Cliff 1982, 1986). The deposits with crushed jade are concentrated in Operation 34, toward the western end of the residential zone. Given the practice of smashing and dispersing jade during termination rituals associated with stone architecture, it is reasonable to suspect that similar behavior and disposal might have taken place with the termination of perishable residential structures or a residential zone. In conclusion, the jade was deposited in residential areas as a part of termination ritual and was not included in the trash when the trash was deposited. The position of several fragments of jade ear flares and beads from the surface and uppermost portions of the Feature 1A residential zone supports this interpretation. Cliff (1982) has suggested that the fragments in that zone may not have been deposited in a ritual associated with the abandonment of the area, but rather with either (1) the construction of Structures 2A-Sub.5-1st and 2A-Sub.7-1st, or (2) ritual activity conducted at nearby Structure 2A-Sub.4-1st.

Associated with this residential zone is a masonry feature, Structure 2A-Sub.2-1st-B and C, of Late Preclassic date, which, on the basis of form and the nature of sediments at its base, has been identified as a wharf or docking facility (Fig. 5) (Cliff 1982, 1986; Freidel 1979).

Within or around Feature 1A, which includes the docking facility, were 108 jade pieces. Fifty-nine were bead fragments representing 35 different beads, in addition to 5 complete beads. Ten ear flare fragments represent 7 different flares. The original form of 31 additional fragments, many of which show signs of polish, cannot be identified. The midden deposits of Feature 1A yielded three celt objects, all of them broken. One was made of chloromelanite and has batter marks on its poll end. The second fragment, dark-green jadeite with gray mottling, is the bit end of an axe, which shows edge damage. The third is a poll fragment of very fine quality blue-green jade with some batter

marks. These pieces may have been used to smash the beads, flares, and vessels and were then themselves broken and scattered about.

The percentages of artifact forms from the Cerros termination rituals containing jade are shown in table 10. The ratios of beads to ear flares, approximately four to one, from Structure 4B and Feature 1A are very similar. Approximately one-half of the beads from each deposit are an elongated form, tubular, barrel, or collared. The remainder are spherical or subspherical. Ear flare assemblages consisting of a flare, two elongated beads (one a counterweight), and two rounded beads may have been selected for sacrifice. Similar ratios from 4B and 1A support this argument. The flare-to-bead ratio is different for Structure 2A-Sub.4-1st, possibly because of the small sample size from this deposit.

COMPARISONS: The practice of intentionally smashing jade artifacts is well documented at the site of Chichén Itzá in Yucatán, Mexico, where over five thousand artifacts of jade have been retrieved from the Cenote of Sacrifice (Proskouriakoff 1974). A great many of these specimens were deliberately smashed prior to deposit in the cenote. Others show signs of heat damage and may have been shattered when they came into contact with the cool cenote water.

The bib and helmet head pendants salvaged from the Cenote of Sacrifice at Chichén Itzá show no signs of intentional damage. Proskouriakoff (1974) suggests that this circumstance might be the result of offerings made prior to the establishment of the cult of sacrifice.

Although bib and helmet head pendants are present in a cache at Cerros, they are absent from the deposits resulting from termination rituals. Hammond (personal communication 1982) suggests that bib head pendants are deity images and thus functioned quite differently from the items smashed, which are objects of

TABLE 10

Jade Artifact Forms from Termination Rituals

Form	From Structure 4B (%)	From Feature 1A (%)	From Structure 2A-Sub. 4-1st (%)
Beads	83.3	79.6	60.0
Ear flares	16.7	14.3	40.0
Celts	0.0	6.1	0.0
	n = 36	n = 49	n = 10

personal adornment (beads and ear flares). Hammond also points out that beads and ear flares are found whole in dedicatory caches, and that the act of smashing jade in termination rituals parallels the smashing of the structures themselves. So, it appears that the artifact form and the event may have dictated the destruction or preservation of an artifact.

The smashing and dispersal of ceramics and jade can also be referred to as a form of termination offering. The term "termination offering" was first coined by Coe (1959) in reference to a deposit on Structure K-5-2nd at Piedras Negras, where open-base vertical flange censers were smashed at the time of structure abandonment. Coe (1959) notes that, despite careful excavation of this termination offering, pieces of censers were missing. This was also the case with many of the Cerros deposits resulting from termination ritual. Similar burned termination offerings were recognized at Kaminaljuyu (Kidder, Jennings, and Shook 1946). Smashed jade was not present in either of those cases.

A layer of intentionally deposited decomposed limestone or marl, 30 cm to 40 cm thick, was observed in the chamber of Burial 10 at Piedras Negras (Coe 1959). The presence of charcoal lenses within the marl suggests that fires had been built on it before the final height was reached. Many artifacts were recovered from this white layer above the floor. Those of jade were intentionally smashed. This Late Classic burial chamber had been opened and its principal interment removed; possibly to be reburied elsewhere. Before the chamber was resealed, marl was scattered about, fires ignited, and artifacts deposited (Coe 1959). This deposit, associated with the abandonment of a burial chamber, is quite similar to the deposits at Cerros containing marl that were associated with the abandonment of monumental architecture.

Potter (1980, 1982) describes an unstructured enigmatic deposit overlying a Late Classic structure in Operation 2012 at the site of Colha in Northern Belize. This medium gray-brown deposit contains smashed Tepeu 3 vessels, human bone, and occasional pieces of broken jade. The deposit may represent a Late or Terminal Classic example of the termination rituals observed at Cerros.

Hammond (1982, 1986) reports two kinds of jade bead deposition associated with the abandonment of Middle Preclassic structures ca. 400 B.C. at the site of Cuello in Northern Belize. Plaster façades were stripped from the buildings, and in one case whole beads were scattered in the scar of the stripped façade. In the other case, whole beads were carefully arranged in a circular pattern in the courtyard floor. In both, the beads are intact, suggesting that the practice of smashing jade in termination ritual is an innovation of the Late Preclassic (Hammond personal communication 1982).

SUMMARY: The vast majority of Cerros jades were broken and recovered from contexts that deviate from previously reported patterns of jade disposal. There were three locations at Cerros, Structures 2A-Sub.4-1st, 4B, and Feature1A, where several jade artifacts were intentionally smashed and scattered about. That activity took place during the abandonment of masonry and perishable structures and has been interpreted as being a part of termination ritual and a form of termination offering (Garber 1981, 1983; Robertson 1983).

At the time of the conquest, the Spanish noted that jade beads were used as money (Tozzer 1941). It is reasonable to suspect that they might have served a similar function in pre-Columbian times as well (Blom 1932; Coe 1965a). At Cerros, certain jade forms, possibly ear flare assemblages, were considered appropriate for sacrifice by destruction, while others were not.

Jades recovered from dedicatory caches are usually intact, whereas those recovered from termination ritual sites are usually broken. Therefore, whole jades are associated with structure completion or dedication, and broken jades are associated with abandonment and destruction. Beads and flares were recovered from both contexts.

Destruction of a valuable material has important economic implications. Demanding tribute for the purpose of stockpiling might have been deemed unacceptable by the support population. Public sacrifice of goods might have been more acceptable to those providing the tribute. By sacrificing jade items, the elite of Cerros raised their prestige through conspicuous consumption and at the same time removed some jade from circulation, thus maintaining its value.

4. THE WORKED BONE INDUSTRY

During the excavations at Cerros 155 pieces of worked bone were recovered. During the faunal analysis by Carr (1985) 89 of those were identified in the general faunal collection and were omitted in the original study of the artifacts (Garber 1981). Descriptions of those additional specimens have been provided by Sorayya Carr (personal communication 1987). Because they were not initially identified as artifacts, they do not have SF numbers and will be referred to by their CM1 catalog number.

Ninety percent of the bone artifacts come from Feature 1A, an occurrence that may be attributed more to a greater preservative environment there than to spatially distinct disposal patterns. Deposits at Feature 1A consist of compact layers of clay, sand, and marl that inhibit the permeation of water, thereby preserving artifacts sealed within. In contrast, many other Cerros deposits are composed of dry-laid construction fill, humus, or sandy loam, which are much more susceptible to water infiltration.

Six human teeth were recovered from Cache 7, a Late Postclassic cache on Structure 4A. These have been identified as unerupted permanent teeth. Upper and lower teeth were present, including two mandibular molars, a mandibular premolar, a maxillar premolar, a shovel-shaped incisor, and a canine. No mandible or maxilla fragments accompanied the teeth, which were from an individual between three and five years of age. None of the teeth showed any signs of having been drilled for suspension. It is possible that a complete cranium was deposited in the cache, but that soil conditions destroyed everything but the teeth, which resisted weathering and disintegration. Alternatively, they might have been extracted and deposited in the cache. The former interpretation seems more likely, especially since shark teeth found in this cache were very poorly preserved, with little of the bony portions intact.

The destructive potential of the soil in which this cache was embedded accounts for the absence of bone artifacts in many other Cerros structures and features. The same applies to nonartifactual bone as well.

ARTIFACT FORM: Bead
SUBFORM: Disk (Fig. 16b, j)
FREQUENCY: 20
MATERIAL: Vertebrae of undetermined species
DATING: Late Preclassic
CONTEXT: Domestic debris 19
Termination ritual 1

COMMENT: The beads are smooth and show occasional light polish. Each side is naturally concave. The holes vary from less than 0.1 cm to 0.7 cm, some with no alteration of the naturally located central hole, and others intentionally enlarged to accommodate a thicker string.

Most of the beads are whole and have a U-shaped groove, which encircles the outer edge. They appear to be ground-out natural depressions. Some have been split along, or to the side of, the groove, forming two beads from one vertebrae. All are round and vary in diameter from 1.5 cm to 0.6 cm.

ARTIFACT FORM: Bead
SUBFORM: Tubular (Fig. 16c, d)
FREQUENCY: 5
MATERIAL: Bone of undetermined species
DATING: Late Preclassic
CONTEXT: Domestic debris 4
In floor 1

COMMENT: SF-420 is a portion of a tubular bead whose exterior surface has been smoothed and shows light sheen. It may have been made on a phalanx. It was burned after breakage, but a portion of the hole rim is intact.

SF-767 is generally tubular, but the sides are not parallel (Fig. 16c). One end is expanding and bulbous while the other end is tapered. The central portion of the shaft has parallel sides. This form is quite common among the coral beads in the Cerros collection. The hole has been biconically enlarged and is slightly off center. Its surface is heavily eroded, obscuring any signs of polish. Like the vast majority of coral beads of this form, it is complete.

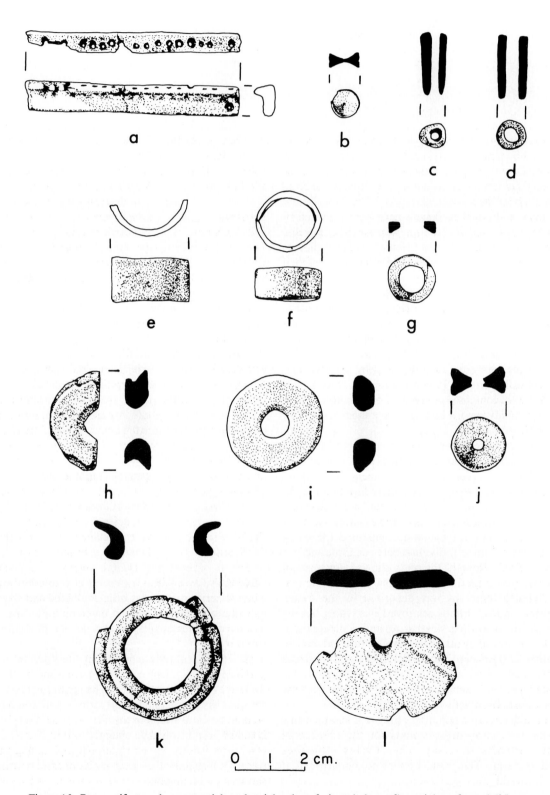

Figure 16. Bone artifacts. a, bar pectoral; b, c, d, g, j, beads; e, f, rings; h, k, ear flares; i, l, perforated disks.

SF-871 is a complete bead made from a long bone and has a suspension hole, which is the enlarged natural marrow cavity (Fig. 16d). Both ends are highly polished and have striations from manufacture. The sides are slightly eroded but also show some polish.

SF-1395 is a broken tubular bead with a rounded end. Like SF-420, it was heavily burned after breakage.

SF-2001 is a bead with a recent break. The suspension hole is the natural marrow cavity, which was smoothed and expanded. The intact end was shaped by cutting and is beveled toward the exterior. Its exterior surface is polished.

Some of these beads, although found in domestic debris, may have been deposited as a part of a termination ritual.

SUMMARY: Bead
FREQUENCY: Total of all subforms   25
DATING: Late Preclassic   25
CONTEXT: Domestic debris   23
                 Termination ritual   1
                 In floor   1

ARTIFACT FORM: Pendant
SUBFORM: Canine (Fig. 17c, d, e, f, g)
FREQUENCY: 7
MATERIAL: Peccary canine   2
                 Dog canine   1
                 Undetermined species
                   canine   4
DATING: Late Preclassic   6
                 Late Postclassic   1
CONTEXT: Domestic debris   5
                 Fall   1
                 Pit fill   1

COMMENT: SF-258 and CM1-14614 are peccary canines with root tips that have been biconically drilled (Fig. 17g). CM1-14614 has an incomplete second drill hole.

Four of the pendants are canines of undetermined species and are considerably smaller than the above specimens. The biconical drill holes are located in the root tip.

CM1-12917 is a dog canine that has an encircling groove between the root and crown, probably placed in an attempt to separate the two. A portion of the crown is missing. This breakage may have occurred during this procedure.

ARTIFACT FORM: Pendant
SUBFORM: Shark tooth (Fig. 17a)
FREQUENCY: 6
MATERIAL: Shark tooth
DATING: Late Preclassic   2
                 Late Postclassic   4
CONTEXT: Cache   4
                 Domestic debris   2

COMMENT: SF-1383 and CM1-7410 are well-preserved teeth, each with two biconical drill holes, one on each tang portion of the root (Fig. 17a). Each drill hole is 0.1 cm in diameter. They are Late Preclassic in date and appeared in a context of domestic debris.

SF-795 (A–D) are four poorly preserved shark teeth found in Cache 7, a Late Postclassic cache on Structure 4A. Only small splinters of the bony portions were preserved. Although none have drill holes, it is assumed that the poorly preserved bases were drilled for suspension, since they were associated with many shell and jade beads.

ARTIFACT FORM: Pendant
SUBFORM: Drilled bar (Fig. 16a)
FREQUENCY: 1
DATING: Late Preclassic
CONTEXT: Domestic debris

COMMENT: SF-1163 is bar-shaped in outline and L-shaped in section. Both exterior surfaces are polished and the interior faces have been smoothed. The piece has fifteen complete holes and four incomplete ones toward the broken end. All holes except one are on the short portion of the L. This one is located near the corner of the piece and extends from the outside surface to the inside surface. Fourteen holes are biconically drilled, and, of the remaining four, it is difficult to say whether they are uniconical or biconical. The holes range from 0.1 cm to 0.2 cm in diameter. The piece probably functioned as a central element in a bar pectoral composite necklace, from which several beads were suspended. Proskouriakoff (1974: 85) describes a very similar jade form for later time periods.

ARTIFACT FORM: Pendant
SUBFORM: Jaw (Fig. 17b)
FREQUENCY: 1
MATERIAL: Ray jaw of undetermined
                   species
DATING: Unknown
CONTEXT: Beach near Feature 1A

COMMENT: The jaw portion of SF-281 is 4.0 cm long. The biconical drill hole is located immediately below the teeth in the bony portion and is located equidistant from the ends.

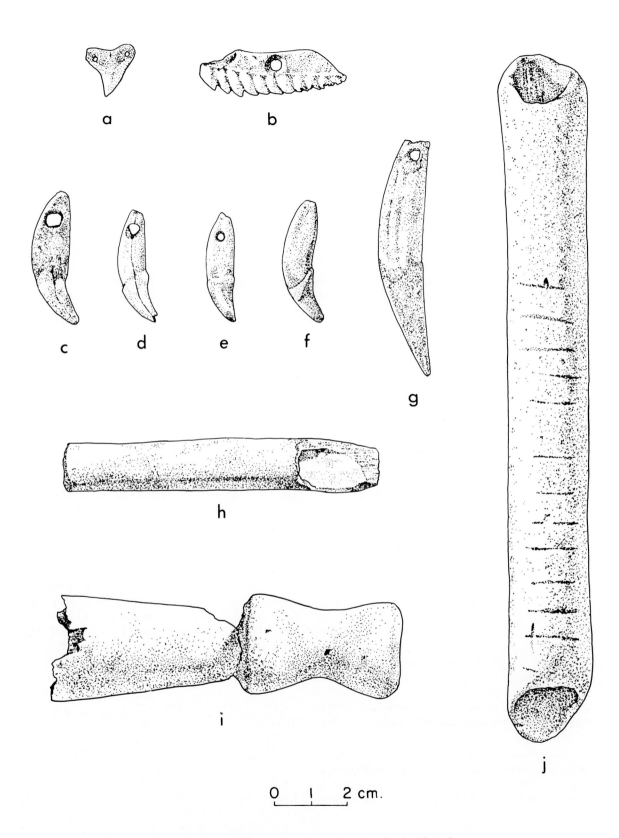

Figure 17. Bone artifacts. a–g, tooth pendants; h, tube; i, whistle; j, rasp.

SUMMARY: Pendant
FREQUENCY: Total of all subforms 15
DATING: Late Preclassic 9
Late Postclassic 5
Unknown 1
CONTEXT: Domestic debris 8
Cache 4
Fall 1
Pit fill 1
Beach near Feature 1A 1

ARTIFACT FORM: Ring (Fig. 16e, f)
FREQUENCY: 2
MATERIAL: Long bone of
undetermined species
DATING: Late Preclassic
CONTEXT: Burial 1
Domestic debris 1

COMMENT: SF-121 is complete and was found in association with Burial 8. It is oval and appears warped (Fig. 16f). The edges are rounded and slightly polished, but its surfaces are badly weathered. The interior surface has encircling striations, probably due to cleaning out of the central cavity during manufacture.

SF-819 is one-half of a bone ring with an estimated diameter of 2.2 cm (Fig. 16e). The edges are flat to slightly rounded. Its outside surface is polished and lightly striated. It was recovered from domestic debris.

ARTIFACT FORM: Ear flare (Fig. 16h, k)
FREQUENCY: 2
MATERIAL: Bone of undetermined
species
DATING: Late Preclassic
CONTEXT: Domestic debris 1
Burial 1

COMMENT: SF-120 appeared in Burial 8. While only 80% of the specimen survived, it was, nevertheless, in a good state of preservation despite its being brittle. Both the flat ventral side and the flaring dorsal side, which angle toward the central throat (Fig. 16k), are polished. The rim of the bone was carefully ground.

SF-344 consists of a fragmented ear flare found in a deposit of domestic debris. While erosion has defaced its surface, enough remains intact to reveal some polish. A U-shaped groove encircles the outer or exterior side of the flare (Fig. 16h).

ARTIFACT FORM: Stingray spine
FREQUENCY: 2

MATERIAL: *Urolophus jamaicensis*
DATING: Late Preclassic
CONTEXT: Domestic debris 1
Pit fill 1

COMMENT: Neither of these finds, both of them broken, shows any evidence of modification or usage, although stingray spines such as these often functioned as bloodletters.

ARTIFACT FORM: Pointed bone tool
(Fig. 18a–h)
FREQUENCY: 46
DATING: Late Preclassic
CONTEXT: Domestic debris 35
Pit fill 8
Burial 2
Construction fill without
rubble 1

COMMENT: SF-11 is broken. Its surface is badly eroded, although some use polish can be observed at the broken tip and along the shaft.

Both ends of SF-473 are broken. It tapers toward one end. Some polish is present on the shaft, and it appears fire hardened.

SF-533 is a complete specimen that is 10.7 cm long with a sharp off-center point.

SF-551 is broken into three pieces, although the complete specimen is represented and is 12.0 cm long. The entire tool has been fire hardened. The point section is circular, the midsection is lenticular, and the butt end is triangular. Its entire shaft is highly polished.

SF-842 is whole except for the tip. The shaft has light use polish, and the butt end has been lightly ground.

The tip end of SF-884 is broken. The complete butt end is unusual in that it exhibits a U-shaped notch. This notch may have been ground for a special function, such as weaving. Both the tip and butt ends exhibit use polish and may have been fire hardened.

SF-1364 is a midsection that has polish on the shaft and appears to have been fire hardened. The tip end exhibits heavy use polish but does not appear to have been used after it was snapped.

SF-1413 is complete but fragmented and poorly preserved. The tip is off-center and was produced by cutting or grinding a bevel, producing a knifelike point. The piece is too poorly preserved to show polish.

SF-548 was fashioned from the distal end of a tibia from a white-tailed deer. Its tip is not present; however, the break is fresh and probably occurred during excavation. Cut marks are present along its edge and

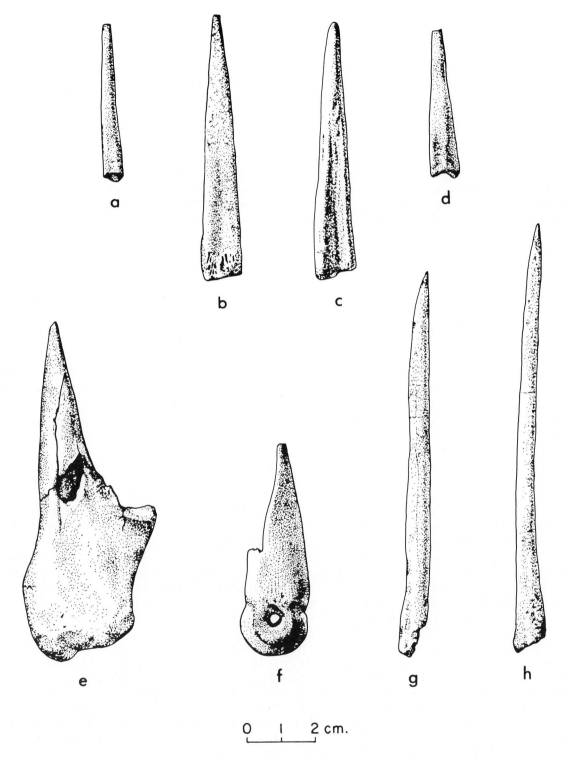

Figure 18. Pointed bone tools.

probably result from shaping during the removal of the anterior surface.

SF-699 is broken on the butt end. Its point is blunt and was smoothed and polished on both edges.

SF-1187 was made from a white-tailed deer ulna. Its tip is chipped, and it is difficult to determine whether it was sharp or blunt (Fig. 18e). Use polish can be observed on the tipmost 2.5 cm of the piece. Numerous striations encircling the tip are also present. This indicates that the tool was used to bore, rather than in a thrusting or piercing fashion.

SF-1318 was made from the end portion of a white-tailed deer long bone. A hole, presumably for suspension, was drilled through the head of the bone (Fig. 18f). It tapers abruptly toward the tip end, which is broken. Smoothing striations and shaping cut marks can be observed on several areas of this specimen.

CM1-10026 is a needle with a broken tip made from an unidentified long bone. The shaft has use polish and striations. The large end is 0.5 cm in diameter. A portion surrounding the drill hole is missing and thus the exact hole diameter cannot be determined.

ARTIFACT FORM: Pointed antler tool
                        (Fig. 19)
FREQUENCY: 4
MATERIAL: *Odocoileus virginianus*
DATING: Late Preclassic
CONTEXT: Pit fill   2
                        Burial   1
                        Domestic debris 1

COMMENT: SF-546 has three utilized areas (Fig. 19a). It was made from the basal portion of an *Odocoileus virginianus* (white-tailed deer) antler and has a portion of the cranium attached. The most prominent area of utilization is a spike fashioned from the ascending element of the antler. The tip area of this spike was fire hardened, as evidenced by a darkened area. The tip area also shows signs of polish from use or shaping. The protrusion at the base of the antler was fashioned to produce two semipointed nubs, which show signs of smoothing but not of fire hardening. The utilized areas are approximately 0.7 cm long. The large spike appears to have functioned as a punch or awl. The smaller nubs are blunt, and it is not clear how these functioned.

SF-547 was fashioned from the base of an antler and the ascending curved portion. The tip is broken and was not recovered. The piece has been sharpened by carving and scraping, as evidenced by numerous longitudinal striations. Light use polish is present on the tipmost half of the specimen. Although it is impossible to determine if the tip was sharp or blunt, because there is polish toward the tip end, it probably functioned as a punch or awl.

SF-695 is the tip portion of a broken antler tool and was shaped to a rounded, blunt point. It exhibits facets from shaping by carving and grinding, but no polish is present. Because the tip looks roughened and damaged, it may have functioned as a tine in working chert or obsidian.

SF-914 was fashioned from the base and ascending portion of an antler. A portion of the cranium is attached to the antler base. It has two working points (Fig. 19b). The largest was fashioned from the main ascending portion of the antler. This tip area was deliberately shaped and was lightly polished. The second working area was fashioned from the nub near the base of the antler. This point is rounded and blunt. This nub was smoothed down and also shows polish. This protrusion would aid in firmly gripping the piece while using the larger punch. This find is in two pieces and was broken sometime prior to excavation. Both SF-546 and SF-547 were recovered from a pit, Feature 1A-9, along with chert debris, obsidian blades, large sherds, shell, fish bone, and SF-105, the distal end of a dark green reworked chloromelanite axe.

ARTIFACT FORM: Rasp (Fig. 17j)
FREQUENCY: 1
MATERIAL: Femur—*Homo sapiens*
DATING: Probably Late Preclassic
CONTEXT: Beach near Feature 1A

COMMENT: Thirteen grooves can be observed on SF-280. More may have been present when it was complete. The grooves are 1.9 cm to 1.2 cm long and most are 0.2 cm wide and 0.1 deep. It is weathered and may be water rolled. Similar specimens have been found throughout the Maya Lowlands.

ARTIFACT FORM: Whistle (Fig. 17i)
FREQUENCY: 1
MATERIAL: Long bone—mammal of
                            undetermined species
DATING: Late Preclassic
CONTEXT: Pit fill

COMMENT: The unbroken end of SF-524 is spool-shaped and has a carefully rounded opening 1.5 cm in diameter. This opening extends through the piece, utilizing the natural central cavity that was cleaned out and enlarged. The spool-like end is 4.3 cm long and

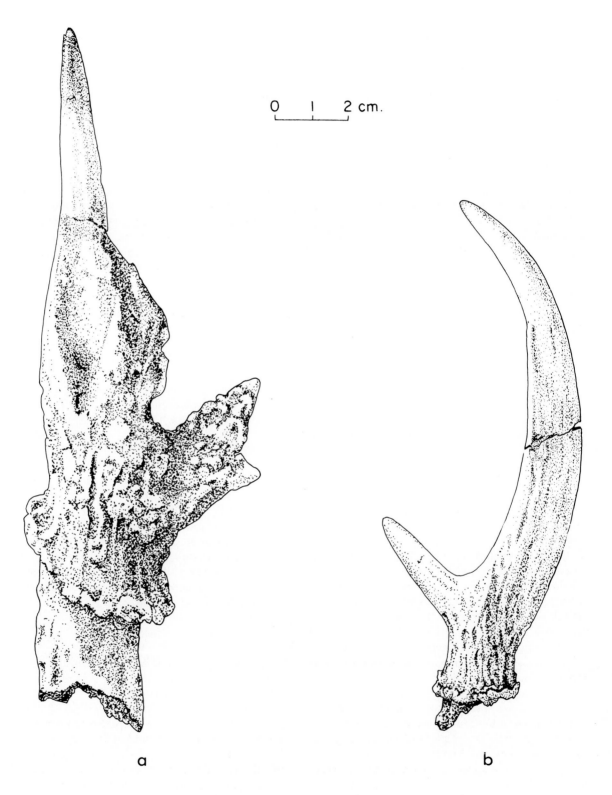

Figure 19. Antler tools. a, SF-546; b, SF-914.

2.2 cm to 2.5 cm in diameter at its constricted portion. It has a hole 1.1 cm by 1.7 cm in the constricted portion of the spool. This hole connects with the hole extending through the piece. The remainder of the specimen is cone-shaped, with the constricted end adjacent to the spool. This constricted end is 1.9 cm in diameter, and the expanded end is 2.9 cm in diameter. A portion of the expanded end rim is present. The surface is weathered, but polish can be observed. Identification as a whistle is based on form. The mouthpiece is the spool-shaped end. Because some fragments are missing and because the interior is heavily encrusted, the piece is no longer functional as a whistle. It was found in Feature 1A-8, a pit that might have functioned as a cache pit for Structure 2A-Sub.1-2nd (Cliff 1982).

ARTIFACT FORM:	Tube (Fig. 17h)	
FREQUENCY:		2
MATERIAL:	Long bone—mammal of undetermined species	2
DATING:	Late Preclassic	
CONTEXT:	Beach near Feature 1A	1
	Domestic debris	1

COMMENT: SF-470 is a broken bone tube. The intact end has been shaped by cutting and is beveled toward the exterior (Fig. 17h). The surface of the bone exhibits dull polish.

SF-1231 is also worked on one end, although the other end is whole and unaltered. The worked end appears to have been cut by the incision of an encircling groove, which is beveled toward the exterior. The surface of the bone is heavily weathered but shows signs of light smoothing. The function of these bone tubes is problematical.

ARTIFACT FORM:	Perforated bone	
SUBFORM:	Disks (Fig. 16i)	
FREQUENCY:		2
MATERIAL:	Bone of undetermined species	
DATING:	Unknown	
CONTEXT:	Surface	1
	Beach	1

COMMENT: SF-532 is one-half of a disk with a centrally located biconical drill hole. Its edges are ground and beveled toward one face.

SF-1087 is whole. It has a centrally located biconically drilled hole (Fig. 16i). One surface is flat and exhibits many pores. The edges are beveled toward

this face. The function of these perforated disks cannot be determined.

ARTIFACT FORM:	Perforated bone	
SUBFORM:	Unmodified	
FREQUENCY:		4
MATERIAL:	Turtle	3
	Fox	1
DATING:	Late Preclassic	
CONTEXT:	Domestic debris	

COMMENT: Other than the perforation holes, these specimens show no other signs of modification. CM1-1995 is a complete turtle nuchal with a centrally located uniconical drill hole. It is 2.1 cm by 2.3 cm. CM1-11966 has been broken into several pieces but was probably a complete shell at the time of use. It has a uniconical drill hole in the central portion of the nuchal. The third perforated turtle bone has no catalog number and is a plastron fragment with a uniconical hole drilled from the outer surface.

CM1-707 is a nearly complete left frontal of a fox skull. It has an angled drill hole toward one edge.

MISCELLANEOUS WORKED PIECES

FREQUENCY:		49
MATERIAL:	Undetermined	32
	Odocoileus virginianus	9
	Turtle species unidentified	3
	Canine familiaris	2
	Magama americana	1
	Tayassu tajacu	1
	Trinchechus manatus	1
DATING:	Late Preclassic	45
	Early Classic	1
	Late Postclassic	2
	Unknown	1
CONTEXT:	Domestic debris	40
	Pit fill	3
	Humus	2
	Beach near Feature 1A	1
	Burial	1
	On floor	1
	Unknown	1

COMMENT: The specimens included in this category include a wide range of worked bones. Evidence for their having been worked includes grinding striations, polish, batter, and splitting. The vast majority appear to represent unfinished tools, broken tools, or debitage produced during tool manufacture.

5. THE WORKED SHELL INDUSTRY

One hundred and sixty objects of worked shell were recovered from Cerros. Because of their small size, many specimens, particularly beads, could not be identified as to genus or species. Shell identifications are provided whenever possible. Anthony Andrews identified some of the finds during visits to the site in the 1978 and 1979 field seasons.

Some of the shell artifacts belong to the genus *Spondylus*. Four almost complete shells came from a Late Preclassic cache on Structure 6B. These shells are currently housed in Belmopan, Belize. The *Spondylus* artifacts curated at Southern Methodist University are too fragmentary or too altered to make a species identification.

Some of the finds identified as conch were done so on the basis of their pink color, characteristic of many conch species, while others were identified on the basis of form.

Although division of artifacts by industry often separates functionally similar specimens such as jade and shell beads, each had its own distinct pattern of disposal. This will be discussed in detail in the summary section on shell beads.

ARTIFACT FORM: BEAD

The shell beads recovered from Cerros were divided according to subform. The frequencies and percentages of these subforms appear in table 11. Unlike the polished stone beads, the shell beads covaried between material and subform due to the suitability of certain materials for specific forms. This is discussed in the "Comment" section of the various subforms. More detailed comparison between polished stone and worked shell beads takes place in the summary section on shell beads.

Cerros shell beads exhibit varying degrees of polish. For the most part, this is due to the raw material, as certain kinds of shell can be highly polished, whereas others can only be smoothed. Many of the disk beads were uniconically drilled, but the elongated beads, such as the tubular and flared subforms, were drilled biconically.

TABLE 11

Shell Bead Subforms

Subform	Frequency	%
Disk	53	57.2
Rectangular	11	12.1
Tubular	9	9.9
Flared	9	9.9
Effigy	2	2.2
Subspherical	2	2.2
Wedge	1	1.1
Triangular	1	1.1
Elongated bipoint	1	1.1
Teardrop	1	1.1
Unknown	1	
Total	91	

Twenty Cerros beads have a short, shallow groove on one of their drill hole surfaces. They are less than 0.1 cm deep and wide and rarely exceed 0.3 cm in length. Many are visible only with the aid of a 10× lens. They may have been ground intentionally to secure the bead during the drilling stage. All but one were on disk beads. That one is on a subspherical bead. Similar grooves also appear on some of the polished stone beads (see chapter 3).

ARTIFACT FORM:	Bead	
SUBFORM:	Disk (Fig. 20l, 21j)	
FREQUENCY:		53
MATERIAL:	Conch	13
	Spondylus	12
	Coral	2
	Dentallium	1
	Unknown	25
DATING:	Late Preclassic	49
	Late Postclassic	3
	Unknown	1
CONTEXT:	Domestic debris	34
	Cache	14
	Burial	3
	Pit fill	1
	Fall	1

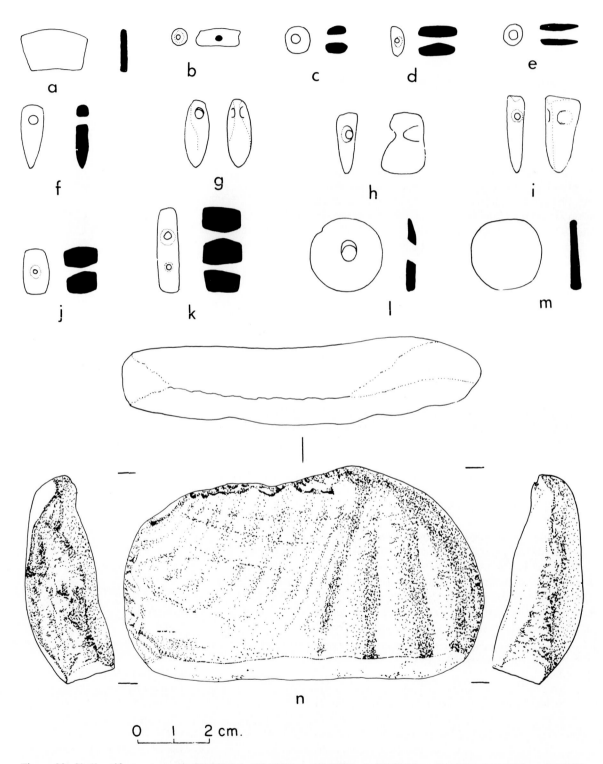

Figure 20. Shell artifacts. a, mosaic SF-738B; b, SF-736B; c, SF-73f91; d, SF-655C; e, SF-739B; f, SF-796; g, SF-734D; h, SF-734A; i, SF-734C; j, SF-655C; k, SF-1053; l, SF-737A; m, SF-738A; n, SF-42.

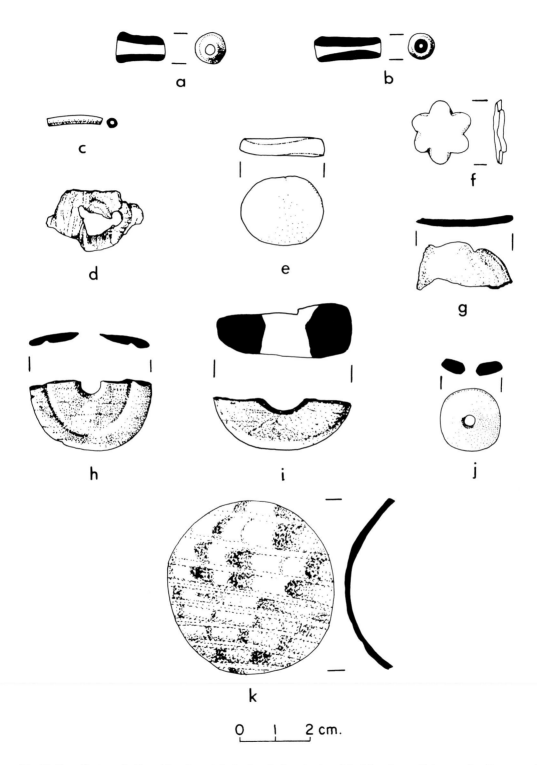

Figure 21. Shell artifacts. a, b, flared beads; c, tubular bead; d, cutout; e, f, h, i, k, adorno disks; g, miscellaneous piece; j, disk bead.

COMMENT: Disk beads are those that have parallel drill surfaces and a diameter that is greater than the length of the drill hole. With the exception of one bead, SF-919, all of the shell beads that exhibit a groove on the drill hole surface are of the disk subform. Disk beads are the most common subform of shell bead in the Late Preclassic period at Cerros. This subform is relatively rare in the Late Postclassic.

ARTIFACT FORM: Bead
SUBFORM: Rectangular
                 (Fig. 20d, j, k)
FREQUENCY: 11
MATERIAL: *Spondylus:*   10
                 Unknown   1
DATING: Late Postclassic
CONTEXT: Cache

COMMENT: Rectangular beads are so shaped in plan and flattened in section. Some have slightly convex sides (Fig. 20j). SF-1053 has two parallel, biconically drilled holes, which run the width of the bead (Fig. 20k). One face is orange, the other is white. Even though many shell beads were recovered from Late Preclassic deposits, none were of the rectangular subform. At Cerros this subform is restricted to the Late Postclassic period.

ARTIFACT FORM: Bead
SUBFORM: Tubular
                 (Figs. 20b, e, 21c)
FREQUENCY: 9
MATERIAL: *Spondylus*   4
                 Dentallium   4
                 Unknown   1
DATING: Late Preclassic   5
                 Late Postclassic   3
                 Unknown   1
CONTEXT: Domestic debris   3
                 Cache   4
                 Beach near Feature 1A 1
                 Construction fill without
                    rubble   1

COMMENT: Tubular beads have parallel sides and a hole length that is greater than the bead diameter.

It should be noted that the beads made of dentallium have a natural hole and, because of the shell form, are natural tubular beads. When cut into very short sections, like SF-1389, the bead is then a disk bead. Some of the dentallium tubular beads show light grinding on the sides and ends. Dentallium beads are rare in

the Maya area; the only other reported occurrence is at Barton Ramie (Willey et al. 1965).

SF-736B has two drill holes (Fig. 20b). The main drill hole is biconical and runs the length of the piece. The second hole is perpendicular to the main hole and enters the bead equidistant from its ends. This hole intersects with the main hole but does not pierce through the other side.

ARTIFACT FORM: Bead
SUBFORM: Flared (Figs. 21a, b, 22a)
FREQUENCY: 9
MATERIAL: Coral
DATING: Late Preclassic
CONTEXT: Domestic debris

COMMENT: These beads exhibit slight to very pronounced flares. The bulges at one end of the coral pieces may be natural. If so, this bulge is intentionally enhanced by grinding on some of the specimens. All are biconically drilled. The flared coral beads are very similar to SF-145, a flared jade bead found in association with an ear spool. Flared beads are frequently depicted on stelae and in the codices, protruding from the center of an ear spool or other flare.

ARTIFACT FORM: Bead
SUBFORM: Effigy
FREQUENCY: 2
MATERIAL: Coral
DATING: Late Preclassic
CONTEXT: Domestic debris

COMMENT: Both SF-61 and SF-71A represent birds in profile. Each has a crest, beak, bulging chest, and tail. The eye on each is represented by a biconically drilled hole.

ARTIFACT FORM: Bead (Fig. 20c)
SUBFORM: Subspherical
FREQUENCY: 2
MATERIAL: Unknown
DATING: Late Preclassic
CONTEXT: Construction fill without
                    rubble   1
                 Domestic debris   1

COMMENT: Subspherical beads have a diameter that is greater than the length of their drill hole. Subspherical shell beads are relatively rare. This is probably due to the nature of the raw material, as shell is more conducive to making disks.

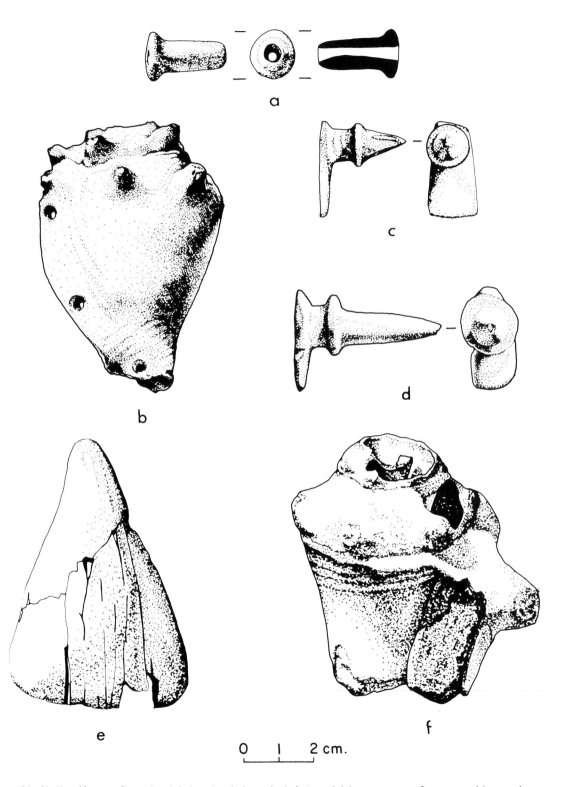

Figure 22. Shell artifacts. a, flared bead; b, largely whole worked piece; c, d, labrets; e, scoop; f, trumpet with ceramic mute.

ARTIFACT FORM: Bead
SUBFORM: Wedge (Fig. 20h)
FREQUENCY: 1
MATERIAL: Unknown
DATING: Late Postclassic
CONTEXT: Cache

COMMENT: SF-734A is wedge-shaped in section and axe-shaped in plan. One side is off-white, the other is purple. Like the wedge-shaped polished stone beads, this subform is Late Postclassic.

ARTIFACT FORM: Bead
SUBFORM: Triangular (Fig. 20i)
FREQUENCY: 1
MATERIAL: *Spondylus*
DATING: Late Postclassic
CONTEXT: Cache

COMMENT: All four faces of SF-734C are triangular. The biconical drill hole is at the wide end.

ARTIFACT FORM: Bead
SUBFORM: Elongated Bipoint (Fig. 20g)
FREQUENCY: 1
MATERIAL: *Spondylus*
DATING: Late Postclassic
CONTEXT: Cache

COMMENT: SF-734D is shaped very much like a human canine. The biconical drill hole is located at one end.

ARTIFACT FORM: Bead
SUBFORM: Teardrop (Fig. 20f)
FREQUENCY: 1
MATERIAL: *Spondylus*
DATING: Late Postclassic
CONTEXT: Cache

COMMENT: In outline SF-796 is shaped like a teardrop. The drill hole is located toward the rounded end. Both drilling surfaces are flat.

ARTIFACT FORM: Bead
SUBFORM: Unknown
FREQUENCY: 1
MATERIAL: Conch
DATING: Unknown, probably Late Preclassic
CONTEXT: Beach near Feature 1A

COMMENT: SF-1070j is a drill hole rim fragment.

SUMMARY: Beads
FREQUENCY: Total of all subforms and those
                    of unknown form   91
MATERIAL: *Spondylus*   29
            Conch   14
            Coral   13
            Dentallium   5
            Unknown   30
DATING: Late Preclassic   67
          Late Postclassic   21
          Unknown   3
CONTEXT: Domestic debris   49
           Cache   33
           Burial   3
           Beach near Feature 1A   2
           Construction fill without
                    rubble   2
           Fall   1
           Pit fill   1

COMMENT: Table 12 clearly shows that, although there is overlap in the subforms of stone and shell beads, there are preferred subforms for each of the two raw material groupings. Most notable is that disk beads account for over half of the shell beads, whereas they account for less than 3.0% of the stone beads. Subspherical and barrel subforms are common in the stone specimens and rare in shell. No doubt, this is due to the

TABLE 12

Stone and Shell Bead Subforms

Subform	Shell (%)	Stone (%)
Disk	57.8	2.9
Rectangular	12.2	1.0
Tubular	11.1	23.1
Flared	11.1	1.0
Effigy	2.2	0.0
Subspherical	1.1	21.2
Wedge	1.1	3.8
Triangular	1.1	0.0
Elongated bipoint	1.1	0.0
Teardrop	1.1	0.0
Barrel	0.0	31.7
Spherical	0.0	6.7
Collared	0.0	5.8
Irregular	0.0	2.9
	n = 90	n = 104

nature of the raw material. Disks can be easily removed with a tubular drill from most kinds of shell or can be fashioned from laminar fragments. Spherical, subspherical, and barrel forms are more easily manufactured from a raw material that is in chunks, blocks, or pebbles, such as jadeite or other greenstones.

Table 13 lists the percentages of the various subforms of shell beads for each time period at Cerros. A notable difference between the Late Preclassic and the Late Postclassic is the relatively high percentage of disk beads in the Late Preclassic and the relatively high percentage of rectangular beads in the Late Postclassic. These differences may be a reflection of changes in subform preference, although it should be kept in mind that a majority of the Late Postclassic beads came from a cache context, whereas the Late Preclassic beads came from a wide variety of contexts. As was the case with stone beads, there is a high percentage of rectangular subforms during the Late Postclassic.

No shell beads were recovered from any of the Cerros Early Classic deposits; however, several Early Classic jade beads were found. This is the result of differential patterns of disposal for stone versus shell beads. Table 14 shows the percentages of selected contexts from which stone and shell beads have been recovered. Contexts that have relatively small, statistically insignificant percentages are not shown. There is a complete absence of shell beads in deposits resulting from termination rituals associated with the destruction and abandonment of monumental architecture.

TABLE 14

Context Percentages for Stone and Shell Beads

Context	Stone (%)	Shell (%)
Domestic debris	39.6	53.8
Termination ritual	34.7	0.0
Cache	12.5	36.3
Beach near Feature 1A	7.6	2.2
	n = 144	n = 91

Many of the stone beads recovered from within domestic debris might have been deposited as a part of termination ritual associated with domestic architecture (see the discussion at the end of chapter 3 on patterns of jade disposal and termination ritual). Many of the shell beads were recovered from the same deposits of domestic debris as were the stone beads and thus may have been a part of the termination of the associated domestic structures.

Jade beads and shell beads were deposited quite differently. Shell beads were not appropriate for inclusion in the termination ritual associated with monumental architecture, but might have been sacrificed in the abandonment of a domestic structure. Perhaps the less-expensive shell, along with some jade, was appropriate for the abandonment of a private domestic structure. In those deposits, shell beads were found whole, as opposed to the jade beads, which were intentionally smashed.

TABLE 13

Shell Bead Subform Percentages by Period

Subform	Late Preclassic (%)	Late Postclassic (%)
Disk	71.6	14.3
Rectangular	0.0	52.4
Tubular	9.0	14.3
Flared	14.9	0.0
Effigy	3.0	0.0
Subspherical	1.5	0.0
Wedge	0.0	4.8
Triangular	0.0	4.8
Elongated bipoint	0.0	4.8
Teardrop	0.0	4.8
	n = 67	n = 21

ARTIFACT FORM:	Adorno	
SUBFORM:	Disk (Fig. 20m, 21e, f, h, i, k)	
FREQUENCY:		18
DATING:	Late Preclassic	15
	Early Classic	2
	Unknown	1
CONTEXT:	Cache	11
	Domestic debris	5
	Beach near Feature 1A	1
	Humus	1

COMMENT: SF-163, SF-164, SF-165, SF-166, SF-167, and SF-168 are oval or round in outline and have from one to five holes drilled near their edges. All are fragile and have lustrous, pearly-white surfaces. They may have functioned as mirror backs, as several specular hematite mirror fragments were recovered from Cache 1, which also contained these disks. Cache 1 is a Late Preclassic dedicatory cache on the summit of Structure 6B. SF-172A-E are fragments of similar shell with ground edges and drill holes and might also have been disks when whole.

Two pieces, SF-1254 and SF-1255, are very similar in size and shape. They are very thin and fragile and each has a very small drill hole near its edge. They are ovoid in outline and their edges have been ground. They probably functioned as ornaments sewn onto clothing.

SF-124 is one-half of a perforated *Spondylus* disk (Fig. 21h). Encircling the centrally located 0.6 cm diameter hole is a groove 2.5 cm in diameter. This groove is on its concave surface. This specimen is very similar to one recovered from Colha (Dreiss 1982).

SF-921 is one-half of a carefully made doughnut-shaped ornament manufactured from an off-white shell of undetermined species. The central hole has been biconically drilled (Fig. 21i).

SF-1844 and SF-738A are similar in size. Both are round or slightly oval. SF-1844 is of a dull gray shell (Fig. 21e). SF-738A was recovered from a cache and is of *Spondylus* (Fig. 20m). One surface is orange, the other is white. SF-1378 is flower-shaped in outline and has six carefully ground petals (Fig. 21f). It has a natural luster.

SF-1402 is circular in outline and has been cut from a trident shell (Fig. 21k). It is curved and may have functioned as a scoop or potter's scraper.

ARTIFACT FORM: Adorno
SUBFORM: Unspecified
(Fig. 23a, b, g)
FREQUENCY: 4
DATING: Late Preclassic 3
Late Postclassic 1
CONTEXT: Pit fill 1
Fall 1
Humus/fall 1
Construction fill with
rubble 1

COMMENT: SF-417 is a fragment of a *Spondylus* shell pendant of unknown shape. Its edge is angled, and it has a drill hole very close to its edge (Fig. 23b).

SF-701 is a triangular-shaped pendant. One corner has been broken off. The drill hole is uniconical. A V-shaped groove crosses the piece. SF-1412 is also a triangular-shaped pendant. It is gray and has two biconical drill holes along the short end of the piece (Fig. 23g). Neither face shows any signs of polish.

SF-1946 was manufactured from a univalve of undetermined species. It is a representation of a face (Fig. 23a). The eyes were formed by two drill holes, each 0.2 cm to 0.3 cm in diameter. The mouth was formed by a saw mark 0.8 cm long, but the cut has pierced the shell for only 0.4 cm. The top of the mouth is straight, whereas the bottom is curved, giving the face a smiling appearance. There is no nose. The apex or spiral of the shell is on the upper left corner of the face (looking toward the face) and looks like a side knot of hair or headdress. SF-158, a jade head pendant, exhibits a similar projection. On the reverse side of the shell are two holes, each 0.3 cm in diameter, drilled presumably for suspension or fastening to a garment. Similar "face" shells of *Oliva* have been reported from Yucatán sites (Andrews 1969; Eaton 1978; Phillips 1979; Proskouriakoff 1962).

ARTIFACT FORM: Largely whole worked
shells
SUBFORM: Tinkler (Fig. 23e, f)
FREQUENCY: 7
MATERIAL: *Oliva*
DATING: Late Preclassic
CONTEXT: Domestic debris 4
Pit fill 2
Construction fill with
rubble 1

COMMENT: The spire was removed from all of these specimens by sawing and grinding. They have up to three drill holes, and two have none. These are either incomplete or were suspended by running a knotted cord up through the center (Suárez 1974). Tinklers are common Maya artifacts and have been recovered throughout the Maya Lowlands (Phillips 1979).

ARTIFACT FORM: Largely whole worked shell
SUBFORM: Univalve (Fig. 22b)
FREQUENCY: 1
MATERIAL: Conch
DATING: Unknown
CONTEXT: Beach

COMMENT: SF-1469 was made from a pearly white univalve. The exterior lip was cut or broken off and ground smooth. Three uniconically drilled holes were drilled along this edge. The ventral half of the shell is not present and appears to have been broken off rather than sawn off, as no saw marks can be observed.

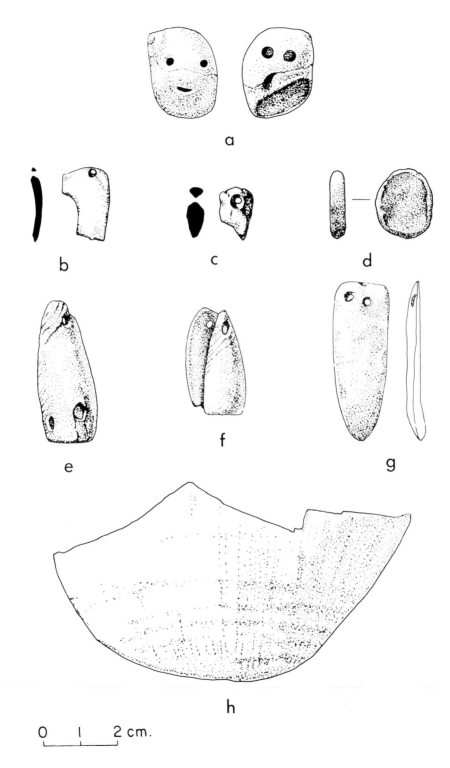

Figure 23. Shell artifacts. a, adorno face; b, adorno; c, bead; d, adorno disk; e, f, tinklers; g, pendant; h, miscellaneous worked piece.

ARTIFACT FORM: Largely whole worked
                  shell
SUBFORM: Bivalve
FREQUENCY: 5
MATERIAL: *Spondylus*   4
                  Unknown   1
DATING: Late Preclassic
CONTEXT: Cache   4
                  Burial   1

COMMENT: The four *Spondylus* shells were recovered from Cache 1 on Structure 6B. Three have two drill holes, and the other has three. All of the drill holes are located near the valve. The holes vary from 0.4 cm to 0.7 cm in diameter. The bivalve area on each shell shows signs of having been shaped by grinding.

SF-446 is a small gray shell with two holes, each 0.3 cm in diameter drilled in the valve area. There are no signs of any attempts to smooth or polish this specimen.

ARTIFACT FORM: Axe
SUBFORM: Oval (Fig. 20n)
FREQUENCY: 2
MATERIAL: Conch
DATING: Late Preclassic   1
                  Unknown   1
CONTEXT: Domestic debris   1
                  Beach near Feature 1A   1

COMMENT: SF-42 was made from the flared edge area of a large conch. It is ovoid in outline. One end has been bifacially worked and shows heavy batter (Fig. 20n).

SF-1468 is also oval in outline. All edges show use and alteration, although these patterns are difficult to assess because the piece has been water rolled. Smoothing is present along one long edge, possibly as a result of hafting. Similar finds are reported from several Lowland Maya sites (Andrews 1969; Ball 1977b; Dreiss 1982; Eaton 1976; Phillips 1979; Piña Chan 1968).

ARTIFACT FORM: Trumpet (Fig. 22f)
FREQUENCY: 2
MATERIAL: *Strombus gigas*
DATING: Late Postclassic   1
                  Unknown   1
CONTEXT: Cache   1
                  Humus/fall   1

COMMENT: The apex of SF-666A was removed by breakage along a suture that was lightly ground (Fig. 22f). A portion of the exterior lip was sawed off and lightly ground. The anterior portion of the shell was also removed. A worked sherd mute was found in place in the lip opening. This ground rim fragment (SF-666B) is triangular in section.

The apex and exterior lip of SF-975 were broken off. This breakage, which may have occurred as a result of natural agents, prevents the piece's functioning as a trumpet.

ARTIFACT FORM: Scoop (Fig. 22e)
FREQUENCY: 2
MATERIAL: Gastropod
DATING: Late Preclassic
CONTEXT: Domestic debris

COMMENT: Both SF-529 and SF-530 are triangular in outline. The working edge of SF-529 was carefully ground down; it is quite sharp and is beveled toward the exterior (Fig. 22e). It may have functioned as a scraper. It appears to have been made on a water-rolled piece of shell.

The working edge of SF-530 is also beveled toward the exterior, but does not exhibit the sharpness of SF-529. All scoops reported from other Lowland Maya sites are of Classic or Late Postclassic date.

ARTIFACT FORM: Labret (Fig. 22c, d)
FREQUENCY: 2
MATERIAL: Unknown
DATING: Late Postclassic
CONTEXT: Fall   1
                  Humus   1

COMMENT: SF-816 and SF-1536 are very similar in form (Fig. 22c, d). SF-1536 exhibits a longer spike. Both were carefully smoothed and polished.

ARTIFACT FORM: Mosaic
SUBFORM: Trapezoidal (Fig. 20a)
FREQUENCY: 4
MATERIAL: *Spondylus*
DATING: Late Preclassic
CONTEXT: Cache

COMMENT: All have one convex edge with an opposing concave edge. Both faces are flat on each piece. The edges are beveled toward one face.

ARTIFACT FORM: Cutout (Fig. 21d)
FREQUENCY: 1
MATERIAL: Unknown
DATING: Late Preclassic
CONTEXT: Cache

COMMENT: SF-984 is semicircular in outline, with two tangs, one on each side. The central part of the piece was cut out and resembles an animal head with rounded ears.

MISCELLANEOUS PIECES

Four of these, SF-218, SF-270, SF-528, and SF-1379, have drill holes, but the complete form cannot be determined because of breakage or incomplete stage of manufacture.

Six pieces, SF-443, SF-529B, SF-1248, SF-1533, SF-1543, and SF-1774, show evidence of having been ground or sawed, but the original or complete form cannot be determined (Fig. 23h).

SF-626 is a piece of black coral. Striations run the length of the piece. These may be the result of polishing.

SF-1838 is a columella of a fossil conch. The anterior end is rounded. It may have been used as a pick.

SF-1890, SF-1901, and SF-1942 are lip portions of large conch shells. SF-1890 may be a part of a termination offering associated with the burial of Structure 5C-1st. It was found in an area of construction fill that contained several smashed vessels.

SF-282 is a carefully shaped piece of *Spondylus*. Its original form cannot be determined because of its broken condition. The carefully worked edge has a V-shaped notch and gentle curves (Fig. 21g).

SF-625 is triangular in outline. It is a *Spondylus* piece that was ground on both faces. One face exhibits five grooves approximately 0.4 cm long, which extend from the edge inward. These grooves appear to be the remains of the natural grooves on the shell edge. It appears to be broken; however, at Piedras Negras thirteen of these *Spondylus* dentate ornaments were recovered from a burial (Coe 1959).

6. THE REWORKED CERAMIC SHERD INDUSTRY

This industry includes all artifacts made from ceramic sherds. Worked sherd artifacts were shaped by drilling, grinding, cutting, and flaking.

ARTIFACT FORM: Disk (Fig. 24e)
FREQUENCY: 248
DATING:
Late Preclassic 217
Early Classic 15
Late Postclassic 9
Unknown 7
CONTEXT:
Termination ritual 70
Domestic debris 53
Construction fill with
  rubble 42
Humus/fall 25
Fall 11
Cache 11
In floor 8
Beach near Feature 1A 8
Humus 7
Pit fill 6
Unknown 5
On floor 1
Construction fill without
  rubble 1

COMMENT: The disks were shaped by flaking and/or grinding. Some disks were very carefully ground, while others show signs of flaking, which leaves a scalloped edge. Most of the flaked forms are unifacial and were struck from the exterior convex surface. No doubt, this was a preventive measure to avoid accidental breakage during manufacture. Table 15 summarizes the ceramic type frequencies of the Cerros sherd disks.

Figure 25 presents the frequency distribution of the sherd disk diameters. The disks range in diameter from 1.4 cm to 15.0 cm. Many are broken and are represented only by portions. For these, the diameters were estimated. Willey (1972) divides the disks from Altar de Sacrificios into two categories, large and small. He does not state whether the distribution is bimodal. Eighty-seven large disks were recovered from Altar de Sacrificios. Many of those came from Structure B-1. Of

TABLE 15

Ceramic Type Frequencies of the Cerros Sherd Disks

Ceramic Type	Frequency
Cabro Red: Cabro variety	40
Cabro/Canxun Transitional	27
Canop Red on Red Trickle: Canop variety	11
Canxun Red: Canxun variety	11
Chactoc Dichrome: Chactoc variety	1
Chamah Washed: Chamah variety	4
Cockscomb Buff: Cockscomb variety	4
Crabboe Washed: Crabboe variety	1
Encanto Striated	1
Hole Dull	4
Hole Dull variety 1	
Hukup variety 3	
Kuxche Orange: Kuxche variety	7
Lanillo Groove Incised: Lanillo variety	1
Matamore Dichrome	13
Matamore variety 9	
Shipyard variety 4	
Nictaa Buff: Nictaa variety	2
Paila Unslipped: variety unspecified	3
Pixoy Usulutan: Pixoy variety	3
Poknoboy Striped: Poknoboy variety	3
Sapote Striated	21
Chichem variety 9	
Sapote variety 12	
Sangre Red: Sangre variety	1
Savannah Bank Usulutan: Variety unspecified	7
Sierra Red	5
Sierra variety 2	
Xaibe variety 3	
Taciste Washed: Taciste variety	1
Teabox Unslipped: Teabox variety	5
Tinta Usulutan: Tinta variety	1
Tuk Red on Red Trickle: Tuk variety	1
Yaxnik through the slip incised: Yaxnik variety	3
Zapatista Trickle on Cream Brown: Zoon variety	5
Zorra Black on Red: Zorra variety	1

those, twenty-eight were in a cache and forty-six were in the structure near the cache. Willey states that the depositional context of the latter was uncertain. Most of the small disks from Altar de Sacrificios came from structure fill or refuse; none came from caches

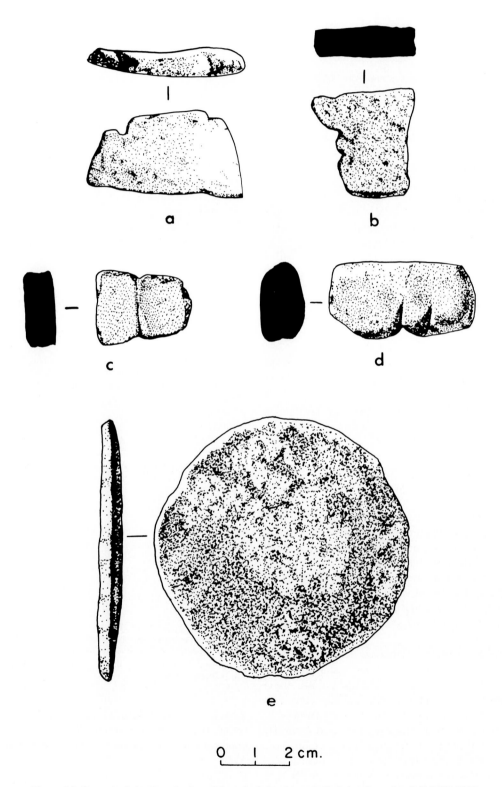

Figure 24. Reworked sherds. a, b, d, multinotched sherds; c, girdled sherds; e, sherd disk SF-1640.

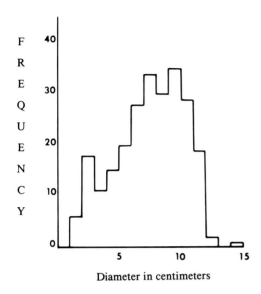

Figure 25. Frequency distribution of sherd disk diameters.

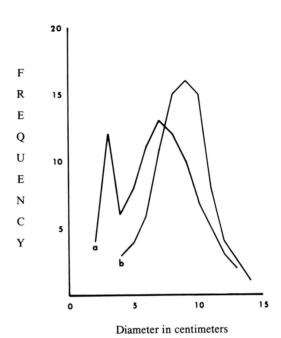

Figure 26. Frequency distributions of sherd disk diameters from two deposit types. curve a, domestic debris; curve b, cache, construction fill and termination ritual.

or burials. Generally, there seems to be a differential pattern of deposition for the large and small disks at Altar de Sacrificios. Large disks are those between 6.5 cm and 13.5 cm in diameter. The range of sizes for small disks was not given.

Although frequency distribution of the Cerros sherd disk diameters is not bimodal, smaller disks show a different pattern of deposition than do larger ones. Two kinds of disks may be present in the sample, and their distinctness, with respect to diameter, may be masked by overlapping distributions.

Figure 26 shows the diameter distributions of sherd disks from two deposit types at Cerros. Curve b is clearly unimodal and represents the disks from caches, construction fill, and deposits resulting from termination ritual. Table 16 indicates that 90% of the disks from those deposits have diameters larger than 5.0 cm. This same pattern of deposition characterized the Altar de Sacrificios specimens, where the larger disks came from caches or cache associations.

Willey et al. (1965) suggest that large disks functioned as lids for narrow-mouthed vessels. This functional assessment is confirmed by SF-157, SF-249, SF-252, SF-256, and SF-854, which were recovered, *in situ,* atop narrow-mouthed vessels in three caches at Cerros. One of those vessel forms has been referred to as "beer mugs" and may have functioned as a beverage container (Robertson-Freidel 1980). The mouth diameter of Cerros beer mugs varies between

TABLE 16

Percentages of Large and Small Disks by Context

Disk Diameter	Construction Fill; Termination Ritual; Cache (%)	Domestic Debris (%)	Humus, Fall; Humus/Fall (%)
Greater than 5.0 cm	90.2	67.9	60.4
Equal to or less than 5.0 cm	9.8	32.1	39.6
	n = 123	n = 53	n = 43

8.0 cm to 12.0 cm. The diameters of the disks found *in situ* approximate the mouth diameters of the corresponding vessels. Four beer mugs and five sherd disks were recovered from Cache 1, a Late Preclassic dedicatory cache on the summit of Structure 6B. One disk, SF-157, was found directly on a beer mug, three others immediately adjacent to beer mugs, and a fifth with a mouthed vessel with three strap handles that probably functioned as a serving vessel for pouring liquid into beer mugs (Robertson-Freidel 1980).

Several sherd disks appeared in deposits attributed to termination ritual. Beer mugs, or their fragments, were also common in those deposits. Beer mugs and their lids were common features of termination rituals and dedicatory offerings.

The forty-six large disks from Structure B-1, at Altar de Sacrificios, found near Cache 40, may have been a part of a termination ritual deposit. Many of the deposits at Cerros resulting from termination rituals resemble scattered or disjointed caches. Coe (1965a) refers to them as termination offerings associated with structure abandonment as opposed to structure dedication.

Curve *a* of Fig. 26 represents the diameter distribution of sherd disks recovered from domestic debris. This distribution curve is bimodal. As noted in chapter 3, many of the artifacts from the domestic debris of Feature 1A may relate to termination rituals associated with the abandonment of the residential structures rather than to the domestic debris itself. If the sherd disks used in the termination of the residential structures were relatively large, as was the case with those in the termination rituals of monumental architecture, then the percentage of the smaller disks actually associated with the domestic debris would be higher than that indicated in Table 16.

Necked globular jars sometimes exhibit a wear pattern that could have been caused by repeated use of a sherd lid. This pattern consists of a clearly defined ring where the slip has worn off on the inside edge of the rim. Sherd disks (SF-249, SF-252, SF-256) were found *in situ* on globular jars in Cache 2 on Structure 4B. This wear pattern did not occur on beer mugs.

The disks on beer mugs may have served as plugs that were sealed with wax or gum. Were that the case, beer mugs could have been vessels for storage and transport, presumably for beverages, as mentioned earlier. Alternatively, beer mugs were vessels for serving a beverage, perhaps *balche,* with lids to keep the liquid warm or dust free until consumed. This latter interpretation could account for the presence of many burned stone spheroids and stone disks in the termination deposit on Structure 2A-Sub.4-1st. Those disks and spheroids may have been used as pot rests for the preparation of hot liquids to be consumed during the ritual.

Some of the disks have linear contusions and/or cut marks on the central area of one face, usually the exterior surface (Fig. 24e). Sometimes these are peck marks in a line or lines. Similar marks have been observed on

a disk from Barton Ramie (Willey et al. 1965: Fig. 260a). These marks may be signs of wear on the vessels from which the disks were made. Alternatively, they may be related to use as lids on globular jars. Placing a sturdy material such as palm fronds over the lid and down the neck and then tying a cord around the neck would secure the lid to the vessel. The lid could then be removed by cutting the cord, leaving cut marks on the jar neck, or by cutting the fronds strap wrapped over the lid, leaving cut marks on the disk. Both kinds of marks have been observed on Cerros specimens.

Some of the disks have features of particular interest. SF-945 and SF-1322 have prominent striped designs and biconical drill holes very close to their edges. The holes are 0.6 cm and 0.2 cm in diameter, respectively. Both were drilled after being shaped into disks. They may have been large pendants.

SF-1329, SF-1344, and SF-1353, found in Feature 1A, the nucleated residential area, are ceramic disks with strap handles Two additional disks, both from Structure 2A-Sub.4-1st, also have strap handles. Those two disks have not been cataloged as artifacts and thus lack SF numbers.

SF-597 and SF-1313 have incised graffiti. The incising was done prior to disk shaping and was probably put on the vessels when whole. The graffito on SF-597 is at the edge of the piece and appears to be a sun motif. It consists of an incised arc with eight incised extending rays. The graffito on SF-1313 is also a sun motif, but it encompasses the entire disk. The disk was shaped in such a manner as to encompass most of the design. It included two concentric circles with eight sets of rays each with six to eight parallel lines filling a triangular-shaped zone. The incising was done in such a manner that the buff-colored paste showed through. This specimen has been identified as Yaxnik through the Slip Incised: Yaxnik variety (Robertson-Freidel, personal communication, 1980).

Willey et al. (1965) suggest that the small disks functioned as gaming pieces. Because the small disks were disposed of differently from large disks, it seems likely that they served a different purpose. However, SF-664, 3.1 cm in diameter, was recovered *in situ* on the opening of a Late Postclassic censer in Cache 6 on Structure 4A. It did function as a lid. The small Postclassic disks recovered at Mayapán may have had a similar function (Proskouriakoff 1962). No Late Preclassic vessels from Cerros had openings small enough to accommodate the smaller disks. It seems likely, then, that the small Late Preclassic disks did not function as lids.

The 248 disks listed do not represent the total number found. At least 40 more were recovered, but not cataloged as artifacts. Most of these uncataloged disks are from deposits resulting from termination ritual and are of the larger variety.

Table 17 shows the percentages of the time periods for the large and small disks from Cerros. Most came from Late Preclassic contexts.

ARTIFACT FORM: Mariposa (Figs. 27, 28, 29)
SUBFORM: Notched sherd
FREQUENCY: 333
MATERIAL: Sherd
DATING: Late Preclassic 65
Early Classic 103
Late Postclassic 161
Unknown 4
CONTEXT: Humus 106
Humus/fall 105
Domestic debris 66
Fall 31
Construction fill with rubble 15
Construction fill without rubble 5
Surface 1
In floor 1
Pit fill 1
Beach near Feature 1A 1
Unknown 1

COMMENT: The word *mariposa* (Spanish for butterfly) is used to describe notched, butterfly-shaped artifacts from the Maya area. Mariposas may be fashioned

TABLE 17

Percentages by Period for Large and Small Sherd Disks

Period	Disk Diameter	
	Less than or equal to 5.0 cm (%)	Greater than 5.0 cm (%)
Late Preclassic	77.6	89.9
Early Classic	10.2	5.1
Late Postclassic	10.2	2.0
Unknown	2.0	3.0
	n = 49	n = 198

from sherds, molded clay, or stone. No stone mariposas were found at Cerros, although Eaton (1976) reports several from sites on the northern coast of Yucatán, Mexico.

The most common mariposas are those made from sherds. They have been reported from sites throughout the Maya area, including Altar de Sacrificios (Willey 1972), Barton Ramie (Willey et al. 1965), Cancún (Andrews et al. 1974), Colha (Gillis 1982), Cozumel (Phillips 1979), Dzibilchaltún (Andrews et al. 1974), Macanche (Bullard 1973), Mayapan (Proskouriakoff 1962), San Juan (Guderjan, Garber, and Smith 1988), Seibal (Willey 1972), Yaxha (Rice 1976), and several sites on the northern Yucatán coast (Eaton 1976, 1978). Excavations at Cerros yielded 333 sherd mariposas. U-and V-shaped notches were made by cutting and grinding and are usually 0.2 to 0.5 cm deep. A majority of them, 231 (69.4%), have a notch on each end; that is, the notches are on the short dimension. Side-notched mariposas (56 were found at Cerros) are indented along the long dimension but are not as common as the end-notched form. Forty-two could not be determined as to side or end notching, and four were square or end/side notched. Those with one notch or more than two notches do occur, although they are relatively rare. SF-1495, SF-1896, and SF-1909 have three notches: a notch on both ends, and one notch on the side.

SF-442 has a pair of notches on each side (Fig. 29j), the notches of each pair 2.5 cm apart. This specimen weighs 35.3 gm and is one of the heavier Cerros notched mariposas. SF-338 is broken; however, assuming symmetry, it would also have had a pair of notches on each side.

Eaton (1976) and Phillips (1978, 1979) have argued strongly that notched ceramic pieces functioned as net weights. Their argument is based on suitability of form, wear pattern, and distribution. Some of the older fishermen on Ambergris Cay, Belize, still use throw nets with notched sherd weights (personal observation 1986). Other proposed functions include weft weights, warp weights, and door hangings (Kent and Nelson 1976; Pollock et al. 1962), although there is little supportive evidence.

Most of the notched sherds are heavily worn, probably because they were used as net weights. SF-794, SF-934B, SF-934F, and SF-934K have stripes of slip between the two notches. Striping is observed on notched sherds from other sites and has been interpreted as the result of a cord tied between the notches,

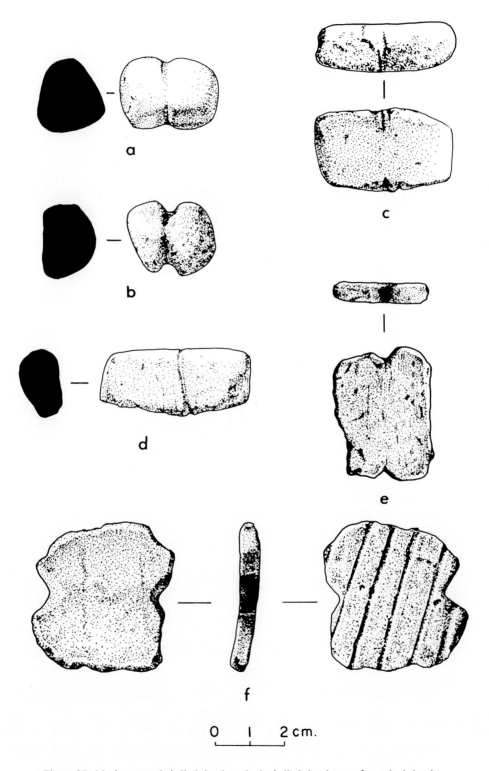

Figure 27. Mariposas and girdled sherds. a, b, d, girdled sherds; c, e, f, notched sherds.

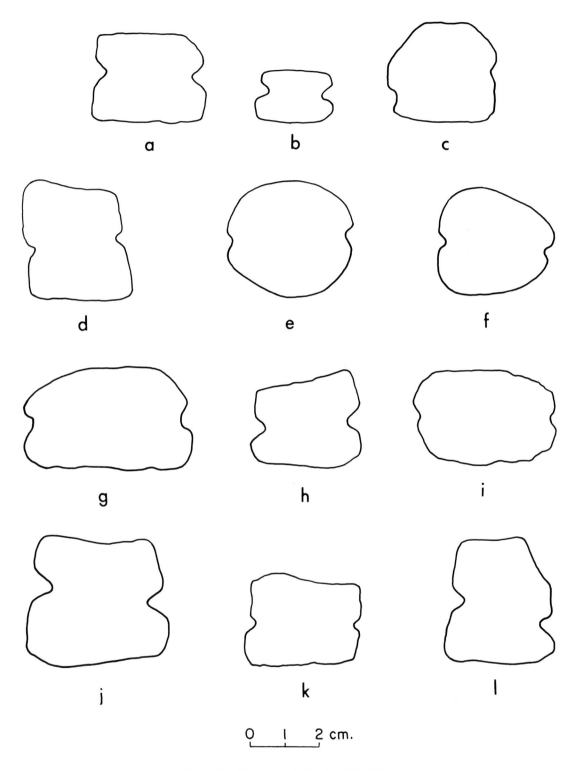

Figure 28. Mariposas. End-notched sherds.

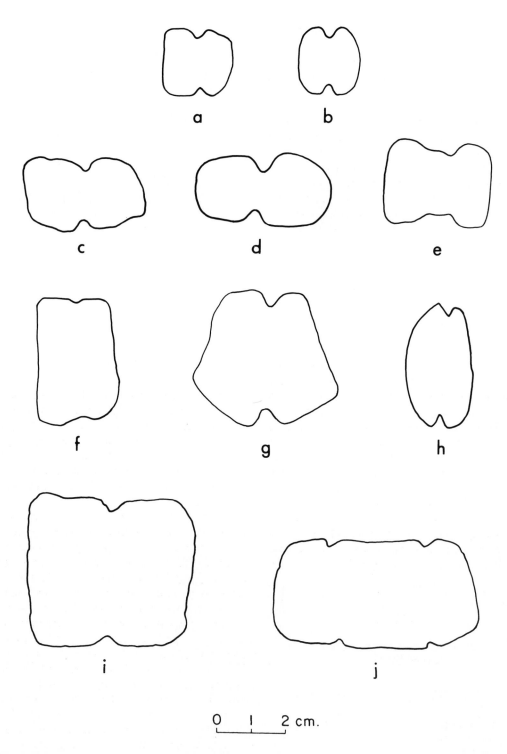

Figure 29. Mariposas. a, b, f, g, h, end-notched sherds; c, d, i, side-notched sherds; e, spool-shaped notched sherd; j, multiple-notched sherd.

which prevented slip loss during net use (Eaton 1976; Phillips 1978, 1979).

Cerros notched sherd mariposas reveal considerable variation in shape. This variation has been described by noting the edge or end shape in relation to the axis of the piece, which is defined as a line connecting the two notches (Garber 1981). The following terms define side or end shapes: straight parallel, straight slant, convex, convex-concave, angled, and irregular. Straight parallel means that the edge is straight and parallel to the axis. Straight slant means that the edge is straight but that it is not parallel to the axis. Convex-concave indicates a wavy edge. Some edges contain an angle, and others are irregular. The frequencies of edge shapes for mariposas are listed in table 18.

The majority appear to have been casually shaped, as only a few show any signs of edge grinding. Table 19 lists cross-tabulations of the various edge shapes for Cerros notched sherd mariposas. Edge shape combinations are not random but dependent. Although convex edges and straight parallel edges are common, a convex edge occurs more frequently with another convex edge than it does with a straight parallel edge. Although most edges were not carefully ground, table 19 indicates that either they were carefully shaped or sherds were carefully selected. Phillips (1979) notes that for the notched sherds from Cozumel, the shape of the potsherd for the most part determined the final shape of the sinker. This may have been the case with the Cerros notched sherds, but if so, certain sherd shapes were selected. There is no evidence to suggest that a particular type or types of pottery were preferred over others for making sherd mariposas. The types used represent the usual cross-section of sherds from the site at which they are found, suggesting that the makers used whatever was available.

TABLE 18

Frequencies of Sherd Mariposa Edge Forms

Edge Form	Frequency
Convex	283
Straight parallel	248
Straight slant	92
Angled	6
Convex-concave	3
Irregular	2

TABLE 19

Frequencies of Edge Form Combinations on Sherd Mariposas

Edge Forms	Frequency
SP SP	89
SP SS	28
SS SS	24
SP Cv	39
SS Cv	12
Cv Cv	116
SS Ag	4
Ag Ag	1
SP CC	3
Ir Ir	1

Note: SP = straight parallel
SS = straight slant
Cv = convex
Ag = angled
CC = convex-concave
Ir = irregular

Figure 30 illustrates the weight distributions of the Cerros unbroken sherd mariposas. The weights of four specimens could not be shown: 30.9 gm, 35.3 gm, 45.0 gm, and 49.0 gm. Although the average weight is 6.7 gm, the mode is between 3.0 gm and 4.0 gm. Distribution curve *A* is very similar in shape to the distribution curve for the weight of the notched sherds from Cozumel (Phillips 1979: 72).

Although the distribution curves are similar in shape, there is an important difference between them. The Cerros curve peaks between 3.0 gm and 4.0 gm, whereas the Cozumel curve peaks between 4.0 gm and 5.0 gm. This difference may be due to the different water turbulence for which the weights were made. The turbulence of Corozal Bay is less than that of the coast of Cozumel. There is some evidence to suggest that during the Late Preclassic, Cerros was situated on a lagoon or slow-moving body of water, making the waters even less turbulent than today (Scarborough 1980; Robertson-Freidel 1980). In either case, the immediate environment at Cerros would not have required as heavy a net weight as that required at Cozumel. Eaton (1976) notes that some sites along the Yucatán coast have sherd and pebble mariposas and others have only sherd specimens. This disparity may represent an adaptation to different microenvironmental zones.

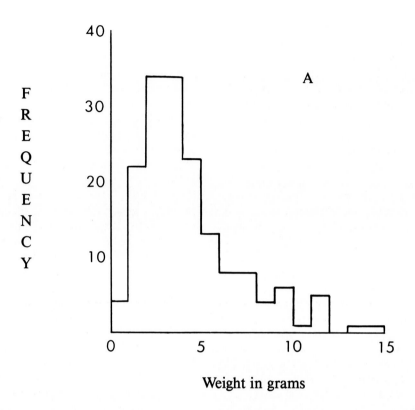

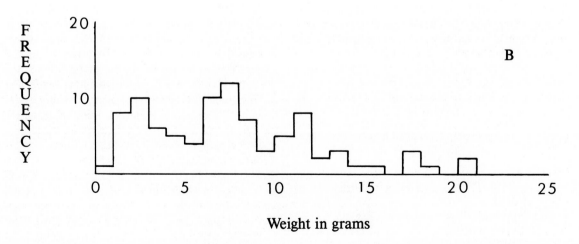

Figure 30. Frequency distribution for the weights of the Cerros mariposas. A, Postclassic mariposas; B, Late Preclassic and Classic mariposas.

Several of the mariposas could have functioned as line weights. End-notched forms were usually found in groups and could have been weights from a net. The less common side-notched forms were often single occurrences in a deposit and may have been line weights. The same may be true for the relatively heavy specimens and for those with more than two notches.

ARTIFACT FORM: Girdled sherds (Figs. 24c,
                      27a, b, d)
FREQUENCY: 4
MATERIAL: Sherd
DATING: Late Preclassic 2
                  Early Classic 1
                  Unknown 1
CONTEXT: Humus/fall 1
                  Termination ritual 1
                  Beach near Feature 1A 1
                  Pit fill 1

COMMENT: SF-125, SF-410, and SF-1465 are similar to the notched sherd mariposas. All have been made on rim sherds, and each has an encircling groove. They might have served a function related to mariposas but were used on lines or nets that required a sure knot, thus necessitating the encircling groove.

SF-1650 is also similar to a mariposa. It has two parallel flat surfaces with notches on the sides; however, unlike a mariposa, the notches are connected by a carefully ground V-shaped groove on each side (Fig. 24c). This groove is 0.1 cm to 0.2 cm deep and 0.2 cm to 0.3 cm wide. It may have functioned as a net or line weight; however, it was recovered from a marl deposit associated with the termination and abandonment of Structure 2A-Sub.4-1st. The unique form of this specimen and its association with ritual debris suggest that it may have functioned in some way other than as a mariposa.

ARTIFACT FORM: Partially perforated disk
                      (Fig. 31d, f, g, 32e)
FREQUENCY: 4
MATERIAL: Sherd
DATING: Late Preclassic
CONTEXT: Domestic debris 2
                  Construction fill with
                      rubble 1
                  Fall 1

COMMENT: The edges of these artifacts were flaked and ground. Each has a centrally located depression, which extends approximately half way through the sherd. The maximum diameters of those depressions are as follows: SF-39, 1.0 cm; SF-371, 0.9 cm; SF-777, 0.5 cm; and SF-1406, 0.6 cm. They vary in section from semicircular to cone-shaped. Artifacts of this kind have been referred to as unfinished spindle whorls (Willey et al. 1965).

All of the partially perforated disks from Cerros are from Late Preclassic deposits. No Late Preclassic centrally perforated sherd disks or molded ceramic spindle whorls were found at Cerros, and thus it is unlikely that the partially perforated disks are unfinished spindle whorls. Coe (1959) states that similar partially perforated disks from Piedras Negras may have functioned as hand-held distaffs to be used with a bow drill. The partial perforations would be largely due to use, although a small depression would have to be drilled initially to prevent the staff from slipping.

ARTIFACT FORM: Centrally perforated disk
                      (Fig. 31e)
FREQUENCY: 1
MATERIAL: Reworked sherd
DATING: Early Classic
CONTEXT: Domestic debris

COMMENT: SF-1286 is a sherd disk 4.9 cm in diameter with a biconical perforation 0.6 cm in diameter. It may have functioned as a spindle whorl; however, no Late Preclassic or Early Classic molded spindle whorls were found at Cerros.

ARTIFACT FORM: Pendant (Figs. 31a,
                      b, c, 32h)
FREQUENCY: 4
MATERIAL: Sherd
DATING: Late Preclassic
CONTEXT: Domestic debris 3
                  In floor 1

COMMENT: SF-375 is circular in outline and has a biconical drill hole, which was drilled from the sherd edge to meet with a hole drilled from the unslipped face (Fig. 31c). Its edges were carefully ground.

SF-435 is also circular in outline and has a biconically drilled hole very close to its edge. Its edges were carefully ground and are slightly beveled toward the unslipped interior face (Fig. 32h).

SF-616 is square in outline and all four edges were roughly ground (Fig. 31b). Its biconically drilled hole is located toward one of the corners.

SF-836 is broken and, as a result, its complete shape cannot be determined (Fig. 31a). The hole was

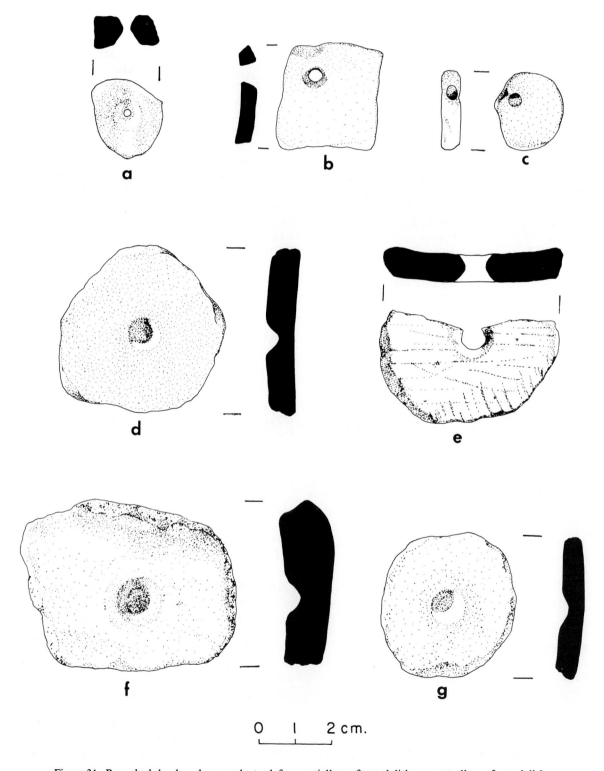

Figure 31. Reworked sherds. a, b, c, pendants; d, f, g, partially perforated disks; e, centrally perforated disk.

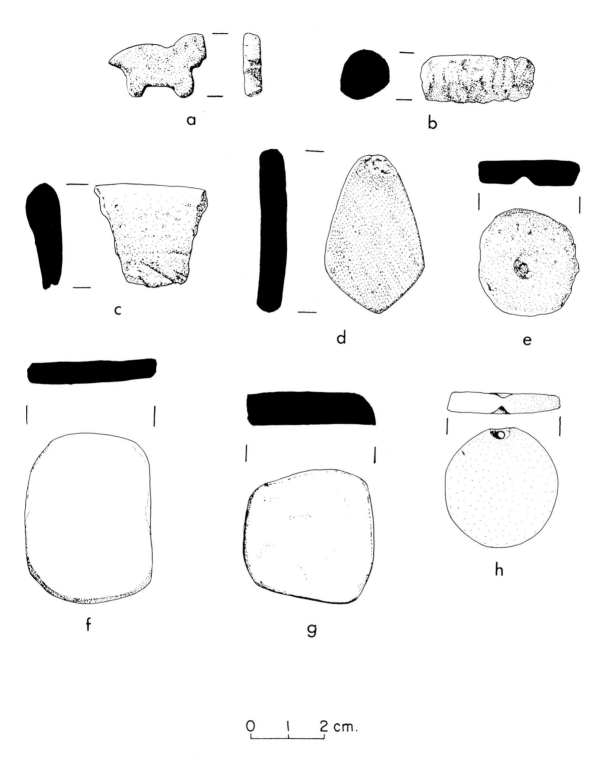

Figure 32. Reworked sherds. a, animal effigy; b, c, cut rim sherds; d, f, g, geometrics; e, partially perforated disk; h, pendant.

biconically drilled and the portion of the unbroken worked edge was carefully ground.

ARTIFACT FORM: Geometrics (Fig. 32d, f, g)
FREQUENCY: 4
MATERIAL: Sherd
DATING: Late Preclassic
CONTEXT: Domestic debris 2
　　　　　　　Cache 1
　　　　　　　In floor 1
COMMENT: SF-143 is square and has carefully ground edges. Because it is flat and has no curve, it may not be a reworked sherd. It was found in Cache 1, a Late Preclassic dedicatory cache on Structure 6B.

SF-440 is trapezoidal in outline. Two of its edges are carefully ground and beveled toward the unslipped surface. The other two edges were lightly ground (Fig. 32g).

SF-1349 is generally rectangular in outline. Its sides and ends are slightly convex and the corners are lightly rounded. All edges were carefully ground (Fig. 32f).

SF-1371 is teardrop-shaped and its edges were carefully ground (Fig. 32d).

The function of these finds could not be determined. Possibilities include gaming pieces, trinkets, or unfinished pendants. SF-143 is probably too large to have been a pendant, and its cache association is suggestive of a ritual function.

ARTIFACT FORM: Animal effigy (Fig. 32a)
FREQUENCY: 1
MATERIAL: Sherd
DATING: Late Preclassic
CONTEXT: Construction fill
COMMENT: SF-1779 is a representation of an animal in profile. Its back and tail are formed by a single arc. The tail is a short, fat, pointed stub. The front and back legs are short, rounded stubs. The head is rounded and has projections for the ear, nose, and chin. It was carefully shaped by grinding and cutting. Small cut marks define the mouth, throat, chest, and abdomen. It may have been deposited intentionally in construction fill or could have fallen from the fill above.

ARTIFACT FORM: Ground sherds
FREQUENCY: 10
DATING: Late Preclassic
CONTEXT: Cache
COMMENT: SF-173 A-J are sherd fragments each of which has at least two ground edges forming an approximate right angle. All have flecks of crystalline specular hematite included as temper. These flecks are planar and reflective, giving the sherds a glimmering appearance. Sherds or vessels with inclusions of this kind have not been found in other deposits at Cerros (Robertson-Freidel, personal communication 1980). Two of the specimens fit together along breaks in a manner that clearly shows that they were ground down after they were broken apart.

In the discussion of termination ritual at the end of chapter 3, it was suggested that some of the artifact fragments smashed during the ritual were curated for deposition elsewhere. Ground fragments of jade and ground sherds are occasionally found in dedicatory caches and may be curated fragments. Specular hematite mirror fragments are found at Cerros in association with dedication and termination offerings. The ground sherds that contain specular hematite were found in a dedicatory cache, but may have once been a part of a termination ritual.

ARTIFACT FORM: Cut rim sherd (Fig. 32b, c)
FREQUENCY: 2
DATING: Late Preclassic
CONTEXT: Termination ritual
COMMENT: SF-613 is a sherd from an everted rim dish. Three V-shaped cuts are on the end opposite the rim (Fig. 32c).

SF-1499 is cylindrical in shape. Numerous grooves are present that extend perpendicular to the longitudinal axis (Fig. 32b). Each is approximately 0.6 cm long, 0.1 cm wide, and 0.05 cm deep.

The function of these finds could not be determined, but because of the grooves, SF-1499 may have been used with thin cord or string. SF-1650, a girdled sherd, was also found in a deposit resulting from termination ritual and is well suited to use with string as well.

7. MISCELLANEOUS INDUSTRIES

The molded clay, worked plaster, ground metal, pounded metal, and cast metal industries have only a few artifacts. Because of the small number of specimens in each industry, they are presented in a single chapter.

THE MOLDED CLAY INDUSTRY

Several stages were involved in the manufacture of molded clay artifacts, including clay preparation, shaping, and firing. Of the molded clay pieces, only 7.0% are Late Preclassic, even though Late Preclassic artifacts account for 70.8% of the Cerros artifact collection. The ceramic vessels have been analyzed in other works (Robertson 1986; Robertson-Freidel 1980).

ARTIFACT FORM:	Mariposa (Fig. 33a–g)	
SUBFORM:	Molded	
FREQUENCY:		32
MATERIAL:	Molded clay	
DATING:	Late Preclassic	2
	Early Classic	1
	Late Postclassic	29
CONTEXT:	Domestic debris	14
	Fall	10
	Humus	1
	Humus/fall	7

COMMENT: Mariposas that have been molded from clay are much less common than those made from sherds, but they do occur at several sites in the Maya area, including Altar de Sacrificios (Willey 1972), Barton Ramie (Willey et al. 1965), Colha (Gillis 1982), Cozumel (Phillips 1979), Lubaantun (Hammond 1975), and Macanche (Bullard 1973). Willey et al. (1965) refer to these as "specially made notched pendants" to distinguish them from the notched sherds. Thirty-two were recovered at Cerros (Fig. 33a–g). This is the largest sample reported from any Maya site.

On all of the Cerros specimens, the notches were cut when the clay was wet. All have convex sides making them round or oval in outline, except SF-934S, which has sides that are parallel to its axis. Twenty-eight are end notched, four are end/side notched or round. Their average weight is 2.4 gm. This is considerably lighter than the average weight of notched sherds, which is 6.7 gm. Their shape suggests use as toggles for clothing, although they were frequently found with notched sherds, suggesting their use as fishing equipment on lines or nets.

ARTIFACT FORM:	Bead (Fig. 33h–k)	
FREQUENCY:		11
MATERIAL:	Molded clay	
DATING:	Late Preclassic	1
	Late Postclassic	10
CONTEXT:	Humus	5
	Domestic debris	4
	Humus/fall	2

COMMENT: All of the beads are unslipped. Colors include red buff, orange buff, pale orange, off-white, and buff. On all beads the hole appears to have been punched when the clay was still wet. Subforms include barrel, spherical, and subspherical.

The one Late Preclassic ceramic bead, SF-1381, is considerably smaller than the rest, off-white, and made of untempered clay or possibly plaster. The Late Postclassic beads are tempered with heavy grit.

ARTIFACT FORM:	Spindle whorl	
	(Fig. 34a–h)	
FREQUENCY:		11
MATERIAL:	Molded clay	
DATING:	Late Postclassic	6
	Unknown	5
CONTEXT:	Beach	4
	Humus	4
	Domestic debris	2
	Unknown	1

COMMENT: No ceramic spindle whorls were recovered from any of the Cerros Late Preclassic deposits. Four of the five whorls listed as being of unknown date are probably Late Postclassic, as they were recovered from the beach in areas where many Late Postclassic sherds were observed.

SF-265 is decorated on one face (Fig. 34e). The decoration, partially worn down by water rolling,

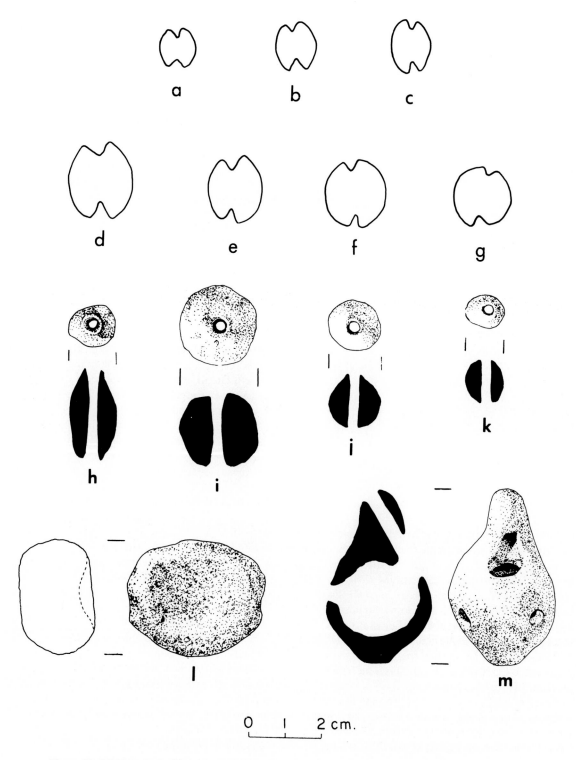

Figure 33. Molded clay artifacts. a–g, mariposas; h–k, beads; 1, oval piece with depression; m, whistle.

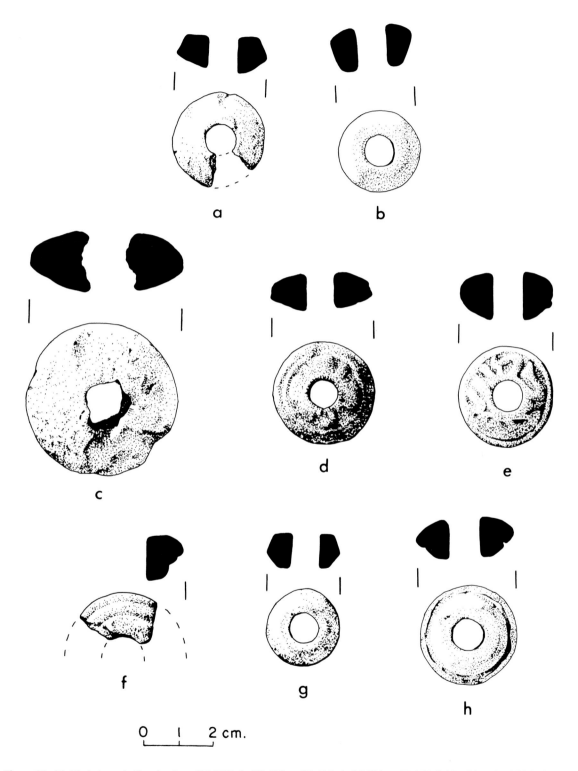

Figure 34. Molded clay spindle whorls. a, SF-1192; b, SF-685; c, SF-585; d, SF-376; e, SF-265; f, SF-174; g, SF-266; h, SF-72.

consists of three legs, each bent at the knee, extending out from the central hole. Also included in the design is a loop and protrusion.

SF-376 is also decorated on one face (Fig. 34d). This design is a representation of a flower composed of eight alternating large and small petals.

SF-585 is heavier and larger than the others (Fig. 34c). It may have functioned on a staff that required a relatively heavy whorl, such as a pump drill.

ARTIFACT FORM: Whistle (Fig. 33m)
FREQUENCY: 1
MATERIAL: Molded clay
DATING: Late Preclassic
CONTEXT: Burial
COMMENT: SF-694 is pear-shaped and off-white. Its surface is rough to the touch due to heavy temper. The tapered end forms the mouth-piece, which opens over a circular vent in the chamber. There are three vent holes in the body of the piece: two on the same surface as the main vent and one on the bottom. When blown, it emits a shrill noise. The pitch can be changed by covering and uncovering the vent holes with the fingers. All holes appear to have been punched in the clay while wet. Whistles of similar form have been recovered from Chalchuapa in El Salvador (Sheets 1978) and Cuello in Northern Belize (Hammond 1982).

ARTIFACT FORM: Sphere
FREQUENCY: 1
MATERIAL: Molded clay
DATING: Late Postclassic
CONTEXT: Humus
COMMENT: SF-557 is an orange clay ball that was probably a rattle in the foot of a vessel. It is irregular in shape, although it is approximately round. Late Post-classic vessels with rattle feet are commonly found throughout the Maya Lowlands.

ARTIFACT FORM: Oval piece with depression (Fig. 33l)
FREQUENCY: 1
MATERIAL: Molded clay
DATING: Early Classic
CONTEXT: Humus/fall
COMMENT: SF-1868 is ovoid in shape and one face has a depression that is 2.6 cm long, 1.8 cm wide, and 0.4 cm deep. This depression appears thumb pressed and not abraded or worn. The entire specimen is burned, and its function could not be determined.

THE WORKED PLASTER INDUSTRY

The working and making of plaster was an important industry at Cerros, as evidenced by the molded plaster designs on Structures 6B, 5C-1st, 5C-2nd, 29B, 11B, and the numerous plaster floors and surfaces throughout the site. This discussion deals only with the portable plaster artifacts. Five such objects were recovered during the excavations.

ARTIFACT FORM: Spiral (Uaxamacatl) (Fig. 35h, i)
FREQUENCY: 4
DATING: Late Postclassic
CONTEXT: Humus/fall 3
Humus 1
COMMENT: These specimens are hollow cones with spiral slits. Each appears to have been molded, not carved. SF-1032 is larger than the others, with an estimated basal diameter of 4.0 cm (Fig. 35i). The others have an estimated basal diameter of approximately 2.0 cm. The function of these pieces is not readily apparent, but they may have been ornaments suspended on knotted cords similar to undrilled *Oliva* tinklers. All were recovered near the surface of monumental architecture. Artifacts of this kind have not been reported from other sites.

ARTIFACT FORM: Dome with hole (Fig. 35g)
FREQUENCY: 1
DATING: Early Classic
CONTEXT: On floor
COMMENT: SF-808 is a fragment of an artifact of unknown shape. It is hollow and dome-shaped. There is a hole in the end, which is 0.5 cm in diameter. The hole was pierced when the plaster was wet. The function of this piece could not be determined. Artifacts of this kind have not been reported from other sites.

THE GROUND METAL INDUSTRY

The identification of the Cerros ground metal fragments as specular hematite was made by Michael J. Holdaway, Department of Geology, Southern Methodist University. Identification was made through the use of x-ray diffraction. When compared visually with other known samples of specular hematite, the Cerros specimens are much flatter (Holdaway, personal communication 1980). They have naturally

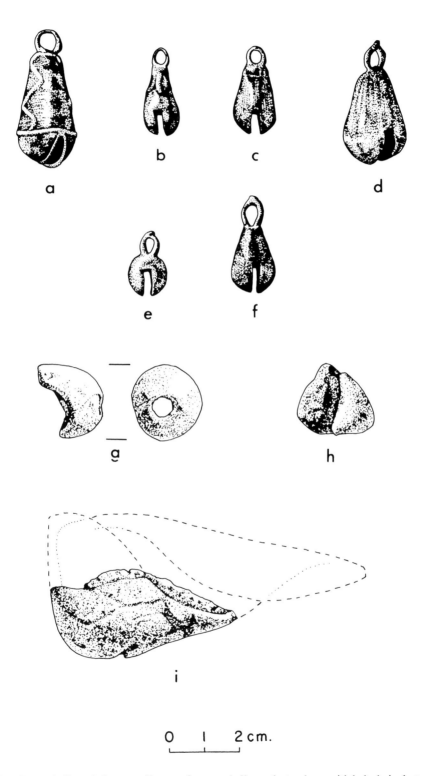

Figure 35. Copper bells and plaster artifacts. a–f, copper bells; g, plaster dome with hole; h, i, plaster spirals.

reflective surfaces with excellent reflective qualities and are bluish-gray in color. Grinding, when evident, is only on the edges. The thin sheets were shaped by grinding and careful breaking of the edges. They are very fragile and are less than 0.1 cm in thickness. Most are less than 1.0 cm in length and width.

ARTIFACT FORM: Mirror fragments
FREQUENCY: 119
MATERIAL: Specular hematite
DATING: Late Preclassic
CONTEXT: Cache   98
                Burial   11
                Domestic debris   8
                Termination ritual   2

COMMENT: Twelve fragments, SF-985 A–L, were found in Cache 9, a Late Preclassic dedicatory cache on Structure 5C-1st. Nine of these fragments fit together to form an incomplete mirror, which is 3.5 cm by 1.8 cm.

Many of the fragments making up SF-148 fit together. SF-148 was recovered from a Late Preclassic dedicatory cache on Structure 6B. At least three mirrors are represented by these fragments, and as many as six mirrors does not seem unlikely. Six shell disks and five disk fragments were recovered in this cache. They may have functioned as backings for the mirrors. Because so many of the fragments fit together along breaks, it is reasonable to suspect that at one time the mirrors were whole and were not mosaics. Mirrors are important symbols of kingship in the Classic period (Schele and Miller 1983). The contents of this cache, which included mirrors, polished stone heads, ear flares, and *Spondylus* shells, may be the insignia worn by a high-status individual or king (Freidel and Schele 1988).

Although eight fragments like the crushed jade, were recovered from domestic debris, these fragments might have been deposited into the domestic debris as a part of termination rituals associated with the abandonment of the domestic architecture and associated middens.

SF-1076 is semicircular. It would have been 1.0 cm in diameter. Its curved edge was ground to its present shape. Similar fragments have been reported from caches and a burial at Uaxactun (Kidder 1947; Ricketson and Ricketson 1937). Fragments of specular hematite have been reported from San José, Tikal, Piedras Negras, and Kaminaljuyu (Coe 1959; Kidder, Jennings, and Shook 1946; Thompson 1939,

1970). Specular hematite fragments have also been recovered from Classic contexts at Altun Ha and Lamanai (personal communication to David Freidel from David Pendergast, 1981).

Specular hematite can be easily crushed and when mixed with water forms a purple-red pigment. This pigment is sometimes used on ceramic vessels (Thompson 1970). It is assumed that rare flat specular hematite was kept in mirror form and not ground for pigment.

Specular hematite crystals do not occur naturally in the Maya Lowlands (Thompson 1970: 142–143). A specific source in Mesoamerica for these crystals or mirrors is not known, but in other areas of the world they are known to occur only in volcanic settings (Palache 1932; Ricketson and Ricketson 1937).

The rarity and value of these crystals is apparent from their pattern of disposal: they are found only in burials, dedicatory caches, and termination offerings.

Although some mirror fragments were recovered from Feature 1A, all were from the uppermost levels of this feature. These fragments may not relate to the abandonment of individual structures, but may be associated with the abandonment of the entire residential zone prior to its burial by the construction of the Feature 2A plaza. Cliff (1982) suggests that the presence of crushed jade and mirror fragments in this area may relate to the construction of Structures 2A-Sub.5-1st and 2A-Sub.7-1st or to ritual activities conducted at nearby Structure 2A-Sub.4-1st. In the summary discussion of shell beads it was suggested that shell beads were included in the termination rituals of domestic structures but were never included in the termination of public monumental architecture. More exotic materials, such as jade and specular hematite, might have been more appropriate for those rituals. The abandonment of a significant portion of the Feature 1A zone may be more closely related to the termination of a public structure than it is to a private dwelling. This would account for the presence of very rare items such as specular hematite mirrors in the uppermost levels of Feature 1A.

THE POUNDED METAL INDUSTRY

This industry includes items of gold and tumbaga, a gold-copper mixture.

ARTIFACT FORM: Disk
FREQUENCY: 3

MATERIAL: Tumbaga
DATING: Late Postclassic
CONTEXT: Cache

COMMENT: SF-718 is 6.8 cm in diameter and slightly less than 0.1 cm thick. It exhibits a central raised area, which is 2.5 cm in diameter. This area bulges out approximately 0.1 cm. At the edge of this bulge are 2 pairs of holes that have been punched into the disk. The holes of one pair are 0.3 cm apart, those of the other are 0.4 cm apart. Adhering to the back of the disk are fragments of a tan woven fabric. Within the perforations in the disk are fragments of thread that was used to secure the disk to the fabric. A detailed analysis of the fabric is currently being conducted (Walker, personal communication 1986).

SF-719 and SF-720 are very similar to SF-718, except that they are in a fragmentary condition. The edges flare out from a central raised area approximately 2.5 cm in diameter. Both disks are between 6.0 cm and 7.0 cm in diameter.

ARTIFACT FORM: Foil
FREQUENCY: 1
MATERIAL: Gold
DATING: Late Postclassic
CONTEXT: Cache

COMMENT: SF-622 is approximately 1.0 cm long and 0.5 cm wide. It is very thin and fragile. It was found inside SF-663, a Bacab ceramic vessel.

ARTIFACT FORM: Scroll
FREQUENCY: 1
MATERIAL: Gold
DATING: Late Postclassic
CONTEXT: Cache

COMMENT: SF-721 is 2.8 cm long by 1.2 cm wide by 0.05 cm thick. The piece appears to have been a wire that was bent into its scroll shape and hammered flat. The piece is broken, and the complete form can not be determined.

THE CAST METAL INDUSTRY

The artifacts of this industry are copper bells made by the lost wax technique.

ARTIFACT FORM: Bell (Fig. 35a–f)
FREQUENCY: 17
MATERIAL: Copper

DATING: Late Postclassic
CONTEXT: Cache   16
                      Humus   1

COMMENT: The Cerros copper bells show a wide range of shapes and designs. Two schemes have been devised to categorize the variability (Bray 1977; Pendergast 1962). Represented at Cerros are Bray's types a, e, f, h, m, and n, and Pendergast's types 1A1ai, 1C1a, 1D1a, 1D4a, 1D5a, 1D6a, and 1D7a. In addition to these is one bell that is not of a type described by Pendergast or Bray. This bell is pear-shaped and has a wirework calyx that attaches the suspension ring to the resonator body (Fig. 35b). It is similar to Pendergast's type 1A3. Table 20 shows the frequencies of the various bell types at Cerros. Conservation and a detailed analysis of the Cerros copper bells is currently being conducted (Walker, personal communication 1986).

THE CHIPPED STONE INDUSTRY: GENERAL COMMENTS

The chipped stone industry is not included in this monograph as it is the subject of separate analyses (Lewenstein 1984, 1986, 1987; Mitchum 1986). These analyses indicate that very little primary reduction took place at Cerros and that nearly all of the tools were imported in finished or nearly finished form (Mitchum 1986). A large chipped stone tool production center has been located at the site of Colha in Belize (Hester 1979; Hester, Eaton, and Shafer 1980; Hester, Shafer, and Eaton 1982; Wilk 1975). It has been suggested that Cerros was one of the sites importing chipped stone tools from Colha (Hester 1981; Hester, Shafer, and Eaton 1982; Shafer 1981).

TABLE 20

Frequencies of Copper Bell Types

Description	Frequency
Pear-shaped, plain	9
Globular, plain	2
Pear-shaped, simulated wirework	2
Pear-shaped, plain, reinforced lip	1
Pear-shaped, simulated wirework, geometric designs	1
Pear-shaped, simulated wirework, geometric designs, and reinforced lip	1
Pear-shaped, wirework calyx below suspension loop	1

The vast majority of chipped stone at Cerros is gray, brown, and banded brown chert. Chert of this coloration is available near Rancho Creek where Colha is located (Hazeldon 1973).

Approximately 4% of the chipped stone from Cerros is obsidian. Obsidian has been found in Late Preclassic and Late Postclassic deposits. Blades are the common artifact form, although no Late Preclassic blade cores have been recovered. Debitage and debris were present in Preclassic and Postclassic deposits, although only in amounts to suggest final shaping and minor reworking.

8. CONCLUSION

As stated in the Introduction, the objectives of this study are (1) to examine the extent of trade at Cerros as evidenced in the artifacts; (2) to examine the changes that Cerros as a community underwent from the Late Preclassic through the Postclassic periods; (3) to examine patterns of artifact consumption and disposal, thus illuminating the behavioral systems that contributed to the configuration of the archaeological record; and (4) to describe the Cerros artifact collection. The success of each of these expectations is evaluated below.

THE CERROS ARTIFACT DATA

The organization of the formal presentation of artifact data followed that of many previous investigators (Coe 1959; Kidder 1947; Kidder, Jennings, and Shook 1946; Phillips 1979; Proskouriakoff 1962, 1974; Ricketson and Ricketson 1937; Rovner 1975; Sheets 1978; Smith and Kidder 1951; Willey 1972, 1978; Willey et al. 1965). In addition, this organizational scheme is easy to use for comparative purposes by future investigators.

Because of the large amount of Classic and Postclassic overburden that often overlies Preclassic remains, Late Preclassic data are scarce (Willey 1977). The absence of major Classic and Postclassic constructions at Cerros rendered the Late Preclassic material easily accessible. As a result, the excavations at Cerros have yielded one of the largest and most variable samples of Late Preclassic artifacts so far recovered from a single site. For this reason, Cerros should provide a valuable data bank to be drawn on by future investigators.

In consulting artifact reports it is sometimes difficult or impossible to obtain certain kinds of information regarding a particular artifact, because limitations in preparation time and funds restrict the formal data presentation. The data forms, presented in Appendix B, were devised to present a maximum of recorded information. It is hoped that this manner of data presentation will give researchers easy access to data that would not otherwise be available had it been presented only in the traditional summarizing fashion and, at the same time, that it will make a methodological contribution in presenting one way to deal with large data sets.

CERROS AS A TRADE CENTER

The raw materials of the Cerros artifacts can be divided into three groups: (1) those that are available in the area surrounding the site, that is, Northern Belize and the adjacent portions of Mexico; (2) those that are available within the Maya Lowlands; and (3) those that are available outside the Maya Lowlands.

Artifacts of materials available only from areas outside the Lowlands include manos and metates of andesite and rhyolite; various ornaments of jade; mirrors of specular hematite; items of copper, gold, and tumbaga; and artifacts of obsidian. Pumice may also have been imported, but in all likelihood, the pumice utilized was that which floats in from Highland sources and is easily obtained on the Belize coast and cays (Graham 1987). The nearest source for these non-Lowland materials is southern Guatemala, 400 km from Cerros.

Artifacts of materials available within the Lowlands but not within the immediate vicinity of Cerros include ground stone tools of quartzite and pegmatite. The nearest source for these materials is the Maya Mountains in West-Central Belize, approximately 150 km from Cerros (Graham 1987; Sidrys and Andresen 1976; Thompson 1964).

Artifacts of materials available locally in Northern Belize and adjacent areas of Mexico make up the majority of artifacts recovered. Some of the shell items may have been imported, but most, if not all, were probably available in Northern Belize.

Manos and metates were made from materials obtained from all three locations. Table 21 shows the percentages of those tools from each source area for the major time periods at Cerros. This table shows that during the Late Preclassic, no manos or metates (or any other ground stone forms) entered Cerros by way of long-distance trade. During the Late Preclassic, trade contacts with volcanic areas were in existence, as evidenced by the recovery of numerous pieces of

TABLE 21

Manos and Metates by Source for Each Period

Source	Late Preclassic (%)	Early Classic (%)	Late Postclassic (%)
Local	28.8	45.9	29.6
Maya Mountains	71.2	48.6	63.0
Long Distance	0.0	5.4	7.4
	n = 52	n = 37	n = 30

jade, specular hematite, and obsidian. The existence of extensive contacts is also manifest in the monumental art of Cerros (Freidel 1977, 1978b, 1979; Schele and Miller 1986).

None of the utilitarian or domestic artifacts of a Late Preclassic date were made from materials obtained through long-distance trade. A possible exception is the pumice used to manufacture the nine Late Preclassic abraders. As previously noted, low-density pumice floats in from Highland sources. Thus, all artifacts produced from exotic materials were either ornamental or nonutilitarian in nature. Many of them were associated with the dedication or ritual abandonment of public architecture. If Cerros were indeed a station for transshipment of nonperishable utilitarian goods, it is reasonable to expect that some of those items would have remained in the local inventory. Of the items dealt with in this study, Late Preclassic long-distance trade was restricted to elitist material culture of an ornamental or nonutilitarian nature. This should not diminish the significance of long-distance contacts in the evolution and development of a complex society. It does demonstrate, however, that subsistence-related or cultural ecology–type trade systems are not the only long-distance trade systems that can be investigated.

Table 21 reveals that 71.2% of Late Preclassic manos, metates, and fragments came from the Maya Mountains, the closest source of quartzite, about 150 km to the south. Cerros and other Late Preclassic sites of similar size, such as Nohmul, Aventura, San Estevan, Lamani, and El Posito, may have functioned as redistribution centers for these and other regional products in Northern Belize. Cerros may also have served as a mercantile hub for transporting products shipped inland by way of the New River. These possibilities can be proved only as more Late Preclassic data from interior and Yucatecan coastal sites become available.

From its size and location, Late Preclassic Cerros emerges as a seat of power and locus for exchange. In terms of material culture, long-distance contacts were restricted to goods relevant to elitist activities. This provided the basis for participation in a wide-ranging interaction sphere. It may have been this participation that enabled Cerros to control the distribution of regional goods.

Rathje (1971, 1972) proposes that basalt, obsidian, and salt had to be imported by long-distance trade to the Lowland Maya area, because those items were essential to the subsistence economy in the Lowland jungle. According to this model, centralized authority evolved in response to the need to organize and maintain long-distance trade routes to ensure the constant flow of goods. Several investigators have questioned the indispensability of obsidian and basalt to Lowland subsistence (Freidel 1978b; Rice 1976; Sanders 1973; Tourtellot and Sabloff 1972). Hammond (1975) and Rice (1976) note that nonutilitarian exotic goods were present as early as the Middle Preclassic.

Freidel (1978b) presents a model that stresses the role long-distance trade played in the development and demise of Late Preclassic Cerros. Briefly stated, the model is as follows. During the Preclassic, trade was mainly coastal. Two distinct interaction spheres had evolved, one in northern Yucatán and the other in the south, including the Petén and Belize. Salt was transported from north to south by way of coastal sites such as Cerros. Exotics from the highlands moved from south to north in exchange for salt. According to this model, the northern and southern spheres attempted to gain control of each other's monopoly. Cerros was abandoned because interior land trade routes had developed after the north-south conflict, which led to eventual domination by the south.

Sanders (1973) and Rice (1976) feel that importation of nonutilitarian exotics was probably organized from the source and provided little stimulus for the evolution of complex society. Although acquisition from the source may not have been an important organizational stimulus, once acquired, these objects could have been the subject of sociocultural manipulation in the Lowlands.

Long-distance exchange, on the other hand, usually dealt with the restricted functional, prestige artifacts which served in behavior relating and coordinating individuals and groups within the socio-cultural system itself (Tourtellot and

Sabloff 1972: 128). . . . These substances would probably not have been market items but rather were exchanges directly between the elites of separate communities as an expression of sociopolitical links (Tourtellot and Sabloff 1972: 132).

Although Tourtellot and Sabloff recognize those internal manipulations, they state that trade in nonutilitarian goods was only of secondary importance in bringing about changes in the level of sociocultural organization from ranked to state society.

Freidel (1978*b*) and Freidel and Schele (1982, 1988) argue that trade in nonutilitarian goods was important in the development of Lowland Maya complex society, because such goods figured prominently in the symbol systems of power.

Given: Social relationships are dependent on knowledge of the participants' socioeconomic status (Goodenough 1963; Goffman 1959).

Then: Increasing population is accompanied by an increased number of social encounters in which knowledge of social status is not based on personal familiarity and hence in which social status must be symbolized (Goffman 1959; Merton 1957). . . . Given: Material culture provides an essential symbolic medium for the expression of social-status distinctions (Mauss 1967; Renfrew 1975; Binford 1972).

Then: Increasing population is accompanied by an increase in the number and complexity of material symbols capable of expressing social-status distinctions (Freidel 1978*b:* 252).

In addition to sociopolitical functions, exotic material must have served important economic functions as well. Population growth and increased communication and interaction would have necessitated the formulation of standards of exchange. At the time of Spanish contact, jade beads functioned as money (Tozzer 1941). Certain forms of jade and obsidian and possibly other exotics no doubt served similar functions in Pre-Columbian times (Garber 1981, 1983). Exotics were not only trinkets for the elites and material indicators of status, but some forms were probably currency or monetary units with standardized equivalencies as well. The Late Preclassic period is characterized by increased interaction and information flow and the establishment of many administrative centers. Exotics are necessary in such a situation because they provide the medium for expression of status and prestige and for the establishment of standardized value systems

that crosscut local economies (Freidel 1977, 1978*b,* 1979). Standardized value systems and symbols would have provided the basis of interaction between the elites of major centers. Exotic goods manipulated in this manner permitted an expansive interaction sphere within the Maya Lowlands.

Sanders and Price (1968) and Tourtellot and Sabloff (1972) note that the diverse environments of the Highlands necessitated trade and market systems in which a broad range of goods was regularly exchanged. It is this necessity for trade, a result of environmental diversity, that contributed to the evolution of complex society in highland environments (Sanders and Price 1968). For years the Maya Lowlands were perceived as a homogeneous resource zone. Since the late 1970s, this view has changed, and environmental diversity and differential resource distribution are regarded as important factors in seeking an explanation for the evolution of complex society in the Lowlands (Graham 1987). Lowland trade in exotics may have generated standardized value systems, which aided in the establishment of a Lowland cultural sphere unlike the Highlands that can be described as a group of individualized states. Consequently, investigation of sociocultural manipulation of nonutilitarian exotics is an essential component in gaining an understanding of the evolution of Maya civilization.

CERROS: A CHANGING COMMUNITY

Cerros operated as a locus of activity during the Late Preclassic, Early Classic, and Late Postclassic periods. The nature of this occupation shifted dramatically. During the Late Preclassic, Cerros was a center of political, religious, and elitist interaction, as well as a locus for domestic activity. No monumental architecture at Cerros has been dated to any period other than the Late Preclassic.

During the Early Classic, Cerros ceased to function as an elitist center but continued as a location for mundane, domestic activity (Scarborough and Robertson 1986). In the dispersed settlement zone Structures 10, 46, and 84 were constructed during the Early Classic. The remainder of the Early Classic deposits consist of cultural debris on or just below the surface of structures built during the Late Preclassic. With the exception of a cache and associated rituals on Structure 4B (Walker 1986), no jade or specular hematite artifacts have been recovered from any of the Classic period deposits at Cerros. The scarcity of nonutilitarian exotic material culture during the Early and Late Classic periods is taken as evidence of the lack of elitism during these periods at Cerros. No monumental constructions dating to the Classic period have been observed. During the Classic period, after Cerros declined as a political and/or economic center, utilitarian objects fashioned from raw materials obtained through long-distance trade were imported to Cerros. These were absent in Late Preclassic deposits.

Although Early Classic nonutilitarian goods are rare at Cerros, they have been found in numerous Classic period sites in Belize (Hammond 1973, 1975, 1979; Pendergast 1976, 1979, 1981; Thompson 1931, 1939, 1964; Willey et al. 1965). Importation of exotic utilitarian items during the Classic, an activity apparently absent in the Late Preclassic, indicates expansion of long-distance contacts and of the categories of items traded.

The discovery of a large Late Postclassic cache containing highly prized exotics including jade, gold, and tumbaga suggests the reemergence at Cerros of elitist activity. This elitism did not include the construction of monumental architecture. Many artifacts relating to Late Postclassic domestic activities have been recovered on many smaller mounds.

The presence of mariposas can be taken as evidence of a reliance, in part, at least, on fish resources. This, of course, assumes that their functional identification as net weights is correct. From the mariposa data, it can be seen that there is a significant increase in the number of mariposas from the Late Preclassic through the Postclassic. Although it could be argued that this is a factor of sampling, other correlative domestic items such as manos and metates decrease from the Late Preclassic to the Late Postclassic. Over 50% of the mariposas date to the Late Postclassic, whereas fewer than 20% of the manos and metates are of corresponding age. Although fishing with mariposa-weighted nets is not the only means of catching fish, an increase in the frequency of mariposas constitutes evidence for an increase in this form of fishing and might indicate an increased reliance on fish as a food source. An increase in this method of fishing, or in fishing in general, is very large when one considers the much-greater quantity of Late Preclassic domestic debris recovered compared to Late Postclassic. Silting in of the Cerros canal system would have rendered the raised-field system of agriculture inoperable. This supports the argument that fishing increased in importance during the Late Postclassic at Cerros.

PATTERNS OF ARTIFACT CONSUMPTION AND DISPOSAL

One of the objectives of this study was to examine the patterns of artifact consumption and disposal in order to illuminate the behavioral systems that contributed to the configuration of the archaeological record. Patterns of consumption can be discerned through an examination of context. The different ways of discarding artifacts determine, for the most part, the location or context in which they are found, except when natural processes such as erosion, settling, and uprooting intervene.

A typology of contexts was devised that reflects the behavior associated with particular deposits. Contextual designations were made on the basis of associated features and artifacts. In many deposits, the feature associations were unclear. A great many Classic and Postclassic artifacts came from the surface or from the humus or fall. Although many of these are probably domestic debris, their lack of association with domestic features relegated them to listing by matrix. Other deposits were more clearly understood and could be listed contextually under headings, such as cache, burial, or domestic debris, which indicate their associated behavior.

An analysis of this sort led to the examination of a contextual setting that has received little attention or has gone unrecognized at other sites: termination ritual. In dealing with the Cerros ceramics, Robertson-Freidel (1980) recognizes deposits resulting from the termination of monumental architecture as one of the sources from which the sherds came.

Termination ritual varies from deposit to deposit, but can consist of removing plaster façading, burning ceremonial fires, smashing jade artifacts, scattering marl, preparing and consuming a ceremonial beverage, and smashing vessels. One or more of these features may be absent from a given deposit, but all consistently include the scattering about of marl, burning, and the smashing of artifacts. Termination ritual has been identified on Structures 29B, 5C, 2A-Sub.4-1st, 4B, 3B and the Feature 1A residential zone.

The artifacts from Cerros that are clearly associated with termination ritual include jade beads, jade flares, sherd disks, bone beads, specular hematite mirrors, armatures, doughnut stones, stone disks, stone spheroids, and miscellaneous pieces. Of all the Late Preclassic finds at Cerros, 43.1% were recovered from the marl and were associated with the termination ritual of monumental architecture. If the numerous burned disks and spheroids are excluded, the figure drops to 17.8%, still an impressive figure when one considers that marl accounts for less than 5.0% of the fill excavated at Cerros. Not included as termination ritual artifacts are the numerous finds from Feature 1A that are surely associated with the abandonment of domestic architecture recovered in domestic debris.

Even though extensive deposits of domestic refuse have been excavated, the above figures and discussion attest to the previously unrecognized relatively high expenditures of time, labor, and material culture investment associated with the abandonment of monumental and domestic architecture.

An analysis of this context led to a definition of a form of artifact disposal not reported at other sites. Within this context, patterns were also recognized. No shell beads have been recovered from deposits resulting from the termination and abandonment of monumental architecture; in contrast, jade beads were often found associated with the termination of both domestic and monumental architecture. Frequently, jade beads were intentionally smashed, whereas shell beads were rarely broken. Jade beads and shell beads were consumed quite differently from each other. The less-expensive shell (available locally) was inappropriate to sacrifice in the abandonment of public architecture, but was appropriate for the abandonment of private architecture.

A contextual analysis of the jade artifacts revealed that whole jades were associated with structure completion and dedication, whereas intentionally broken jades were associated with structure abandonment and termination.

Similarly, a contextual analysis of Cerros doughnut stones disclosed that identical artifacts may occur in quite different archaeological settings. Some maintain that doughnut stones were weights for digging sticks and nets, thus accounting for their deposition in domestic debris. They also appear on friezes as design elements of iconographic representation on monumental architecture. They may have been offerings from the lower levels of Maya society. The inclusion of a utilitarian element into the designs of a monumental structure represents a symbolic link between the social extremes of Maya society.

The presence of metates and manos in the construction fill of monumental architecture was quite unexpected, since those items normally appear only in domestic debris. Furthermore, the absence of sherds clearly indicated that the fill itself did not originate as domestic refuse, because sherds are a common component of household debris. One may only conclude that metates and manos were votive offerings placed by workmen in the fill at the time of construction.

Manos and metates are found in many contexts, including construction fill, domestic debris, humus, fall, and on the surface. Those on the surface or in the humus are probably the result of domestic activity at those locations. No manos, metates, or their fragments were recovered from deposits resulting from termination ritual.

Sherd disks appear in several contexts, including structure dedication, structure completion, and domestic debris. There is ample evidence to demonstrate that the larger disks functioned as lids for narrow-mouthed vessels. Although many functioned in similar ways, the contexts in which they were found suggest that they were appropriate for various kinds of activities.

Mariposas usually occur in domestic debris or deposits such as humus or fall. Those found within the humus and fall are probably also domestic refuse, but lack clear association with domestic features. No mariposas appeared in caches or deposits resulting from termination ritual.

The role of Cerros as a community changed drastically over time. These changes are reflected in the artifact assemblages and contexts in which they are found.

The Late Preclassic deposits at Cerros exhibit a wide range of artifact types and contexts. The behavior reflected by these contexts is in sharp contrast to that recognized from the Early Classic period at Cerros, which implies predominantly domestic activities. At the end of the Late Preclassic, Cerros ceased to function as a center for political, religious, and elitist activity, but it continued through the Early Classic as a locus for more mundane activities.

Several artifacts relating to Late Postclassic domestic activities have been recovered. As evidenced by a large Late Postclassic cache and numerous censers on several of the mounds, the Late Postclassic period witnessed the reemergence of elitist activity.

An examination of artifact deposition, in conjunction with categorization and description of artifact types as defined by material, technology, and form, is essential in obtaining an understanding of the functions of various artifacts and the behavioral systems that account for their deposition.

APPENDICES

Appendix A
Key to Data Form Symbols

A-1: Key to Abbreviations on Data Form Headings

Abbreviation	Meaning
Cond.	Condition
Cont.	Context
C	Catalog number - CM1
Dia.	Diameter
Feat.	Feature or structure
Ln	Length (cm)
Mat.	Material
SF	Small Find catalog number
Th	Thickness (cm)
Wd	Width (cm)

A-2: Alphabetical Symbols for Condition, Form, and Material of Artifacts Listed on Data Forms

Symbol		Symbol	
A	Anvil	Pg	Pegmatite
Ag	Angled	Pt	Pentagonal
An	Anvil-pounder	Pu	Pumice
At	Antler	Q	Quartzite
B	Broken	R	Rectangular
BC	Black coral	Rb	Rhomboid
BL	Bilobed	Rh	Rhyolite
Bl	Barrel	S	Spool
Bn	Basin	Sc	Schist
Bv	Bivalve	Sd	Sandstone
C	Circular	Sf	Spherical
Ca	Canine	Sh	Sherd
CC	Convex-concave	Sl	Slab
Ch	Chert	SN	Side notch
Cl	Coral	SP	Straight parallel
Cm	Chloromelanite	Sp	Spondylus
Cn	Conch	Sq	Square
Co	Collared	Sr	Serpentine
Cr	Crescent	SS	Straight slant
Cv	Convex	Ss	Subspherical
Cy	Cylindrical	ST	Shark tooth
Dk	Disk	T	Tinkler
Dm	Domed	TD	Teardrop
Dn	Dentallium	To	Tooth
Do	Dolomite	Tp	Trapezoidal
Ef	Effigy	Tq	Turquoise
El	Elongated	Tr	Triangular
EN	End notch	TS	Trident shell
ES	End/side notch	Tu	Tubular
FB	Flared bead	Ul	Ulna
FC	Fossil coral	Uv	Univalve
FJ	Fish jaw	W	Whole
Fl	Flower	Wd	Wedge
Fu	Fuschite	Y	Yes
FV	Fish vertebra		
GB	Grinding basin		
Gs	Gastropod		
Ir	Irregular		
Ja	Jadeite		
L	Limestone		
Lg	Legged		
Mb	Marble		
MC	Molded clay		
MP	Metapodial		
N	No		
Oh	Overhang		
Ol	Oliva		
Ov	Oval		
PC	Plano-convex		

A-3: Numeric Symbols for Context on Data Forms

    1   Surface
    2   Humus
    3   Humus/fall
    4   Fall
    5   Termination ritual
    6   Slump
    7   On floor
    8   In floor
    9   Construction fill with rubble
    10 Construction fill without rubble
    11 Domestic debris
    12 Cache
    13 Burial
    14 Pit fill
    15 Beach near Feature 1A
    16 Beach
    17 Unknown or mixed

A-4: Numeric Symbols for Chronological Placement on Data Forms

Symbol	Chronological Placement
1	Late Preclassic - Phase 1, Ixtabi
2	Late Preclassic - Phase 2, C'oh
2/3	Late Preclassic - Phase 2-3, transition
3	Late Preclassic - Phase 3, Tulix
1-3	Late Preclassic - Phase 1, 2, or 3
4	Early Classic
5	Late Classic
6	Classic
7	Late Postclassic
8	Unknown

Appendix B
Data Forms

B-1: Manos

SF	Feat.	Cond.	Form	Mat.	Date	Cont.	Ln	Wd	Th	Dia.	Hole Dia.
4	1A/2A	B	Ov	Ch	8	15		8.2	5.6		
12	1A	B	Ov	Q	1-3	13		7.6	5.2		
32	1A	B	PC	Q	1-3	11		7.2	4.1		
95	1A	B	Tr	Mb	1-3	11		7.6	3.5		
128	6A	B	Ov	Q	7	1		7.6	4.9		
213	2A	B	Ov	FC	7	1		8.3	5.3		
214	2A	B	R	Q	7	1	10.2	8.0	5.2		
263	2A	B	PC	Q	7	1		7.5	5.1		
378	33A	B	C	An	7	2		6.6			
396	1A	B	Ov	FC	1-3	14			5.9		
397	1A	B	PC	Q	1-3	14		7.1			
447	4A	B	Ov	Q	7	3		6.6	4.9		
537	1A	B	Ov	Q	1-3	13		7.9	5.4		
558	11B	B	PC	L	7	2	6.4	6.0	3.0		
559	11B	B	Oh	Do	7	2		7.0	3.1		
690	4A	B	C	L	1-3	9		4.5			
807	10C	B	C	An	6	4		6.6			
837	1A	B	PC	FC	1-3	11	20.2				
863	10C	B	C	Do	1-3	9		8.4			
900	1A	B	PC	FC	1-3	8		8.1	4.4		
956	1A/2A	W	PC	Mb	8	15	13.7	9.8	4.1		
1013		B	Oh	L	7	1		6.0	4.8		
1019	22A	B	Pt	L	7	1		5.7	4.8		
1025	112A	B	PC	Q	7	1		7.4	4.4		
1031	5C	B	Ov	Q	7	3			6.0		
1048	4A	B	PC	Q	1-3	9	7.0	6.2			
1050	4A	B	PC	Mb	1-3	9			3.3		
1095	4A	B	PC	Mb	1-3	9			4.0		
1096	4A	B	PC	Do	1-3	9					
1107	1A/2A	B	Ov	Q	8	15		7.6	4.1		
1108	2A	B	PC	Q	7	1		7.2	4.7		
1129	1A/2A	B	PC	Q	8	15		7.6	5.1		
1263		B	R	Q	8	17		7.2	5.2		
1264	14A	B	Ov	Q	3	9					
1278	1A/2A	B	C	FC	8	15					
1289	46A	B	C	Do	7	3					
1298	46A	B		Do	4	11					
1320	2A	B		L	8	3					
1332	50A	B	Oh	Do	5	14		7.7	5.9		
1342	5C	B	Ov	Q	3	5		7.4	5.7		
1350	1A	B	PC	Mb	1-3	8					

B-1: Manos--continued

SF	Feat.	Cond.	Form	Mat.	Date	Cont.	Ln	Wd	Th	Dia.	Hole Dia.
1372	50B	B	R	L	4	4		5.2	4.0		
1377	50B	B	R	Do	4	2	12.0	6.2	7.0		
1405	4A	B		Q	1-3	9					
1428	1A/2A	B		Q	8	15					
1430	1A	B	Ov	Q	1-3	11		8.0	6.2		
1438	1A/2A	B	PC	Q	8	15		7.6	4.3		
1448		B	C	An	8	16		8.1			
1480	50B	B	C	Ch	4	3					
1574	50B	B		Q	4	3					
1575	29B	B	R	L	7	3		6.3	5.2		
1615	29B	B	Ov	Q	7	3		3.9	5.4		
1644	50B	B	PC	Q	3	9					
1698	50E	B	Ov	Do	4	3			6.0		
1714	50E	B	Oh	Do	3	3			6.4		
1834	34A	B	PC	Do	3	11	7.8	6.9	3.7		
1842	2A	B	C	Q	1-3	10					
1843	50D	B	PC	Q	4	3					
1892	2A	B	R	Q	7	1		6.4	5.3		
1951	50C	B	R	Do	4	3			4.2		

B-2: Metates

SF	Feat.	Cond.	Form	Mat.	Date	Cont.	Ln	Wd	Th	Dia.	Hole Dia.
104	1A	B	Bn	Q	1-3	13					
215	2A	B	Bn	Q	7	1					
246	2A	B	Bn	Pg	7	1					
324	22A	B	Bn	Q	7	4					
368	1A	B	Bn		1-3	11					
383	1A	B	Bn	Q	1-3	11					
457	1A	B	Bn	Q	1-3	11					
467	1A	B	Bn	Q	1-3	11					
475	1A	B	Bn	Q	1-3	14					
538	2A	B	Bn	FC	7	1		14.0			
560	2A	B	Bn	Q	7	2					
589	2A	B	Bn	Q	1-3	9					
623	2A	B	Lg	An	7	1					
630	2A	B	Bn	Q	1-3	9					
760	7A	B	Bn	Q	1-3	4					
790	4A	B	BN	Q	7	2					
859	10C	B	Sl	Do	6	4					
868	5C	B	Sl	Q	3	3					
930	10C	B	Bn	Do	6	2					
976	5A	B	Sl	Q	1-3	9					

B-2: Metates--continued

SF	Feat.	Cond.	Form	Mat.	Date	Cont.	Ln	Wd	Th	Dia.	Hole Dia.
1057	1A/2A	B	Bn	Q	8	15					
1098	4A	B	Bn	Q	1-3	9					
1099	4A	B	Bn	Q	1-3	9					
1100	4A	B	Bn	Q	1-3	9					
1106	4A	B	Bn	Q	1-3	9					
1110	4A	B	Bn	Q	1-3	9					
1118	4A	B	Bn	Q	1-3	9					
1125	1A/2A	B	Bn	Q	8	15					
1196	1A	B	Bn	Q	1-3	11					
1208	76A	B	Bn	Rh	8	17		13.0			
1234	1A	B	Sl	Mb	1-3	11					
1279		B	Bn	Q	8	1					
1281		B	Bn	Q	8	1					
1294	61A	B	Sl	FC	3	4					
1331	94A	B	Bn	Q	7	3					
1333	50B	B	Bn	Q	4	2					
1334	1A	B	Bn	Q	1-3	11					
1404	38A	B	Bn	Q	2						
1429	2A	B	Bn	Q	8	1					
1461	50B	B	Bn	Q	4	3					
1471	2A	B	Sl	Do	8	1					
1509	50B	B	Sl	Do	4	3					
1516	50E	B	Bn	Q	4	4					
1527	2A	B	Bn	Q	7	2					
1578	50A	B	Sl	An	4	2					
1588	50B	B	Sl	Q	4	3					
1600	46A	B	Sl	Do	4	4					
1613	50C	B	Lg	Do	4	3					
1625	50D	B	Bn	Q	4	4					
1668	50D	B	Bn	Q	4	3					
1697	50B	B	Bn	Do	4	3					
1700	50C	B	Bn	L	4	3					
1734	29B	B	Bn	Rh	1-3	4					
1748	50E	B	Bn	Q	4	3					
1760	50C	B	Bn	Q	4	3					
1762	50B	W	Bn	Do	4	1					
1770	1A	B	Bn	Q	1-3	11					
1848	5C	B	Bn	Q	1-3	9					
1867	50C	B	Bn	Q	4	3					
1891	50C	B	Bn	Q	4	3					
1894	50D	B	Bn	Q	4	2					
1903	34A	B	Bn	Do	3	3					
1950	11B	B	Bn	Q	7	12					
1952	50C	B	Bn	Q	4	3					
1953	50E	B	Bn	Q	4	3					
1954	50B	B	Sl	Do	4	3					
1955		B	Bn	Q	8	16					
1956		B	Bn	Q	8	16					
1957		B	Bn	Q	8	16					
1958		B	Bn	Q	8	16					

B-3: Ground stone fragments

SF	Feat.	Cond.	Form	Mat.	Date	Cont.	Ln	Wd	Th	Dia.	Hole Dia.
1042	4A	B		Q	1-3	9					
1082	1A	B			1-3	11					
1227	1A	B		Q	1-3	8					
1228	127A	B		Q	8	17					
1267	1A	B		Q	1-3	11					
1308	1A/2A	B		Q	8	15					
1765	50E	B		Do	4	3					
1859	127A	B		Rh	8	10					

B-4: Armatures

SF	Feat.	Cond.	Form	Mat.	Date	Cont.	Ln	Wd	Th	Dia.	Hole Dia.
1135	29B	B	Ov	L	3	5		5.2	4.0		
1454	29B	W	R	L	3	5	20.6	5.8	3.1		
1455	29B	B	R	L	3	5	19.7	5.3	2.5		
1467	29B	B	Ov	L	3	4		5.2	3.5		
1473	29B	B	C	L	3	5		7.6	5.8		
1476	29B	B	Ov	L	3	5		3.1	2.4		
1486	29B	B	Ov	L	3	4		5.2	4.8		
1487	29B	B	R	L	3	4		4.5	3.2		
1488	29B	B	Ov	L	3	4		6.4	3.9		
1504	29B	W	Ov	L	3	5	15.0	3.5	2.7		
1513	29B	B	Ov	L	3	2		4.9	4.1		
1560	29B	B	Ov	L	3	5		3.4	3.2		
1571	29B	B	R	L	3	4		2.7	2.2		
1576	29B	B	C	L	3	5		9.3	9.3		
1694	29B	B	Ov	L	3	3		3.3	2.8		
1729	29B	B	R	L	3	5		5.6	3.2		
1788	29B	B	Ov	L	3	2		5.2	4.6		
1960	29B	B	Sq	L	3	5		2.5	2.4		
1961	29B	B	Ov	L	3	5		3.5	2.8		

B-5: Doughnut stones

SF	Feat.	Cond.	Form	Mat.	Date	Cont.	Ln	Wd	Th	Dia.	Hole Dia.
5	1A/2A	W		L	8	15			3.0	11.0	1.4
19	1A	W		L	1-3	11			3.3	10.5	1.1
428	33A	W		L	2	11			1.9	6.3	0.5
698	5C	W		L	3	4			2.8	8.1	1.3
714	5C	B		L	3	14			2.9	9.2	1.6
747	5C	W		L	3	5			3.3	9.5	1.3
748	5C	B		L	3	5			3.6	10.0	1.6
865	4A	W		L	3	5			3.3	11.2	0.9
971	4A	B		L	1-3	9			2.3	8.8	0.9
1012	5A	W		L	1-3	4			3.9	11.1	1.0
1044	4A	W		L	1-3	9			2.9	10.6	0.8
1058	4A	W		L	1-3	9			2.2	6.5	0.8
1089	5A	W		L	1-3	9			2.3	9.2	0.9
1109	4A	B		L	1-3	9			2.2	8.1	1.4
1132	5C	B		L	3	5			3.3	8.4	1.2
1133	5C	B		L	3	5			3.5	7.1	
1201	5C	W		L	8	17			3.7	10.6	1.0
1203	5C	W		L	3	5			3.2	12.4	1.2
1256	1A	B		L	1-3	11			2.7	7.4	1.6
1280	1A/2A	W		L	8	15			2.0	7.6	1.0
1376	98A	W		L	3	9			2.5	10.2	1.1
1399	98A	W		L	3	11			3.4	9.6	1.5
1400	98A	W		L	3	11			3.5	10.4	1.2
1401	38A	W		L	2	9			2.7	9.3	1.3
1913	5C	W		L	1-3	9			4.0	12.3	0.9
1947	5C	W		L	1-3	9			2.6	11.9	1.1
1959	4B	W		L	8	3			3.0	10.1	0.8

B-6: Abraders

SF	Feat.	Cond.	Form	Mat.	Date	Cont.	Ln	Wd	Th	Dia.	Hole Dia.
66	9A	B		Sd	7	11					
68	9A	B		Sd	7	11					
76	1A	B	PC	Pu	1-3	11		7.0	5.0		
229	4B	B	Ir	Pu	8	4			3.2		
446	1A	W	Ov	Pu	1-3	11	6.4	6.3	4.5		
814	4B	W	Tr	Pu	8	4	9.0	8.6	4.7		
969	1A	W	PC	Pu	1-3	11	13.5	6.6	5.3		
1051	4A	W	PC	Pu	1-3	9	14.2	10.9	7.1		
1145	1A/2A	W	Ov	Pu	8	15	6.4	4.8	3.8		
1195	1A	B		Pu	1-3	11					
1236	1A	B	Ir	Pu	1-3	8					
1275	112A	B	Ir	Pu	7	3			8.2		
1422	1A	W	Ov	Pu	1-3	11	5.7	4.1	2.9		
1860	5C	W	Ov	Pu	1-3	9	12.5	8.0	5.4		
1932	1A	B		Pu	1-3	11					

B-7: Bark beaters

SF	Feat.	Cond.	Form	Mat.	Date	Cont.	Ln	Wd	Th	Dia.	Hole Dia.
1018	1A	B	Ov	L	8	15			3.8		
1447		B	Ov	L	8	16			4.9		

B-8: Girdled stones

SF	Feat.	Cond.	Form	Mat.	Date	Cont.	Ln	Wd	Th	Dia.	Hole Dia.
806	1A	W	Cy	L	1-3	11	5.8	2.9	2.5		
977	4A	W	Bl	L	7	2	1.0			0.6	
1052	4A	W	Cy	L	1-3	9	6.7	2.9			
1261	1A	W	Bl	L	1-3	11	4.0	1.8	1.5		

B-9: Stone spindle whorls

SF	Feat.	Cond.	Form	Mat.	Date	Cont.	Ln	Wd	Th	Dia.	Hole Dia.
190	9C	W	Dm	L	7	2			1.6	3.4	0.8
1335	1A	W	Ov	L	8	15			1.1	2.5	0.6

B-10: Ground stone pendants

SF	Feat.	Cond.	Form	Mat.	Date	Cont.	Ln	Wd	Th	Dia.	Hole Dia.
576	11B	W	Cr	L	7	2	2.9	2.0	1.3		
902	1A	W	Ov	L	1-3	8	3.6	3.3	0.8		0.3
1258	1A	B	TD	L	1-3	11	4.2	2.5	1.1		0.3

B-11: Pestle-pounders

SF	Feat.	Cond.	Form	Mat.	Date	Cont.	Ln	Wd	Th	Dia.	Hole Dia.
707	1A	W		Sd	1-3	4	5.9	5.2	4.1		
957	1A	W		Q	1-3	11	10.9			8.1	

B-12: Stone with hemispherical depression

SF	Feat.	Cond.	Form	Mat.	Date	Cont.	Ln	Wd	Th	Dia.	Hole Dia.
317	1A	W	Ss	Mb	1-3	11			4.6	5.5	

B-13: Anvil-pounder-grinder

SF	Feat.	Cond.	Form	Mat.	Date	Cont.	Ln	Wd	Th	Dia.	Hole Dia.
1130	5A	W	Ss	Mb	1-3	9	8.4	7.3	7.7		

B-14: Weights with suspension holes

SF	Feat.	Cond.	Form	Mat.	Date	Cont.	Ln	Wd	Th	Dia.	Hole Dia.
1599	112A	W	Ir	L	8	1	23.2	15.6	7.2		2.6
1851	2A	B		L	1-3	11					2.6

B-15: Ground stone figurine

SF	Feat.	Cond.	Form	Mat.	Date	Cont.	Ln	Wd	Th	Dia.	Hole Dia.
1503	50B	W	Tr	L	4	3	10.2	6.7	2.5		

B-16: Polished stone beads

SF	Feat.	Cond.	Form	Mat.	Date	Cont.	Ln	Wd	Th	Dia.	Hole Dia.
113	1A	W	Sf	Ja	1-3	11				0.5	0.1
136	6B	W	Ss	Ja	3	12	0.9			1.2	0.3
137	6B	W	Ss	Ja	3	12	1.0			1.2	0.4
138	6B	W	Ss	Ja	3	12	0.8			1.2	0.3
139	6B	W	Ss	Ja	3	12	0.7			1.1	0.3
140	6B	W	Ss	Ja	3	12	1.1			1.2	0.3
145	6B	W	FB	Ja	3	12	2.2			0.9	0.4
183	4B	B	Tu	Ja	4	4					
185	4B	B	Co	Ja	4	5	3.3			1.3	0.6
219	4B	W	Dk	Ja	4	4	0.4			0.9	0.2
433	33A	B	Tu	Ja	7	2					
539B	4B	B	Sf	Ja	4	5	0.9				
539C	4B	B	Sf	Ja	4	5					
539D	4B	B	Ss	Ja	4	5	0.7				
539E	4B	B	Tu	Ja	4	5					
539F	4B	B	Ss	Ja	4	5					
539G	4B	B	Tu	Ja	4	5					
539H	4B	B	Bl	Ja	4	5					
539I	4B	B		Ja	4	5					
540A	4B	B	Ss	Ja	4	5	0.6			1.0	0.1
540B	4B	B	Ss	Ja	4	5	0.5			0.7	0.1
540C	4B	B	Tu	Ja	4	5					
540D	4B	B	Tu	Ja	4	5					
540E	4B	B	Tu	Ja	4	5					
540F	4B	B	Tu	Ja	4	5					
540G	4B	B	Bl	Ja	4	5					
540H	4B	B	Tu	Ja	4	5					
541A	4B	B	Co	Ja	4	5					
541B	4B	B	Bl	Ja	4	5					
541C	4B	B	Bl	Ja	4	5					
541D	4B	B	Bl	Ja	4	5					
542	4B	B	Sf	Ja	4	5					
543C	4B	W	Ss	Ja	4	5					
543D	4B	B	Ss	Ja	4	5	0.4			0.8	0.1
543E	4B	B	Ss	Ja	4	5	0.4			0.8	0.1
543F	4B	B		Ja	4	5	0.8				
543G	4B	B		Ja	4	5					
543H	4B	B	Tu	Ja	4	5					
543I	4B	B	Bl	Ja	4	5					
543J	4B	B	Bl	Ja	4	5					
543K	4B	B		Ja	4	5					
543L	4B	B		Ja	4	5					
543M	4B	B		Ja	4	5					
543N	4B	B	Co	Ja	4	5					
543O	4B	B		Ja	4	5					
544	4B	W	Sf	Ja	4	5					
545	4B	W	Sf	Ja	4	5					

B-16: Polished stone beads--continued

SF	Feat.	Cond.	Form	Mat.	Date	Cont.	Ln	Wd	Th	Dia.	Hole Dia.
552A	4B	W	Ss	Ja	4	5			0.4	0.6	0.1
552B	4B	W	Tu	Ja	4	5	0.7			0.4	0.2
665A	4B	B	R	Ja	7	12	2.0	1.1	0.7		
665B	4B	W	Wd	Tq	7	12	1.0	1.2	0.7		
704	11B	B	Ss	Ja	1-3	9					
735A	4A	W	Ss	Ja	7	12	0.5			1.0	0.3
735B	4A	W	Wd	Ja	7	12	1.6	1.4	0.8		
736A	4A	W	Ss	Ja	7	12	0.7			1.2	0.2
737D	4A	W	Bl	Ja	7	12	1.6			1.0	0.1
737E	4A	W	Rb	Ja	7	12	1.5	1.1	1.1		0.2
739J	4A	W	Ir	Ja	7	12	1.3	1.0	0.7		0.3
878	7A	B		Ja	1-3	9					0.2
879	4A	W	Ir	Tq	7	12	1.7	1.3	1.1		0.2
922	1A	B	Tu	Ja	1-3	11					
923	1A	W	Ss	Ja	1-3	11	0.3			0.5	0.1
924A	4A	B	Sf	Ja	3	5	1.5			1.5	
924B	4A	B		Ja	3	5					
925	1A	W	Bl	Ja	1-3	11	1.5			0.7	0.1
964	1A	W	Ss	Mb	1-3	11	0.9			1.3	0.2
965A	1A	B		Ja	1-3	11					
983	5C	W	Tu	Ja	3	12	4.9	0.8			0.2
986	4A	W	Wd	Ja	7	2	1.5	1.1	0.6		0.2
994A	1A	B		Ja	1-3	15					
995B	1A	B	Tu	Ja	1-3	15					
995C	1A	B		Ja	1-3	15					
995D	1A	B		Ja	1-3	15					
995E	1A	B	Bl	Ja	1-3	15					
995F	1A	B	Bl	Ja	1-3	15					
995G	1A	B	Dk	Ja	1-3	15					
1065	1A	B	Bl	Ja	1-3	11					
1068	5C	W	Ss	Ja	3	5					
1069	5C	B		Ja	3	5					
1070A	1A	B	Tu	Ja	1-3	15					
1070B	1A	B	Bl	Ja	1-3	15					
1070C	1A	B	Tu	Ja	1-3	15					
1071	1A	W	Dk	Ja	1-3	15	0.3			0.5	0.1
1074A	1A	B	Tu	Ja	1-3	11					
1074B	1A	B	Tu	Ja	1-3	11					
1077A	1A	B		Ja	1-3	11					
1077B	1A	B		Ja	1-3	11					
1077C	1A	B		Ja	1-3	11					
1078	1A	B		Ja	1-3	11					
1080A	1A	W		Ja	1-3	11	0.3			0.6	0.1
1080B	1A	B		Ja	1-3	11					
1083A	1A	B		Ja	1-3	11					
1111A	1A	B	Bl	Ja	1-3	11					
1111B	1A	B	Tu	Ja	1-3	11					
1111C	1A	B		Ja	1-3	11					
1112A	1A	B		Ja	1-3	11					

B-16: Polished stone beads--continued

SF	Feat.	Cond.	Form	Mat.	Date	Cont.	Ln	Wd	Th	Dia.	Hole Dia.
1112B	1A	B		Ja	1-3	11					
1114A	1A	B	Co	Ja	1-3	11					
1114B	1A	B	Co	Ja	1-3	11					
1114C	1A	B	Co	Ja	1-3	11					
1114D	1A	B	Bl	Ja	1-3	11	1.3				
1114E	1A	B	Bl	Ja	1-3	11					
1114F	1A	B	Bl	Ja	1-3	11					
1114G	1A	B		Ja	1-3	11					
1114H	1A	B		Ja	1-3	11					
1114I	1A	B		Ja	1-3	11					
1114J	1A	B		Ja	1-3	11					
1114K	1A	B		Ja	1-3	11					
1114L	1A	B		Ja	1-3	11					
1114M	1A	B		Ja	1-3	11					
1116A	1A	B	Tu	Ja	1-3	11					
1116B	1A	B	Tu	Ja	1-3	11					
1117	1A	W	Ss	Ja	1-3	11	0.2			0.6	0.1
1168	1A	B		Ja	1-3	11					
1169	1A	W	Bl	Ja	1-3	11	0.6			0.5	0.2
1171	1A	B		Ja	1-3	11					
1172D	1A	B	Bl	Ja	1-3	11					
1172E	1A	B	Bl	Ja	1-3	11					
1172F	1A	B	Bl	Ja	1-3	11					
1172G	1A	B	Bl	Ja	1-3	11					
1172H	1A	B	Bl	Ja	1-3	11					
1172I	1A	B	Bl	Ja	1-3	11					
1172J	1A	B	Bl	Ja	1-3	11					
1172K	1A	B	Bl	Ja	1-3	11					
1172L	1A	B	Bl	Ja	1-3	11					
1172M	1A	B	Bl	Ja	1-3	11					
1172N	1A	B	Bl	Ja	1-3	11					
1172O	1A	B	Bl	Ja	1-3	11					
1172P	1A	B	Ss	Ja	1-3	11					
1176	1A	B		Ja	1-3	11					
1186	112A	W	Ss	Ja	7	3	1.5			2.1	0.3
1382	1A	B		Ja	1-3	11					
1386	1A	B		Ja	1-3	11					
1388	1A	B		Ja	1-3	11					
1512	29B	W	Wd	Ja	7	2	4.3	1.6	1.2		0.2
1737A	2A	B		Ja	2/3	5					
1785	2A	B		Ja	2/3	5					
1786	2A	B	Bl	Ja	2/3	5					
1787A	2A	B	Tu	Ja	2/3	5					
1787B	2A	B	Tu	Ja	2/3	5					
1798	2A	B	Bl	Ja	2/3	5					
1808C	2A	B		Ja	2/3	5					
1965	1A	W	Tu	Ja	1-3	12	1.3			0.6	0.2
1967	1A	W	Bl	Ja	1-3	12	0.8			0.6	0.2

B-17: Polished stone ear flares

SF	Feat.	Cond.	Form	Mat.	Date	Cont.	Ln	Wd	Th	Dia.	Hole Dia.
80	1A/2A	B		Ja	8	15				10.0	
142	6B	W		Ja	3	12				3.1	
144	6B	W		Ja	3	12				3.2	
539A	4B	B		Ja	4	5					
540I	4B	B		Ja	4	5					
540J	4B	B		Ja	4	5					
543A	4B	B		Ja	4	5					
543B	4B	B		Ja	4	5					
553	4B	B		Ja	4	5					
874	11B	B		Ja	1-3	9					
875	4A	B		Ja	3	5					
924C	4A	B		Ja	3	5					
995A	1A	B		Fu	1-3	15					
1066	1A	B		Ja	1-3	15					
1070I	1A	B		Ja	1-3	15					
1079A	1A	B		Ja	1-3	11					
1114N	1A	B		Ja	1-3	11					
1172A	1A	B		Ja	1-3	11					
1172B	1A	B		Ja	1-3	11					
1172C	1A	B		Ja	1-3	11					
1178	1A	B		Ja	1-3	11					
1173	2A	B		Ja	2/3	5					
1737B	2A	B		Ja	2/3	5					
1737C	2A	B		Ja	2/3	5					
1737D	2A	B		Ja	2/3	5					
1780A	2A	B		Ja	2/3	5					
1780B	2A	B		Ja	2/3	5					
1781	2A	B		Ja	1-3	11					
1782	2A	B		Ja	2/3	5					
1783	2A	B		Ja	2/3	5					
1807	2A	B		Ja	2/3	5					
1808A	2A	B		Ja	2/3	5					
1808B	2A	B		Ja	2/3	5					
1850	2A	B		Ja	2/3	5					

B-18: Jade head pendants

SF	Feat.	Cond.	Form	Mat.	Date	Cont.	Ln	Wd	Th	Dia.	Hole Dia.
158	6B	W		Ja	3	12	4.0	2.5	1.4		
159	6B	W		Ja	3	12	3.8	2.7	2.3		
160	6B	W		Ja	3	12	5.1	2.6	1.3		
161	6B	W		Ja	3	12	4.3	2.4	1.2		
162	6B	W		Ja	3	12	5.7	5.1	1.0		

B-19: Polished stone celts

SF	Feat.	Cond.	Form	Mat.	Date	Cont.	Ln	Wd	Th	Dia.	Hole Dia.
69		B		Sr	8	16		5.2	2.9		
105	1A	B		Cm	1-3	11		5.8	2.7		
225	1A	B		Ja	1-3	10		4.5	2.7		
429	1A	B		Cm	1-3	14					
605	11B	B	Ov	Sc	7	2	9.9	5.0	2.6		
1190	1A	B		Mb	1-3	11			3.0		
1545	50D	B		Ch	4	3					
1895	127A	B		Ch	8	4					

B-20: Jade spangle

SF	Feat.	Cond.	Form	Mat.	Date	Cont.	Ln	Wd	Th	Dia.	Hole Dia.
146	6B	W		Ja	3	12	2.5	1.4	1.0		

B-21: Ground jade fragments

SF	Feat.	Cond.	Form	Mat.	Date	Cont.	Ln	Wd	Th	Dia.	Hole Dia.
147A	6B	B		Ja	3	12					
147B	6B	B		Ja	3	12					
147C	6B	B		Ja	3	12					
147D	6B	B		Ja	3	12					
147E	6B	B		Ja	3	12					

B-22: Jade mosaics

SF	Feat.	Cond.	Form	Mat.	Date	Cont.	Ln	Wd	Th	Dia.	Hole Dia.
106	5A	W	Cr	Ja	7	1	2.8	1.6	0.3		
147A	6B	W	Ir	Ja	3	12	0.8	0.7	0.3		
147B	6B	W	Ir	Ja	3	12	0.8	0.7	0.3		
147C	6B	W	Ir	Ja	3	12	1.3	0.7	0.3		
147D	6B	W	Ir	Ja	3	12	1.0	0.7	0.3		
147E	6B	W	Ir	Ja	3	12	0.8	0.6	0.3		
171A	6B	W	Ir	Ja	3	12	0.7	0.5	0.3		
171B	6B	W	Ir	Ja	3	12	0.9	0.7	0.3		
171C	6B	W	Cr	Ja	3	12	1.3	0.9	0.3		
171D	6B	W	R	Ja	3	12	1.1	0.7	0.3		
171E	6B	W	Cr	Ja	3	12	1.1	0.7	0.3		
813	4A	W	TP	Ja	7	2	2.3	1.4	0.5		
987	5A	W		Ja	7	3	1.6	1.1	0.4		
1424A	6B	W	Ir	Ja	3	12	1.2	0.9	0.3		
1424B	6B	W	Ir	Ja	3	12	0.9	0.7	0.3		
1424C	6B	W	Ir	Ja	3	12	0.8	0.6	0.2		
1424D	6B	W	Ir	Ja	3	12	0.5	0.4	0.1		

B-23: Unidentifiable polished stone fragments

SF	Feat.	Cond.	Form	Mat.	Date	Cont.	Ln	Wd	Th	Dia.	Hole Dia.
191	4B			Ja	8	4					
961	1A/2A			Ja	1-3	15					
965B	1A			Ja	1-3	11					
994B	1A			Ja	1-3	15					
994C	1A			Ja	1-3	15					
1067	1A			Ja	1-3	15					
1074C	1A			Ja	1-3	11					
1075	1A			Ja	1-3	11					
1079B	1A			Ja	1-3	11					
1080C	1A			Ja	1-3	11					
1081	1A			Ja	1-3	11					
1083A	1A			Ja	1-3	11					
1083B	1A			Ja	1-3	11					
1112C	1A			Ja	1-3	11					
1112D	1A			Ja	1-3	11					
1112E	1A			Ja	1-3	11					
1112F	1A			Ja	1-3	11					
1112G	1A			Ja	1-3	11					
1112H	1A			Ja	1-3	11					
1164	1A			Ja	1-3	11					
1168B	1A			Ja	1-3	11					
1168C	1A			Ja	1-3	11					
1170	1A			Ja	1-3	11					
1172Q	1A			Ja	1-3	11					
1172R	1A			Ja	1-3	11					
1176B	1A			Ja	1-3	11					
1176C	1A			Ja	1-3	11					
1176D	1A			Ja	1-3	11					
1180A	1A			Ja	1-3	11					
1181	1A			Ja	1-3	11					
1390A	1A			Ja	1-3	11					
1390B	1A			Ja	1-3	11					
1737E	2A			Ja	2/3	5					

B-24: Bone beads

SF	Feat.	Cond.	Form	Mat.	Date	Cont.	Ln	Wd	Th	Dia.	Hole Dia.
419	1A	W	Dk	FV	1-3	11			0.4	0.8	
420	1A	B	Tu		1-3	11					
436	1A	W	Dk	FV	1-3	11			0.7	1.5	0.2
439	1A	W	Dk	FV	1-3	5			0.8	1.5	0.3
767	1A	W	Tu		1-3	11	1.7			0.7	0.2
871	1A	W	Tu		1-3	8	1.7			0.9	0.4
941	1A	W	Dk	FV	1-3	11			0.6	1.3	0.4
1123	1A	B	Dk	FV	1-3	11			0.3	1.3	0.7
1167A	1A	W	Dk	FV	1-3	11			0.3	0.6	
1167B	1A	W	Dk	FV	1-3	11			0.3	0.6	
1167C	1A	W	Dk	FV	1-3	11			0.3	0.6	
1167D	1A	W	Dk	FV	1-3	11			0.3	0.6	
1167E	1A	W	Dk	FV	1-3	11			0.3	0.6	
1167F	1A	W	Dk	FV	1-3	11			0.3	0.6	
1167G	1A	W	Dk	FV	1-3	11			0.3	0.6	
1167H	1A	W	Dk	FV	1-3	11			0.3	0.6	
1274A	1A	B	Dk	FV	1-3	11			0.4	1.2	0.1
1274B	1A	B	Dk	FV	1-3	11			0.4	1.1	0.2
1274C	1A	B	Dk	FV	1-3	11			0.3	1.2	0.3
1274D	1A	W	Dk	FV	1-3	11			0.7	1.2	0.1
1375	1A	B	Dk	FV	1-3	11			0.4	1.1	0.2
1395	1A	B	Tu		1-3	11			0.4		
1439	1A	W	Dk	FV	1-3	11			0.3	0.6	0.1
2001	1A	B	Tu	FV	1-3	11					
12516	1A	W	Dk		1-3	11				1.0	

B-25: Bone pendants

SF/C	Feat.	Cond.	Form	Mat.	Date	Cont.	Ln	Wd	Th	Dia.	Hole Dia.
258	1A	W		Ca	3	10	6.3	1.2	0.8		0.2
281	1A/2A	W		FJ	8	1	4.0	1.2	0.9		0.6
795A	4A	W		ST	7	12					
795B	4A	W		ST	7	12					
795C	4A	W		ST	7	12					
795D	4A	W		ST	7	12					
839	1A	W		Ca	1-3	14	3.0	0.8	0.5		0.3
917	1A	W		Ca	1-3	11	3.5	1.0	0.6		0.5
1072	1A	W		Ca	1-3	11	2.9	0.8	0.4		0.2
1163	1A	B			1-3	11	3.6	0.9	0.5		
1383	1A	W		ST	1-3	11	1.2	1.3	0.3		0.1
757	18A	B		To	7	4					
7410	1A	W		ST	1-3	11	1.5	1.9			0.1
12917	1A	B		To	1-3	11					
14614	98A	W		Ca	1-3	11	5.8	2.3			

B-26: Bone rings

SF	Feat.	Cond.	Form	Mat.	Date	Cont.	Ln	Wd	Th	Dia.	Hole Dia.
121	1A	W	C		1-3	13		1.0	0.2	1.6	
819	1A	B	C		1-3	11		1.2	0.2	2.2	

B-27: Bone ear flares

SF	Feat.	Cond.	Form	Mat.	Date	Cont.	Ln	Wd	Th	Dia.	Hole Dia.
120	1A	B			1-3	13				3.7	2.0
344	1A	B			1-3	13				2.7	0.8

B-28: Sting ray spines

C	Feat.	Cond.	Form	Mat.	Date	Cont.	Ln	Wd	Th	Dia.	Hole Dia.
5575	1A	B			1-3	14			0.2		
11400	1A	B			1-3	11			0.2		

B-29: Pointed antler tools

SF	Feat.	Cond.	Form	Mat.	Date	Cont.	Ln	Wd	Th	Dia.	Hole Dia.
546	1A	W		At	1-3	14	17.8	6.4	3.0		
547	1A	B		At	1-3	14	11.5	3.8	2.0		
695	1A	B		At	1-3	13	4.0	1.2	1.1		
914	1A	W		At	1-3	11	14.2	6.0	5.6		

B-30: Bone rasp

SF	Feat.	Cond.	Form	Mat.	Date	Cont.	Ln	Wd	Th	Dia.	Hole Dia.
280	1A	B			1-3	15	18.2			2.4	

B-31: Bone whistle

SF	Feat.	Cond.	Form	Mat.	Date	Cont.	Ln	Wd	Th	Dia.	Hole Dia.
524	1A	B			1-3	14	10.1			3.0	

B-32: Bone tubes

SF	Feat.	Cond.	Form	Mat.	Date	Cont.	Ln	Wd	Th	Dia.	Hole Dia.
470	1A	B	Tu		1-3	15	8.7			1.3	
1231	1A	W			1-3	11	10.5	1.8	1.3		

B-33: Perforated bone, disk

SF	Feat.	Cond.	Form	Mat.	Date	Cont.	Ln	Wd	Th	Dia.	Hole Dia.
532	1A	B	C		8	1			0.5	4.4	0.6
1087	1A	W	C		8	16			0.6	2.7	0.8

B-34: Perforated bone, unmodified

C	Feat.	Cond.	Form	Mat.	Date	Cont.	Ln	Wd	Th	Dia.	Hole Dia.
(No #)	1A	B			1-3	11	2.3	1.0	0.2		
707	1A	B			1-3	13	2.9	1.8	1.1		2.0
1995	5A	W			1-3	11	2.1	2.3			
11966	1A	B			1-3	11					

B-35: Shell beads

SF	Feat.	Cond.	Form	Mat.	Date	Cont.	Ln	Wd	Th	Dia.	Hole Dia.
21	1A	W	Tu	Dn	1-3	10	1.1			0.3	0.2
22	1A	W	FB	Cl	1-3	11	1.4			0.9	0.2
61	1A	W	Ef	Cl	1-3	11	0.5				0.2
71A	1A	W	Ef	Cl	1-3	11	0.9				0.2
71B	1A	W	Dk		1-3	11	0.6			1.2	0.3
71C	1A	W	Dk		1-3	11	0.6			1.0	0.3
71D	1A	W	Dk		1-3	11	0.4			0.9	0.2
71E	1A	W	Dk		1-3	11	0.4			0.7	0.2
71F	1A	W	Dk	Cl	1-3	11	1.2			0.7	0.3
71G	1A	W	Dk	Cl	1-3	11	1.4			0.8	0.3
141	6B	W	Tu	Sp	3	12	1.7			0.6	0.2
273	1A	W	FB	Cl	1-3	11	1.9			1.8	0.3
321		W	Tu		8	15	0.9			0.9	0.3
370A	1A	W	FB	Cl	1-3	11	1.6			0.8	0.3
370B	1A	W	FB	Cl	1-3	11	1.2			0.7	0.2
418	1A	W	FB	Cl	1-3	11	2.2			1.3	0.3
438	1A	B	FB	Cl	1-3	11	1.5			0.8	0.2
471	33A	W	FB	Cl	2	11	2.1			0.8	0.3
665C	4A	W	R	Sp	7	12					0.2
734A	4A	W	Wd		7	12					0.2
734B	4A	W	R	Sp	7	12					0.2
734C	4A	W	Tr	Sp	7	12					0.2
734D	4A	W	El	Sp	7	12					0.2
734E	4A	W	R		7	12					0.3
736B	4A	W	Tu	Sp	7	12					0.2
737A	4A	W	Dk	Sp	7	12	0.2			0.9	0.2
737B	4A	W	R	Sp	7	12					0.2
737C	4A	W	Dk	Sp	7	12	0.5			0.8	0.2
739A	4A	W	R	Sp	7	12	0.5			1.0	0.3
739B	4A	W	Tu	Sp	7	12	1.0			0.6	0.2
739C	4A	W	R	Sp	7	12					0.2
739D	4A	W	R	Sp	7	12					0.3
739E	4A	W	R	Sp	7	12					0.4
739F	4A	W	Tu	Sp	7	12	0.7			0.6	0.2
739G	4A	W	R	Sp	7	12					0.2
739H	4A	W	R	Sp	7	12					0.3
739I	4A	W	Dk	Sp	7	12	0.6			0.8	0.3
741	1A	W	Dk		1-3	11	0.4			0.7	0.1
796	4A	W	TD	Sp	7	12					0.2
877	1A	W	Dk		1-3	11	0.4			1.1	0.2
916	4B	W	Dk	Sp	8	4	0.4			0.8	0.2
919	1A	W	Ss		1-3	10	0.4			0.7	0.2
959	1A	W	FB	Cl	1-3	11	2.0			1.0	0.2
960	1A	W	Ss		1-3	11	0.5			0.9	0.3
1053	4A	W	R	Sp	7	12					
1055	5C	W	Dk	Cn	3	14	0.3			0.8	0.2
1070	1A	B		Cn	8	15					

B-35: Shell beads--continued

SF a.	Feat.	Cond.	Form	Mat.	Date	Cont.	Ln	Wd	Th	Dia.	Hole Di
1088	1A	W	Dk		1-3	11	0.1			0.3	0.1
1136	1A	W	Dk		1-3	11	0.1			0.5	0.1
1166	1A	B	Tu	Dn	1-3	11	0.8			0.3	0.2
1177	1A	W	Tu	Dn	1-3	11	0.9			0.2	0.1
1179	1A	W	Dk		1-3	11	0.2			0.4	0.1
1214	1A	W	Dk	Sp	1-3	11	0.2			0.4	0.1
1215	1A	W	Dk		1-3	11	0.2			0.3	0.2
1216	1A	W	Dk	Sp	1-3	11	0.1			0.4	0.1
1217	1A	W	Dk		1-3	11	0.2			0.4	0.2
1218	1A	W	Dk		1-3	11	0.2			0.3	0.1
1219	1A	W	Dk		1-3	11	0.3			0.5	0.1
1220	1A	W	Dk		1-3	11	0.2			0.3	0.1
1221	1A	W	Dk		1-3	11	0.3			0.5	0.2
1222	1A	W	Dk		1-3	11	0.2			0.3	0.1
1243	1A	W	Tu	Dn	1-3	11	1.7			0.3	0.2
1250	1A	W	Dk		1-3	11	0.2			0.3	0.1
1251	1A	W	Dk	Cn	1-3	11	0.2			0.4	0.1
1252	1A	W	Dk		1-3	11	0.1			0.4	0.2
1253	1A	W	Dk		1-3	11	0.3			0.6	0.2
1273	1A	B	FB	Cl	1-3	11					
1380	1A	W	Dk		1-3	11	0.2			0.5	0.1
1384	1A	W	Dk	Cn	1-3	11	0.2			0.4	0.2
1385A	1A	W	Dk		1-3	11	0.2			0.5	0.2
1385B	1A	W	Dk		1-3	11	0.1			0.3	0.1
1387	1A	W	Dk		1-3	11	0.1			0.3	0.1
1389	1A	W	Dk	Dn	1-3	11	0.1			0.3	0.2
1392	1A	W	Dk	Sp	1-3	11	0.2			0.3	0.2
1393	1A	W	Dk		1-3	11	0.2			0.5	0.2
1394	1A	W	Dk		1-3	11	0.3			0.4	0.2
1396	1A	W	Dk	Sp	1-3	11	0.1			0.4	0.2
1418	1A	W	Dk	Sp	1-3	13	0.2			0.4	0.1
1421	1A	W	Dk	Cn	1-3	13	0.3			0.4	0.2
1966	1A	W	Dk	Sp	1-3	12	0.3			0.5	0.2
1968	1A	W	Dk	Sp	1-3	12	0.3			0.5	0.2
1969	1A	W	Dk	Cn	1-3	12	0.3			0.4	0.1
1970	1A	W	Dk	Cn	1-3	12	0.2			0.4	0.1
1971	1A	W	Dk	Cn	1-3	12	0.2			0.4	0.2
1972	1A	W	Dk	Cn	1-3	12	0.3			0.6	0.1
1973	1A	W	Dk	Cn	1-3	12	0.2			0.4	0.1
1974	1A	W	Dk	Cn	1-3	12	0.3			0.5	0.1
1975	1A	W	Dk	Sp	1-3	12	0.3			0.5	0.2
1976	1A	W	Dk	Cn	1-3	12	0.2			0.5	0.1
1977	1A	W	Dk	Cn	1-3	12	0.2			0.5	0.1
1978	1A	W	Dk	Cn	1-3	13	0.2			0.4	0.2

B-36: Shell adornos

SF	Feat.	Cond.	Form	Mat.	Date	Cont.	Ln	Wd	Th	Dia.	Hole Dia.
124	1A	B	Dk	Sp	8	15				3.4	0.6
163	6B	W	Dk		3	12					
164	6B	W	Dk		3	12					
165	6B	W	Dk		3	12					
166	6B	W	Dk		3	12					
167	6B	B	Dk		3	12					
168	6B	B	Dk		3	12					
172A	6B	B	Dk		3	12					
172B	6B	B	Dk		3	12					
172C	6B	B	Dk		3	12					
172D	6B	B	Dk		3	12					
172E	6B	B	Dk		3	12					
417	1A	B		Sp	1-3	14					0.1
701	11B	B	Tr		1-3	4	1.8	1.7	0.6		0.2
738A	4A	W	C	Sp	7	12					
921	1A	B	Dk		1-3	11			1.5	3.9	1.3
1010	112A	W	Dk		8	1			0.4	1.7	0.3
1254	1A	W	Dk		1-3	11	0.9	0.8	0.1		0.2
1255	1A	B	Dk		1-3	11		1.1	0.1		0.2
1378	46A	W	Fl		4	11			0.2	1.8	
1402	38A	W	Dk	TS	2	11			0.2	4.7	
1412	94A	W	Tr		7	3	4.2	1.6	0.2		0.2
1844	34A	W	Dk	Cn	4	2			0.5	2.3	
1946	50A	W			3	9					

B-37: Largely whole worked shells

SF	Feat.	Cond.	Form	Mat.	Date	Cont.	Ln	Wd	Th	Dia.	Hole Dia.
10	2A	B	T	Ol	3	9					
131	6B	W	Bv	Sp	3	12					
133	6B	W	Bv	Sp	3	12					
134	6B	B	Bv	Sp	3	12					
135	6B	W	Bv	Sp	3	12					
369	1A	W	T	Ol	1-3	11	3.7			1.5	
446	1A	W	Bv		1-3	13					
512A	1A	W	T	Ol	1-3	14	2.3	1.5	1.3		
512B	1A	B	T	Ol	1-3	14	1.9				
809	1A	W	T	Ol	1-3	11	2.0	1.0	1.1		
963	1A	W	T	Ol	1-3	11	2.8				
1259	1A	W	T	Ol	1-3	11	2.5	1.1	1.3		
1469		W	Uv	Cn	8	16					

B-38: Shell axes

SF	Feat.	Cond.	Form	Mat.	Date	Cont.	Ln	Wd	Th	Dia.	Hole Dia.
42	1A	W	Ov	Cn	1-3	11	9.9	5.7	1.9		
1468		W	Ov	Cn	8	15	12.4	6.0	1.8		

B-39: Shell trumpets

SF	Feat.	Cond.	Form	Mat.	Date	Cont.	Ln	Wd	Th	Dia.	Hole Dia.
666A	11B	W		Cn	7	12	7.5	8.0	6.5		
666B	11B	W	Tr	Sh	7	12	3.9	1.9	1.7		
975	5A	W		Cn	8	3	7.4	5.0	4.0		

B-40: Shell scoops

SF	Feat.	Cond.	Form	Mat.	Date	Cont.	Ln	Wd	Th	Dia.	Hole Dia.
529	33A	W	Tr	Gs	2	11	7.5	5.0	1.3		
530	33A	W	Tr	Gs	2	11	5.8	4.9	1.5		

B-41: Shell labrets

SF	Feat.	Cond.	Form	Mat.	Date	Cont.	Ln	Wd	Th	Dia.	Hole Dia.
816	4B	W			8	4					
1536	2A	W			8	2					

B-42: Shell mosaics

SF	Feat.	Cond.	Form	Mat.	Date	Cont.	Ln	Wd	Th	Dia.	Hole Dia.
735C	4A	W	TP	Sp	7	12	1.9	1.1	0.2		
738B	4A	W	TP	Sp	7	12					
738C	4A	W	TP	Sp	7	12					
738D	4A	W	TP	Sp	7	12					

B-43: Shell cutout

SF	Feat.	Cond.	Form	Mat.	Date	Cont.	Ln	Wd	Th	Dia.	Hole Dia.
984	5C				3	12	2.8	1.7	0.4		

B-44: Miscellaneous shell pieces

SF	Feat.	Cond.	Form	Mat.	Date	Cont.	Ln	Wd	Th	Dia.	Hole Dia.
218	2A	B			3	9					
270	1A	B			1-3	10					
282	1A	B	Ir	Sp	8	15					
443	1A	B	C		1-3	11					
528	1A	B			1-3	10					
529B	33A	B			2	11					
625	1A	W	Tr	Sp	1-3	11	2.3	1.1	0.2		
626	1A	B		BC	1-3	14	1.7	0.4	0.3		
650	1A	B		Cn	1-3	9					
1248	1A	B		Sp	1-3	11					
1379	50B	B			4	2					
1533	50E	B			5	4					
1543	50B	B		Cn	4	3					
1774	2A	B		Sp	1-3	11					
1838	34A	B		Cn	3	2					
1857	34A	B		Cn	3	11					
1890	5C	B		Cn	1-3	9					
1901	61C	B		Cn	4	3					
1942	1A	B		Cn	1-3	11					

B-45: Girdled sherds

SF	Feat.	Cond.	Form	Mat.	Date	Cont.	Ln	Wd	Th	Dia.	Hole Dia.
125	1A	W	Tr	Sh	8	15					
410	1A	W		Sh	1-3	13					
1465	50D	W	Bl	Sh	4	3					
1650	2A	W	Bl	Sh	2/3	5					

B-46: Partially perforated sherd disks

SF	Feat.	Cond.	Form	Mat.	Date	Cont.	Ln	Wd	Th	Dia.	Hole Dia.
39	1A	W	Ov	Sh	1-3	11	4.1	3.6	0.6		
371	1A	W	Ov	Sh	1-3	11	4.4	4.5	0.8		
777	11C	W	C	Sh	1-3	4			0.7	2.8	
1406	4A	W	Ov	Sh	1-3	9	5.9	4.5	1.4		

B-47: Centrally perforated sherd disk

SF	Feat.	Cond.	Form	Mat.	Date	Cont.	Ln	Wd	Th	Dia.	Hole Dia.
1286	46A	B	C	Sh	4	11				4.9	0.6

B-48: Sherd pendants

SF	Feat.	Cond.	Form	Mat.	Date	Cont.	Ln	Wd	Th	Dia.	Hole Dia.
375	33A	W	C	Sh	2	11			0.5	2.0	0.3
435	33A	W	C	Sh	2	8			0.5	3.1	0.2
616	1A	W	Sq	Sh	1-3	11	3.4	3.4	0.5		0.3
836	1A	B		Sh	1-3	11					0.2

B-49: Geometric sherds

SF	Feat.	Cond.	Form	Mat.	Date	Cont.	Ln	Wd	Th	Dia.	Hole Dia.
143	6B	W	Sq	Sh	3	12	9.1	9.1	0.8		
440	1A	W	TP	Sh	1-3	11	3.9	3.5	0.8		
1349	1A	W	R	Sh	1-3	8	4.5	3.5	0.6		
1371	16B	W	TD	Sh	2	11	3.6	2.8	0.7		

B-50: Sherd animal effigy

SF	Feat.	Cond.	Form	Mat.	Date	Cont.	Ln	Wd	Th	Dia.	Hole Dia.
1779	34A	W		Sh	3	9	2.8	1.8	0.4		

B-51: Ground sherds

SF	Feat.	Cond.	Form	Mat.	Date	Cont.	Ln	Wd	Th	Dia.	Hole Dia.
173A-J	6B	W		Sh	3	12					

B-52: Cut rim sherds

SF	Feat.	Cond.	Form	Mat.	Date	Cont.	Ln	Wd	Th	Dia.	Hole Dia.
613	1A	W		Sh	3	5					
1499	2A	W		Sh	2/3	5	3.2				

B-53: Molded mariposas

SF	Feat.	Cond.	Form	Subform	Date	Cont.	Weight
57A	18A	W	EN	CvCv	7	4	3.0
57B	18A	W	EN	CvCv	7	4	3.0
58A	18A	B	EN	CvCv	7	4	
58B	18A	W	EN	CvCv	7	4	1.0
59	18A	W	EN	CvCv	7	4	3.0
60	18A	W	EN	CvCv	7	4	1.1
92A	18A	W	EN	CvCv	7	11	3.0
92B	18A	W	EN	CvCv	7	11	2.0
92C	18A	W	EN	CvCv	7	11	2.0
92D	18A	W	EN	CvCv	7	11	2.0
92E	18A	W	EN	CvCv	7	11	2.1
92F	18A	W	EN	CvCv	7	11	3.0
92G	18A	W	EN	CvCv	7	11	2.3
93K	9A	W	EN	CvCv	7	11	1.8
99B	9A	W	ES	CvCv	7	4	2.0
102B	9A	W	EN	CvCv	7	11	1.4
102C	9A	W	ES	CvCv	7	11	1.4
102D	9A	B	EN	Cv	7	11	
116A	9A	B	EN	CvCv	7	11	
116B	9A	W	ES	CvCv	7	11	2.9
116C	9A	W	EN	CvCv	7	11	3.0
563A	11B	W	ES	CvCv	7	2	0.4
563B	11B	W	EN	CvCv	7	2	1.0
575B	11B	W	EN	CvCv	7	2	2.1
600	2A	W	EN	CvCv	7	2	1.8
762	11C	W	EN	CvCv	7	2	1.8
775	11C	W	EN	CvCv	1-3	4	1.2
778	11C	W	EN	CvCv	1-3	4	1.0
929C	10C	W	EN	CvCv	7	2	7.1
934S	2A	W	EN	SPSP	7	2	4.0
939	10C	W	EN	CvCv	6	4	7.6
1272	54A	W	EN	CvCv	7	3	1.6

B-54: Molded clay beads

SF	Feat.	Cond.	Form	Mat.	Date	Cont.	Ln	Wd	Th	Dia.	Hole Dia.
54	9A	W	Bl		7	11	1.1			1.0	0.3
56	9A	W	Bl		7	11	1.5			1.2	0.4
63	9A	W	Sf		7	11				1.5	0.3
70	18A	W	Bl		7	2	2.4			1.3	0.3
556	11B	W	Ss		7	2	1.4			1.6	0.5
610	11B	W	Sf		7	2				1.1	0.3
766	11C	W	Sf		7	2				1.2	0.3
872	11C	B	Sf		7	2				1.2	0.4
873	11C	W	Bl		7	3	1.1			1.0	0.3
1366	46A	W	Ss		7	3	1.8			2.1	0.4
1381	1A	W	Ss		1-3	11	0.3			0.4	0.1

B-55: Molded clay spindle whorls

SF	Feat.	Cond.	Form	Mat.	Date	Cont.	Ln	Wd	Th	Dia.	Hole Dia.
72	9A	W		MC	7	11			1.1	2.8	0.9
79		W		MC	8	17			0.8	2.3	0.8
101	9A	B		MC	7	11			0.9	2.3	0.8
174	11A	B		MC	7	2			1.2		
264		W		MC	8	16			0.7	2.2	0.9
265		W		MC	8	16			1.4	2.8	0.8
266		W		MC	8	16			1.0	2.1	0.9
376	33A	W		MC	7	2			1.0	2.9	0.7
585	11B	W		MC	7	2			1.6	4.4	1.3
685	2A	B		MC	7	2			1.0	2.7	0.8
1192		W		MC	8	16			1.2	2.3	0.9

B-56: Molded clay whistle

SF	Feat.	Cond.	Form	Mat.	Date	Cont.	Ln	Wd	Th	Dia.	Hole Dia.
694	1A	W		MC	1-3	13	4.8				0.3

B-57: Molded clay sphere

SF	Feat.	Cond.	Form	Mat.	Date	Cont.	Ln	Wd	Th	Dia.	Hole Dia.
557	11B	W	Sf	MC	7	2				1.0	

B-58: Molded clay piece with oval depression

SF	Feat.	Cond.	Form	Mat.	Date	Cont.	Ln	Wd	Th	Dia.	Hole Dia.
1868	50C	W	Ov	MC	4	3	3.8	3.1	2.0		

B-59: Plaster spirals

SF	Feat.	Cond.	Form	Mat.	Date	Cont.	Ln	Wd	Th	Dia.	Hole Dia.
655	5C	B			7	3				2.1	1.2
689	5C	B			7	2				1.8	
1032	5C	B			7	3				4.0	
1268	29B	B			7	3					

B-60: Plaster dome with hole

SF	Feat.	Cond.	Form	Mat.	Date	Cont.	Ln	Wd	Th	Dia.	Hole Dia.
808	10C	B	Dm		4	7					0.5

B-61: Specular hematite mirror fragments

SF	Feat.	Cond.	Date	Cont.	No. of fragments
148	6B	B	3	12	86
985	5C	B	3	12	12
1076	1A	B	1-3	11	1
1113	1A	B	1-3	11	2
1115	1A	B	1-3	11	1
1165	1A	B	1-3	11	1
1174	1A	W	1-3	11	1
1175	1A	B	1-3	11	1
1391	1A	B	1-3	11	1
1420	1A	B	1-3	11	11
1778	2A	B	2/3	5	1
1784	2A	B	2/3	5	1

B-62: Tumbaga disks

SF	Feat.	Cond.	Form	Mat.	Date	Cont.	Ln	Wd	Th	Dia.	Hole Dia.
718	4A	W	C		7	12			0.1	6.8	
719	4A	B	C		7	12			0.1	6.5	
720	4A	B	C		7	12			0.1	6.5	

B-63: Gold foil

SF	Feat.	Cond.	Form	Mat.	Date	Cont.	Ln	Wd	Th	Dia.	Hole Dia.
622	4A	B			7	12	1.0	0.5			

B-64: Gold scroll

SF	Feat.	Cond.	Form	Mat.	Date	Cont.	Ln	Wd	Th	Dia.	Hole Dia.
721	4A	B			7	12	2.8	1.2	0.05		

Appendix C
Artifact Associations by Structure

C-1: Feature 1A

LATE PRECLASSIC
Humus, Fall, Humus/Fall, and Fall
    1 pestle-pounder

Domestic debris
    4 manos
    8 metates
    2 ground stone fragments
    2 doughnut stones
    6 abraders
    2 girdled stones
    1 ground stone pendant
    1 pestle pounder
    1 stone with depression
    48 shell beads
    28 unidentified greenstone fragments
    47 sherd disks
    3 shell adornos
    4 largely whole worked shells
    1 shell axe
    1 geometric sherd
    19 specular hematite mirror fragments

    56 greenstone beads or bead fragments
    6 greenstone ear flare fragments
    2 polished stone celts
    4 stone disks
    30 pointed bone tools
    23 bone beads
    6 bone pendants
    1 bone ring
    1 ray spine
    1 pointed antler tools
    1 bone tube
    1 unmodified perforated bone
    1 molded ceramic bead
    2 partially perforated sherd disks
    2 sherd pendants
    27 mariposas
    1 marble bead

Burial
    2 manos
    1 metate
    2 pointed bone tools
    1 unmodified perforated bone
    1 largely whole worked shell
    1 molded ceramic whistle

    1 bone ring
    2 bone ear flares
    1 pointed antler tool
    3 shell beads
    1 girdled sherd

Cache
    2 greenstone beads
    11 shell beads

    1 sherd disk

Pit fill
    2 manos
    1 metate
    1 polished stone celt
    1 bone whistle
    1 shell adorno
    1 mariposa

    1 bone pendant
    1 ray spine
    2 pointed antler tools
    3 sherd disks
    2 largely whole worked shells

In floor
2 manos
1 ground stone fragment
1 abrader
1 ground stone pendant

1 bone bead
7 shell disks
1 geometric sherd
1 stone disk

Construction fill with rubble
4 sherd disks

1 stone spheroid

Construction fill without rubble
1 bone pendant

1 pointed bone tool

Termination ritual
1 stone spheroid
2 stone disks
2 stone disks

1 bone bead
1 cut rim sherd
2 sherd disks

Beach
13 greenstone beads or bead fragments
3 greenstone ear flare fragments
1 bone rasp

1 bone tube
7 sherd disks
4 unidentified greenstone fragments

C-2: Feature 2A

LATE PRECLASSIC
Domestic debris
1 weight with hole
2 greenstone ear flare fragments

1 mariposa
4 sherd disks

Construction fill with rubble
2 metates
2 mariposas

25 sherd disks

Construction fill without rubble
1 mano

1 sherd disk

Termination ritual
7 greenstone bead fragments
11 greenstone ear flare fragments
338 stone spheroids
62 stone disks
2 specular hematite mirror fragments

1 girdled sherd
1 cylindrical sherd
39 sherd disk
1 unidentified greenstone fragment

Pit fill
2 sherd disks

LATE POSTCLASSIC
Humus, Fall, Humus/Fall, and Fall
6 manos
7 metates
1 molded ceramic spindle whorl

4 sherd disks
60 mariposas

C-3: Structure 4A

LATE PRECLASSIC
Construction fill with rubble
6 manos   6 metates
1 ground stone fragment   4 doughnut stones
1 abrader   1 girdled stone
1 sherd disk   1 mariposa
1 partially perforated sherd disk

Termination ritual
1 doughnut stone   2 greenstone bead fragments
2 greenstone ear flare fragments   9 sherd disks

LATE POSTCLASSIC
Humus, Fall, Humus/Fall, and Fall
1 mano   1 metate
1 girdled stone   1 greenstone bead
1 sherd disk   1 mariposa
1 copper bell

Cache
2 greenstone beads   1 sherd disk
21 shell beads   12 bone pendants
1 shell adorno   4 shell mosaics
3 tumbaga disks   1 piece of gold foil
1 gold scroll   1 stone mosaic
16 copper bells   1 turquoise bead

C-4: Structure 4B

LATE PRECLASSIC
Cache
4 sherd disks

EARLY CLASSIC
Humus, Fall, Humus/Fall, and Fall
2 greenstone beads or fragments

Termination Ritual
39 greenstone beads   1 sherd disk
6 greenstone ear flare fragments

LATE POSTCLASSIC
Humus, Fall, Humus/Fall, and Fall
1 mariposa

Cache
1 greenstone bead fragment   1 turquoise bead

C-5: Structure 5A

    LATE PRECLASSIC
      <u>Humus, Fall, Humus/Fall, and Fall</u>
        1 doughnut stone   5 sherd disks

      <u>Construction fill with rubble</u>
        1 metate   1 anvil-pounder
        1 doughnut stone   1 stone spheroid
        3 stone disks   2 sherd disks

      <u>Domestic debris</u>
        4 pointed bone tools   1 perforated bone

      <u>Termination ritual</u>
        2 sherd disks

    LATE POSTCLASSIC
      <u>Humus, Fall, Humus/Fall, and Fall</u>
        1 mariposa   2 greenstone mosaic pieces

C-6: Structure 5C

    LATE PRECLASSIC
      <u>Humus, Fall, Humus/Fall, and Fall</u>
        1 doughnut stone   4 sherd disk
        1 stone spheroid   1 metate

      <u>Termination ritual</u>
        1 mano   5 doughnut stones
        2 greenstone beads or bead fragments   5 stone disks
        10 sherd disks

      <u>Construction fill with rubble</u>
        1 metate   1 stone disk
        2 doughnut stones   1 sherd disk
        1 abrader

      <u>Cache</u>
        1 greenstone bead   1 shell cutout
        12 specular hematite mirror fragments

      <u>Pit fill</u>
        1 doughnut stone   1 stone disk
        1 shell bead

    LATE POSTCLASSIC
      <u>Humus, Fall, Humus/Fall, and Fall</u>
        1 mano   3 plaster spirals

C-7: Structure 6B

    LATE PRECLASSIC
        <u>Humus, Fall, Humus/Fall, and Fall</u>
          1 stone spheroid

        <u>Cache</u>

6 greenstone beads	5 greenstone head pendants
2 greenstone ear flares	1 greenstone spangle
6 sherd disks	11 shell adornos
1 shell bead	1 geometric sherd
4 largely whole unworked shells	14 greenstone mosaic pieces
86 specular hematite mirror fragments	5 ground greenstone fragments

C-8: Structure 7A

    LATE PRECLASSIC
        <u>Humus, Fall, Humus/Fall, and Fall</u>
          1 metate

        <u>Construction fill with rubble</u>

1 greenstone bead fragment	1 mariposa

    LATE POSTCLASSIC
        <u>Humus, Fall, Humus/Fall, and Fall</u>
          16 mariposas

C-9: Structure 9A

    LATE POSTCLASSIC
        <u>Humus, Fall, Humus/Fall, and Fall</u>
          9 mariposas

        <u>Domestic debris</u>

2 abraders	3 molded clay beads
33 mariposas	2 molded clay spindle whorls

C-10: Structure 10C

    LATE PRECLASSIC
      <u>Humus, Fall, Humus/Fall, and Fall</u>
        1 mano

    CLASSIC
      <u>Humus, Fall, Humus/Fall, and Fall</u>
        1 mano   1 stone speheroid
        2 metates   6 mariposas
        1 plaster dome with hole

    POSTCLASSIC
      <u>Humus, Fall, Humus/Fall, and Fall</u>
        8 mariposas

C-11: Structure 11B

    LATE PRECLASSIC
      <u>Construction fill with rubble</u>
        1 greenstone bead fragment   1 stone disk
        1 greenstone ear flare fragment   1 mariposa

      <u>Humus, Fall, Humus/Fall, and Fall</u>
        1 sherd disk   2 mariposas
        1 shell adorno

    LATE POSTCLASSIC
      <u>Humus, Fall, Humus/Fall, and Fall</u>
        2 manos   1 stone disk
        1 ground stone pendant   7 mariposas
        2 molded ceramic beads   1 molded ceramic spindle whorl
        1 molded ceramic sphere

      <u>Cache</u>
        1 metate   2 shell trumpets

C-12: Structure 11C

    LATE PRECLASSIC
      <u>Humus, Fall, Humus/Fall, and Fall</u>
        2 mariposas

      <u>Construction fill with rubble</u>
        1 partially perforated sherd disk

    LATE POSTCLASSIC
      <u>Humus and Fall</u>
        3 molded ceramic beads   1 mariposa

C-13: Structure 22A

    LATE POSTCLASSIC
      <u>Humus, Fall, Humus/Fall, and Fall</u>
        1 mano   7 mariposas
        1 metate

C-14: Structure 29B

    LATE PRECLASSIC
      <u>Humus, Fall, Humus/Fall, and Fall</u>
        8 armatures   1 stone disk
        1 sherd disk   1 metate

      <u>Termination ritual</u>
        11 armatures   5 stone disks
        3 sherd disks

      <u>Construction fill with rubble</u>
        1 sherd disk

      <u>On floor</u>
        1 sherd disk

    LATE POSTCLASSIC
      <u>Humus, Fall, Humus/Fall, and Fall</u>
        2 manos   1 plaster spiral
        1 greenstone bead

C-15: Structure 33A

LATE PRECLASSIC
Domestic debris
1 doughnut stone
1 pointed bone tool
2 shell scoops
1 shell bead

In floor
1 mariposa
1 ceramic spindle whorl

LATE POSTCLASSIC
Humus, Fall, Humus/Fall, and Fall
1 mano
1 mariposa

1 sherd disk
1 mariposa
1 sherd pendant

1 sherd disk
1 sherd pendant

1 greenstone bead fragment

C-16: Structure 34A

LATE PRECLASSIC
Humus, Fall, Humus/Fall, and Fall
1 metate
6 sherd disks

Domestic debris
1 mano

Construction fill with rubble
3 sherd disks
1 sherd animal effigy

EARLY CLASSIC
Humus, Fall, Humus/Fall, and Fall
1 stone disk
2 sherd disks

Construction fill with rubble
2 mariposas

LATE POSTCLASSIC
Humus, Fall, Humus/Fall, and Fall
1 mariposa

11 mariposas

3 mariposas

6 mariposas

1 shell adorno

C-17: Structure 38A

    LATE PRECLASSIC
      Construction fill with rubble
        1 metate   1 doughnut stone

      Domestic debris
        1 shell adorno

    LATE POSTCLASSIC
      Humus, Fall, Humus/Fall, and Fall
        2 stone disks

C-18: Structure 46A

    LATE PRECLASSIC
      Construction fill without rubble
        1 stone spheroid

      Construction fill with rubble
        1 mariposa

    EARLY CLASSIC
      Humus, Fall, Humus/Fall, and Fall
        1 metate   4 mariposas

      Domestic debris
        1 mano   1 shell adorno
        1 molded ceramic spindle whorl   2 mariposas
        1 centrally perforated sherd disk

      Construction fill without rubble
        3 mariposas

    LATE POSTCLASSIC
      Humus, Fall, Humus/Fall, and Fall
        1 molded ceramic bead   1 mano

C-19: Structure 50A

    LATE PRECLASSIC
      <u>Construction fill with rubble</u>
        1 sherd disk   1 shell adorno

    EARLY CLASSIC
      <u>Humus, Fall, Humus/Fall, and Fall</u>
        1 metate   5 sherd disks
        1 stone spheroid

    LATE CLASSIC
      <u>Pit fill</u>
        1 mano

C-20: Structure 50B

    EARLY CLASSIC
      <u>Humus, Fall, Humus/Fall, and Fall</u>
        4 manos   1 ground stone figurine
        7 metates   2 stone spheroids
        3 stone disks   12 sherd disks
        20 mariposas

C-21: Structure 50C

    LATE PRECLASSIC
      <u>Termination ritual</u>
        2 sherd disks

    EARLY CLASSIC
      <u>Humus, Fall, Humus/Fall, and Fall</u>
        1 mano   1 stone spheroid
        6 metates   3 sherd disks
        22 mariposas   1 molded ceramic piece with oval
                                                   depression

C-22: Structure 50D

    LATE PRECLASSIC
        <u>Humus, Fall, Humus/Fall, and Fall</u>
           1 stone disk

        <u>Construction fill with rubble</u>
           1 mariposa

    EARLY CLASSIC
        <u>Humus, Fall, Humus/Fall, and Fall</u>
           1 mano   1 stone spheroid
           3 metates   1 stone disk
           1 polished stone celt   3 sherd disks
         14 mariposas   1 girdled sherd

C-23: Structure 50E

    LATE PRECLASSIC
        <u>Humus, Fall, Humus/Fall, and Fall</u>
           1 mano   1 ground stone fragment
           3 metates   4 sherd disks
           6 mariposas

C-24: Structure 61A

    LATE PRECLASSIC
        <u>Humus, Fall, Humus/Fall, and Fall</u>
           1 metate

    EARLY CLASSIC
        <u>Humus, Fall, Humus/Fall, and Fall</u>
           1 sherd disk   5 mariposas

C-25: Structure 94A

    LATE POSTCLASSIC
        <u>Humus, Fall, Humus/Fall, and Fall</u>
           1 metate   13 mariposas
           1 shell adorno

C-26: Structure 112A

     LATE PRECLASSIC
       <u>Pit fill</u>
          1 sherd disk

     LATE POSTCLASSIC
       <u>Humus, Fall, Humus/Fall, and Fall</u>
          1 mano   1 greenstone bead
          1 metate

C-27: Structure 127A

     LATE PRECLASSIC
       <u>Humus, Fall, Humus/Fall, and Fall</u>
          4 stone disks   1 sherd disk

       <u>Domestic debris</u>
          1 stone disk

       <u>Construction fill with rubble</u>
          1 mariposa

BIBLIOGRAPHY

Adams, Richard E. W., ed., 1977, *The origins of Maya civilization.* University of New Mexico Press, Albuquerque.

Andresen, John M., 1986, Lowland Maya beekeeping, Paper presented at 51st annual meeting of Society for American Archaeology, New Orleans.

Andrews, E. Wyllys, IV, 1959, Dzibilchaltun: lost city of the Maya. *National Geographic* 115(1): 90–109.

———, 1969, *The archaeological use and distribution of Mollusca in the Maya Lowlands.* Middle American Research Institute, Tulane University, Publication 34.

Andrews, E. Wyllys, IV, et al., 1974, *Excavation of an early shell midden on Isla Cancun, Quintana Roo, Mexico.* Middle American Research Institute, Tulane University, Publication 31: 147–197.

Ball, Joseph W., 1977*a, Archaeological ceramics of Becan, Campeche, Mexico.* Middle American Research Institute, Tulane University, Publication 43.

———, 1977*b,* A hypothetical outline of coastal Maya Prehistory: 300 B.C.–A.D. 1200. In *Social process in Maya prehistory: studies in honour of Sir Eric Thompson,* edited by N. Hammond, pp. 167–196. Academic Press, London.

Binford, Lewis R., 1972, Mortuary practices: their study and potential. In *An archaeological perspective,* pp. 208–243. Seminar, New York.

Blom, Frans, 1932, Commerce, trade and monetary units of the Maya. In *Middle American papers: studies relating to research in Mexico, the Central American republics, and the West Indies,* pp. 531–556. Middle American Research Institute, Tulane University, Publication 4.

Bray, Warwick, 1977, Maya metalwork and its external connections. In *Social process in Maya prehistory: studies in honour of Sir Eric Thompson,* edited by N. Hammond, pp. 365–403. Academic Press, London.

Brew, John O., 1946, Archaeology of Alkali Ridge, Southeastern Utah, *Papers of the Peabody Museum of American Archaeology and Ethnology,* Harvard University, Vol. 21.

Bullard, William R., Jr., 1973, Postclassic culture in Central Peten and adjacent British Honduras. In *The Classic Maya collapse,* edited by T. P. Culbert, pp. 221–241. University of New Mexico Press, Albuquerque.

Butzer, Karl W., 1980, Context in archaeology: an alternative perspective. *Journal of Field Archaeology* 7(4): 417–422.

Carr, Helen S., 1986, *Faunal utilization in a Late Preclassic Maya community at Cerros, Belize.* Ph.D. dissertation, Tulane University. University Microfilms, Ann Arbor.

Cliff, Maynard B., 1982, *Lowland Maya nucleation: a case study from northern Belize.* Ph.D. dissertation, Southern Methodist University. University Microfilms, Ann Arbor.

———, 1986, Excavations in the Late Preclassic nucleated village. In *Archaeology at Cerros Belize, Central America, volume 1: an interim report,* edited by R. A. Robertson and D. A. Freidel, pp. 45–63. Southern Methodist University Press, Dallas.

Coe, William R., 1959, *Piedras Negras archaeology: artifacts, caches, and burials.* Museum Monographs, The University Museum, University of Pennsylvania.

———, 1965*a,* Artifacts of the Maya Lowlands. In *Handbook of Middle American Indians,* edited by R. Wauchope and G. R. Willey, Vol. 3, pp. 594–602. University of Texas Press, Austin.

———, 1965*b,* Tikal, Guatemala, and emergent Maya civilization. *Science* 147(3664): 1401–1419.

———, 1965*c,* Tikal: ten years of study of a Maya ruin in the Lowlands of Guatemala. *Expedition* 8: 5–56.

Covarrubias, Miguel, 1957, *Indian art of Mexico and Central America.* Knopf, New York.

Digby, Adrian, 1964, *Maya jade.* British Museum, London.

Dillon, Brian D., 1977, *Salinas de los Nueve Cerros, Guatemala: preliminary archaeological investigations,* edited by J. A. Graham. Studies in Mesoamerican art, archaeology, and ethnohistory, No. 2. Socorro, New Mexico.

Dreiss, Meredith L., 1982, An initial description of shell artifacts from Colha, Belize. In *Archaeology at Colha, Belize,* edited by T. R. Hester, H. J. Shafer, and J. D. Eaton, pp. 206–224. Center for Archaeological Research, University of Texas at San Antonio.

Easby, Elizabeth K., 1961, The Squire jades from Tonina, Chiapas. In *Essays in pre-Columbian art and archaeology,* edited by S. K. Lothrop et al., pp. 60–80. Harvard University, Cambridge.

Easby, Elizabeth K., and John F. Scott, 1970, *Before Cortez: sculpture of Middle America.* Metropolitan Museum of Art, New York.

Eaton, Jack D., 1976, Ancient fishing technology on the Gulf Coast of Yucatan, Mexico. *Bulletin of the Texas Archaeological Society* 47: 231–243.

———, 1978, Archaeological survey of the Yucatan-Campeche coast. In *Studies in the archaeology of coastal Yucatan and Campeche, Mexico,* pp. 1–67. Middle American Research Institute, Tulane University, Publication 46.

Flannery, Kent V., 1968, The Olmec and the Valley of Oaxaca: a model for inter-regional interaction in formative times. In *Dumbarton Oaks Conference on the Olmec,* edited by E. P. Benson, pp. 79–110. Dumbarton Oaks Research Library and Collection, Washington.

Freidel, David A., 1976, *Late Postclassic settlement patterns on Cozumel Island, Quintana Roo, Mexico.* Ph.D. dissertation, Harvard University. University Microfilms, Ann Arbor.

——, 1977, A Late Preclassic monumental mask at Cerros, Northern Belize. *Journal of Field Archaeology* 4: 488–491.

——, 1978*a*, Archaeological investigations at Cerros: a changing Preclassic Lowland Maya community in northern Belize. NSF grant proposal, Southern Methodist University.

——, 1978*b*, Maritime adaptation and the rise of Maya civilization: the view from Cerros, Belize. In *Prehistoric coastal adaptations: the economy and ecology of maritime Middle America,* edited by B. L. Stark and B. Voorhies, pp. 239–265. Academic Press, New York.

——, 1979, Culture areas and interaction spheres: contrasting approaches to the emergence of civilization in the Maya Lowlands. *American Antiquity* 44: 36–54.

——, 1986, The monumental architecture. In *Archaeology at Cerros Belize, Central America, volume 1: an interim report,* edited by R. A. Robertson and D. A. Freidel, pp. 1–22. Southern Methodist University Press, Dallas.

Freidel, David A., and Linda Schele, 1982, Symbol and power: a history of the Lowland Maya cosmogram, Paper presented at the Princeton conference on the origins of Maya iconography, Princeton University.

——, 1988, Kingship in the Late Preclassic Maya Lowlands: the instruments and places of ritual power. *American Anthropologist* 90(3): 547–567.

Garber, James F., 1981, *Material culture and patterns of artifact consumption and disposal at the Maya site of Cerros in Northern Belize.* Ph.D. dissertation, Southern Methodist University. University Microfilms, Ann Arbor.

——, 1983, Patterns of jade consumption and disposal at Cerros, Northern Belize. *American Antiquity* 48(4): 800–807.

——, 1985, Long distance trade and regional exchange at the Maya community of Cerros in Northern Belize. *Mexicon* 7(1): 13–16.

——, 1986, The artifacts. In *Archaeology at Cerros Belize, Central America, volume 1: an interim report,* edited by R. A. Robertson and D. A. Freidel, pp. 117–126. Southern Methodist University Press, Dallas.

Gillis, Judy A., 1982, Analysis of miscellaneous ceramic artifacts from Colha, Belize: 1979–1981. In *Archaeology at Colha, Belize,* edited by T. R. Hester, H. J. Shafer, and J. D. Eaton, pp. 229–250. Center for Archaeological Research, University of Texas at San Antonio.

Goffman, Erving, 1959, *The presentation of self in everyday life.* Doubleday-Anchor Books, New York.

Goodenough, Ward H., 1963, *Cooperation in change.* Russell Sage Foundation, New York.

Graham, Elizabeth, 1987, Resource diversity in Belize and its implications for models of Lowland trade. *American Antiquity* 52(4): 753–767.

Guderjan, Thomas; James F. Garber; and Herman Smith, 1988, San Juan: a Maya trade transshipment point on northern Ambergris Cay, Belize. *Mexicon* 10(2): 35–37.

Hammond, Norman (editor), 1973, *British Museum–Cambridge University Corozal Project, 1973 interim report.* Centre of Latin American Studies, Cambridge University, Cambridge.

——, 1975, *Archaeology in Northern Belize: British Museum–Cambridge University Corozal Project 1974–75 interim report.* Centre of Latin American Studies, Cambridge University, Cambridge.

——, 1977, Ex orient lux: a view from Belize. In *The origins of Maya civilization,* edited by R. E. W. Adams, pp. 45–76. University of New Mexico Press, Albuquerque.

——, 1979, *Cuello Project 1978 interim report.* Archaeological Research Program, Douglass College, Rutgers University, New Brunswick, New Jersey, Publication 1.

——, 1980, The jades from Cuello and related research, Paper presented at the Conference on jade at Dumbarton Oaks, Washington.

——, 1982, *Ancient Maya civilization.* Rutgers University Press, New Brunswick.

——, 1986, The emergence of Maya civilization. *Scientific American* 255(2): 106–115.

Hazeldon, J., 1973, Soils and geology of the Orange Walk and Corozal Districts. *British Museum–Cambridge University Corozal Project, 1973 interim report,* edited by N. Hammond, pp. 74–85. Centre of Latin American Studies, Cambridge University, Cambridge.

Hester, Thomas R. (editor), 1979, *The Colha Project, 1979: a collection of interim papers.* Center for Archaeological Research, University of Texas at San Antonio.

——, 1981, The archaeology of Colha Belize: an overview after three seasons, Paper presented at the 80th annual meeting of the American Anthropological Association, Los Angeles.

Hester, Thomas R.; J. D. Eaton; and Harry J. Shafer (editors), 1980, *The Colha Project, second season, 1980 interim report.* Center for Archaeological Research, University of Texas at San Antonio.

Hester, Thomas R.; Harry J. Shafer; and J. D. Eaton (editors), 1982, *Archaeology at Colha Belize: the 1981 interim report.* Center for Archaeological Research, University of Texas at San Antonio.

Hummer, Anne G., 1983, Ground stone from the Zapotitan valley. In *Archaeology and volcanism in Central America: the Zapotitan valley of El Salvador,* edited by Payson D. Sheets, pp. 229–251. University of Texas Press, Austin.

Joesink-Manderville, L. R. V., and Sylvia Meluzine, 1976, Olmec-Maya relationships: Olmec influence in Yucatan. In *Origins of religious art and iconography in Preclassic Mesoamerica,* edited by H. B. Nicholson, pp. 87–105. UCLA Latin American Publications, Los Angeles.

Kent, Kate P., and Sarah M. Nelson, 1976, Net sinkers or weft weights? *Current Anthropology* 174(1): 152.

Kidder, Alfred V., 1947, *The artifacts of Uaxactun, Guatemala.* Carnegie Institution of Washington, Washington, D.C., Publication 576.

Kidder, Alfred V.; J. D. Jennings; and E. M. Shook, 1946, *Excavations at Kaminaljuyu, Guatemala.* Carnegie Institution of Washington, Washington, D.C., Publication 561.

Lewenstein, Suzanne M., 1984, *Stone tool use at Cerros, a Late Preclassic site on the north coast of Belize.* Ph.D. dissertation, Arizona State University. University Microfilms, Ann Arbor.

———, 1986, Feature 11 and the quest for the elusive domestic structure: a preliminary reconstruction based on chipped stone use. In *Archaeology at Cerros Belize, Central America, volume 1: an interim report,* edited by R. A. Robertson and D. A. Freidel, pp. 65–73. Southern Methodist University Press, Dallas.

———, 1987, *Stone tool use at Cerros: the ethnoarchaeological and use-wear evidence.* University of Texas Press, Austin.

Longyear, John M., III, 1952, Copan ceramics: a study of Southeastern Maya pottery. Carnegie Institution of Washington, Washington, D.C., Publication 597.

MacNeish, Richard S.; Antoinette Nelkin-Turner; and Irmgard W. Johnson, 1967, *The prehistory of the Tehuacan Valley.* Vol. 2, *The non-ceramic artifacts.* D. S. Byers, general editor. University of Texas Press, Austin.

Mauss, Marcel, 1967, *The gift: forms and functions of exchange in archaic societies,* J. Canison, translator. W. W. Norton, New York.

Merton, Robert K., 1957, *Social theory and social structure.* Free Press, Glencoe, Illinois.

Mitchum, Beverly A., 1986, Chipped stone artifacts. In *Archaeology at Cerros Belize, Central America, volume 1: an interim report,* edited by R. A. Robertson and D. A. Freidel, pp. 105–115. Southern Methodist University Press, Dallas.

Palache, Charles, 1932, Zunyite from Guatemala. *American Mineralogist* 17(7): 304–307.

Pendergast, David M., 1962, Metal artifacts in Prehispanic Mesoamerica. *American Antiquity* 27(4): 520–545.

———, 1976, *Altun Ha: a guidebook to the ancient Maya ruins* (2nd rev. ed.). University of Toronto Press, Toronto.

———, 1979, *Excavations at Altun Ha, Belize 1964–1970* (Vol. 1). Royal Ontario Museum, Toronto, Canada.

———, 1981, Lamani, Belize: summary of excavation results, 1974–1980. *Journal of Field Archaeology* 8(1): 29–53.

Phillips, David A., Jr., 1978, Additional notes on the fishing technology of the Yucatan Peninsula, Mexico. *Bulletin of Texas Archaeological Society* 49: 349–354.

———, 1979, *Material culture and trade of the Post-classic Maya.* Ph.D. dissertation, University of Arizona. University Microfilms, Ann Arbor.

Piña Chan, Roman, 1968, *Isla Jaina, la casa en el agua.* Instituto Nacional de Antropología e Historia, Mexico City.

Pollock, H. E. D. et al., 1962, *Mayapán, Yucatán, Mexico.* Carnegie Institution of Washington, Washington, D.C., Publication 619.

Potter, Daniel R., 1980, Archaeological investigations at operation 2012. In *The Colha Project, second season, 1980 interim report,* edited by T. R. Hester, J. D. Eaton, and H. J. Shafer, pp. 173–184. Center for Archaeological Research, University of Texas at San Antonio.

———, 1982, Some results of the second year of excavation at operation 2012. In *Archaeology of Colha Belize: the 1981 interim report,* edited by T. R. Hester, H. J. Shafer, and J. D. Eaton, pp. 98–122. Center for Archaeological Research, University of Texas at San Antonio.

Proskouriakoff, Tatiana, 1954, *Varieties of Classic central Veracruz sculpture.* Carnegie Institution of Washington, Washington, D.C., Publication 58.

———, 1962, The artifacts of Mayapán. In *Mayapán, Yucatán, Mexico,* edited by H. E. D. Pollock et al., pp. 321–442. Carnegie Institution of Washington, Washington, D.C., Publication 619.

———, 1974, Jades from the Cenote of Sacrifice, Chichen Itza, Yucatan. *Memoirs of the Peabody Museum of Archaeology and Ethnology* 10(1).

Rands, Robert L., 1965, Jades of the Maya Lowlands. In *Handbook of Middle American Indians,* edited by R. Wauchope and G. R. Willey, Vol. 3, pp. 561–580. University of Texas Press, Austin.

Rathje, William L., 1970, Socio-political implications of Lowland Maya burials. *World Archaeology* 1: 359–374.

———, 1971, The origin and development of Lowland Classic Maya civilization. *American Antiquity* 36(3): 275–285.

———, 1972, Praise the gods and pass the metates: a hypothesis of the development of Lowland rainforest civilizations in Mesoamerica. In *Contemporary Archaeology: a guide to theory and contributions,* edited by M. P. Leone, pp. 365–392. Southern Illinois University Press, Carbondale.

———, 1977, The Tikal connection. In *The origins of Maya civilization,* edited by R. E. W. Adams. University of New Mexico Press, Albuquerque.

Renfrew, Colin, 1975, Trade as action at a distance: question of integration and communication. In *Ancient civilization and trade,* edited by J. A. Sabloff and C. C. Lamberg-Karlovsky. University of New Mexico Press, Albuquerque.

Rice, Don S., 1976, Middle Preclassic Maya settlement in the central Maya Lowlands. *Journal of Field Archaeology* 3(4): 425–445.

Ricketson, Oliver G., Jr., and Edith Bayles Ricketson, 1937, *Uaxactun, Guatemala: Group E—1926–1931.* Carnegie Institution of Washington, Washington, D.C., Publication 477.

Robertson, Robin A., 1983, Functional analysis and social process in ceramics: the pottery from Cerros, Belize. In *Civilization in the ancient Americas: essays in honor of Gordon R. Willey,* edited by R. M. Leventhal and A. L. Kolata, pp. 105–142. University of New Mexico Press, Albuquerque.

———, 1986, The ceramics. In *Archaeology at Cerros Belize, Central America, volume 1: an interim report,* edited by R. A. Robertson and D. A. Freidel, pp. 89–103. Southern Methodist University Press, Dallas.

Robertson-Freidel, Robin A., 1980, *The ceramics from Cerros: a Late Preclassic site in Northern Belize.* Ph.D. dissertation, Harvard University. University Microfilms, Ann Arbor.

Rovner, Irwin, 1975, *Lithic sequences of the Maya Lowlands.* Ph.D. dissertation, University of Wisconsin. University Microfilms, Ann Arbor.

Roys, Ralph L. (translator and editor), 1933, *The Book of Chilam Balam of Chumayel.* Carnegie Institution of Washington, Washington, D.C., Publication 438.

Ruz Lhuillier, Alberto, 1952, Exploraciones en Palenque. *Anales del Instituto Nacional de Antropología e Historia 6.*

Sabloff, Jeremy A., 1975, *Excavations at Seibal, Department of Peten, Guatemala: ceramics.* Memoirs of the Peabody Museum of Archaeology and Ethnology. Harvard University, Vol. 13(2).

Sanders, William T., 1973, The cultural ecology of the Lowland Maya: a reevaluation. In *The Classic Maya collapse,* edited by T. P. Culbert, pp. 325–365. University of New Mexico Press, Albuquerque.

Sanders, William T., and Barbara J. Price, 1968, *Mesoamerica: the evolution of a civilization.* Random House, New York.

Scarborough, Vernon L., 1980, *The settlement system at a Late Preclassic community: Cerros, Northern Belize.* Ph.D. dissertation, Southern Methodist University. University Microfilms, Ann Arbor.

———, 1986, The dispersed settlement. In *Archaeology at Cerros Belize, Central America, volume 1: an interim report,* edited by R. A. Robertson and D. A. Freidel, pp. 23–43. Southern Methodist University Press, Dallas.

Scarborough, Vernon L. et al., 1982, Two Late Preclassic ballcourts at the Lowland Maya center of Cerros, Northern Belize. *Journal of Field Archaeology* 9(1): 21–34.

Scarborough, Vernon L., and Robin A. Robertson, 1986, Civic and residential settlement at a Late Preclassic Maya center. *Journal of Field Archaeology* 13: 155–175.

Schele, Linda, and Jeffrey H. Miller, 1983, The mirror, the rabbit, and the bundle: "accession" expressions from the Classic Maya inscriptions. *Studies in pre-Columbian art and archaeology* No. 25, Dumbarton Oaks Research Library and Collection, Washington, D.C.

Schele, Linda, and Mary Ellen Miller, 1986, *The blood of kings: dynasty and ritual in Maya art.* Kimball Art Museum, Fort Worth.

Shafer, Harry J., 1981, Maya craft specialization in northern Belize, Paper presented at the 80th annual meeting of the American Anthropological Association, Los Angeles.

Sheets, Payson D., 1978, Part one: artifacts. In *The prehistory of Chalchuapa, El Salvador* (Vol. 2), edited by R. J. Sharer, pp. 1–131. University Monographs, University Museum, University of Pennsylvania.

———, 1979, Maya recovery from volcanic disasters: Illopango and Ceren. *Archaeology* 32(3): 32–42.

Sheets, Payson D. (editor), 1983, *Archaeology and volcanism in Central America: the Zapotitan valley of El Salvador.* University of Texas Press, Austin.

Sidrys, Raymond V., 1976, *Mesoamerica: an archaeological analysis of a low-energy civilization.* Ph.D. dissertation, University of California, Los Angeles. University Microfilms, Ann Arbor.

Sidrys, Raymond V., and John Andresen, 1976, Metate import in Northern Belize. In *Maya lithic studies: papers from the 1976 Belize Field Symposium,* edited by T. R. Hester and N. Hammond, pp. 177–190. Center for Archaeological Research, University of Texas at San Antonio, Special Report No. 4.

Smith, A. Ledyard, and Alfred V. Kidder, 1951, *Excavations at Nebaj, Guatemala.* Carnegie Institution of Washington, Washington, D.C., Publication 594.

Spaulding, Albert C., 1953, Statistical techniques for the discovery of artifact types. *American Antiquity* 18(4): 305–313.

Stone, Doris Z., 1957, *The archaeology of central and southern Honduras.* Papers of the Peabody Museum of Archaeology and Ethnology, Harvard University, Vol. 49(3).

Suárez Diez, Lourdes, 1974, *Técnicas prehispánicas en los objetos de concha.* Instituto Nacional de Antropología e Historia, Collección Científica No. 14, Mexico City.

Thompson, J. Eric S., 1931, *Archaeological investigations in the Southern Cayo District, British Honduras.* Field Museum of Natural History, Publication 301, Anthropological Series Vol. 17(3).

———, 1939, *Excavations at San Jose, British Honduras.* Carnegie Institution of Washington, Washington, D.C., Publication 506.

———, 1950, *Maya hieroglyphic writing: introduction.* Carnegie Institution of Washington, Washington, D.C., Publication 589.

———, 1954, *The rise and fall of Maya Civilization.* University of Oklahoma Press, Norman.

———, 1963, *Maya archaeologist.* University of Oklahoma Press, Norman.

———, 1964, Trade relations between the Maya Highlands and Lowlands. *Estudios de cultura maya* 4: 13–49.

———, 1966, *The rise and fall of Maya civilization* (2nd edition). University of Oklahoma Press, Norman.

———, 1970, *Maya history and religion.* University of Oklahoma Press, Norman.

Tourtellot, Gair, and Jeremy A. Sabloff, 1972, Exchange systems among the ancient Maya. *American Antiquity* 37(1): 126–135.

Tozzer, Alfred M., 1941, *Landa's Relacion de las Cosas de Yucatan: a translation.* Papers of the Peabody Museum of American Archaeology and Ethnology, Harvard University.

Vayda, Andrew P., and Roy Rappaport, 1968, Ecology, cultural and noncultural. In *Introduction to cultural anthropology,* edited by J. Clifton. Houghton Mifflin, Boston.

Walker, Debra, 1986, A context for Maya ritual at Cerros Belize, Paper presented at the Maya hieroglyphics symposium, University of Texas, Austin.

Wilk, Richard, 1975, Superficial examination of structure 100, Colha. In *Archaeology in Northern Belize: British Museum–Cambridge University Corozal Project 1974–75 interim report,* edited by N. Hammond, pp. 152–173. Centre of Latin American Studies, Cambridge University, Cambridge.

Willey, Gordon R., 1972, *The artifacts of Altar de Sacrificios.* Papers of the Peabody Museum of Archaeology and Ethnology. Harvard University, Vol. 64(1).

———, 1977, The rise of Maya civilization: a summary view. In *The origins of Maya civilization,* edited by R. E. W. Adams. University of New Mexico Press, Albuquerque.

———, 1978, Artifacts. In *Excavations at Seibal, Department of Peten, Guatemala,* edited by G. R. Willey, pp. 1–189.

Memoirs of the Peabody Museum of Archaeology and Ethnology. Harvard University, Vol. 14(1).

Willey, Gordon R. et al., 1965, *Prehistoric Maya settlements in the Belize Valley.* Papers of the Peabody Museum of Archaeology and Ethnology. Harvard University, Vol. 54.

Willey, Gordon R.; T. Patrick Culbert; and Richard E. W. Adams (editors), 1967, Maya Lowland ceramics: a report from the 1965 Guatemala City Conference. *American Antiquity* 32: 289–315.

Woodbury, Richard B., 1965, Artifacts of the Guatemalan Highlands. In *Handbook of Middle American Indians,* edited by R. Wauchope and G. R. Willey, Vol. 2, Pt. 1, pp. 163–180. University of Texas Press, Austin.

Woodbury, Richard B., and Audrey S. Trik, 1953, *The ruins of Zaculeu, Guatemala.* United Fruit Co., Boston.

Zier, Christian J., 1980, A Classic-Period Maya agricultural field in Western El Salvador. *Journal of Field Archaeology* 7(1): 65–74.

——, 1983, The Ceren site: a Classic period Maya residence and agricultural field in the Zapotitan valley. In *Archaeology and volcanism in Central America: the Zapotitan valley of El Salvador,* edited by Payson D. Sheets, pp. 119–143. University of Texas Press, Austin.

INDEX